# SHIFTING CLASSES IN TWENTIETH CENTURY BRITAIN

# Shifting Classes in Twentieth Century Britain:

## From Village Street to Downing Street

**Martin Minogue**

YOUCAXTON
PUBLICATIONS

ISBN 978-1-913425-63-0
Published by YouCaxton Publications 2020
YCBN: 01



YouCaxton Publications
www.youcaxton.co.uk

To Nick and Ben,
two fine boys

# Contents

# Acknowledgements


> *Each of us is a snowball growing bigger every moment and in which all our past, and also the past out of which we spring, all the generations behind us, is rolled up, involved*
> Jane Harrison, in Francesca Wade (2020)

Unavoidably, the author of a memoir is centre-stage throughout, but this memoir itself is owed to the framework provided by the close, loving and always supportive family which gave me existence and sustained me through many difficult times. For me, the heroes of the story are that wonderful pair Martin and Josie, our extraordinary father and mother. They are long departed, but my sisters and I still tell each other how lucky we were to have them as brave, resilient, intelligent and funny parents. They also gave me the best possible present of my two dear sisters, Maureen and Sally. Maureen has long been a wonderful family maker, ably assisted by her husband Tom, drawing the rest of us back to proper Yorkshire celebrations, however far flung we might have become. Sally has, for me, quite simply been a wise, generous, and lifelong kindred spirit.

Because the memoir itself stops short in the middle of the twentieth century the rest of my close family scarcely make an appearance, possibly to their great relief. Yet in many ways they are the ones who gave me the motivation to write it, for I wanted them, (and in particular my two much loved sons, Nick and Ben) to have some sense of their roots, a better understanding of a world that produced and shaped them, but no longer exists as it was experienced by their elders. Unhappily, Nick enjoyed a brilliant but all too short life and cannot now read this family story; but he is there in spirit, for the front cover illustration is a painting by him intended to capture the idea of the upward path I pursued. His brother Ben helped me to come through a very dark time: his qualities of resilience, good humour, and love of political argument remind me of my own father, his Grandad, and I can find no greater tribute. He and his wife Sally have always been there for me; even better, they have made me the grandfather of two beautiful and lively girls, Mia and Cleo, who give me joy and make me smile every time I think of them. Nor do I forget what I owe to Liz, mother to Nick and Ben, and Granny to the girls.

I have been lucky too to enjoy the friendships and loving welcomes of all of Maureen's children, Tom, Emma and Michael. I hope this memoir will again bring alive for them their fondly remembered Granny and Grandad Minogue. They have also made sure of the next generation, Tom's sons Thomas and Harry, and Emma and Olivier's daughters Éva, Céleste and Marielle. They all, together with Mia and Cleo, have tremendous and varied qualities, making me feel sure that the future is in safe hands, and that they will take this family story forward in ways impossible to predict. My family: thank you, each and every one of you.

Many people have helped to make this book better than it might have been, a reminder of how fortunate I am in my friends. Both Quentin Skinner and Fred Inglis gave generously of their time, and incisive and perceptive critiques, saving me from egregious errors along the way, but more important did what good friends do, giving warm and highly practical encouragement during the whole process. Through Quentin, I received considerable and well-judged advice on publication possibilities from Jeremy Mynott. Hugh Johnson brought a lawyerly eye to bear on the text and its language, a reminder that one of his functions in life has been to keep me out of the law courts. David McLellan read the whole text with a keen and critical eye and sought to soften some of my sharper judgements. Rex Taylor was full of warm encouragement, and so were Michael and Sally James. I was considerably helped to get family matters and relationships right by my cousin on the paternal side, Tom Minogue, and likewise by my cousin on the maternal side, Joe Burns and his wife Linda.

I have been helped enormously by the careful readings and suggestions of my sister Sally. My wife Sarah has rescued me from several entanglements with computer technology, never failing to put me on the right track from which I so frequently, and with no little bafflement, wandered. Both gave me the loving support that we should all be lucky enough to have.

# Preface

> *Dearly I would love now to leave an account, some kind of brittle and honest-minded history of myself*
> Sebastian Barry: *The Secret Scripture*

> *The present is only ever one day long. The past grows richer and subtler each day as it snakes behind you to the source and centre of your life*
> Barney Norris: *Five Rivers Met On A Wooded Plain*

It seems nowadays that almost everyone is a do-it-yourself family historian. Many factors have come together at the beginning of the twenty-first century to enable this: the rise of the internet, the computerisation of family and other records, the expansion of literacy and numeracy. But perhaps most influential have been the changes in social structures and social relationships that have created in people an urge to know where they come from, to trace and understand their origins, if only to be able to marvel at the social and economic distances some of them have travelled.

It is within this framework that I seek to offer a memoir that is at once personal and at the same time of general significance. Each personal memoir is unique to and for the person writing it, and provides a story which may be of more burning interest to the author's family and friends than to a wider readership. But if a personal story taps into a seam of social experience in ways that illuminate and inform our general understandings and reception of our recent past, then it transcends the personal, and becomes of generic interest. I want to tell here a story that is, of course, an account of my life, or at least its earlier stages, and of my immediate family, especially my parents and their forebears. But I go well beyond simple genealogy, since we need to dig around the roots of the family tree to find out how families actually lived and behaved, the culture they both constructed and inhabited. I also wish to avoid the trap of 'golden age' nostalgia, where we see the past through rose-tinted spectacles, as a time when everything was wonderful and better than it is now, and we say regretfully 'ah, if only things were still like that'.

Life in the past was often grim, and has in innumerable ways improved out of recognition for large numbers of people. So I want to take a clear-eyed look at the past, warts and all so to speak, though recollecting the good things too.

Above all, my aim is to link my personal and family account to the wider economic and social system which has been the dominant framework for that everyday life: the world of work, of social relationships, of improvement and mobility. For me this means, unavoidably, examining social relationships of class and status, and the ways in which these were related to poverty and inequalities, both in our cities and our villages. My father, born in 1911, was a farm labourer, son of an Irish immigrant labourer; both worked on an aristocratic estate in Yorkshire that was positively mediaeval in structure and spirit. My mother, born just after the outbreak of the Great War in 1914, was the daughter of a coal-miner from Wallsend-on-Tyne, who worked in an industry then dominated by a greedy and uncaring owning class. These urban and rural strands of British social history were linked together when my mother became, through the Catholic church's mysterious ways, a kitchen, then house maid on the very estate employing both my grandfather and later my father. My parents would have three children, all of whom went to grammar school: the eldest, I would go to Cambridge and then into the Foreign and Commonwealth Office; Maureen, next in line, would leave school at sixteen, stay at home in Yorkshire, and become the School Secretary at Harrogate Grammar School; Sally, the youngest, would at sixteen win a scholarship to Oxford, then go on to a successful academic career. So the lives and times of my grandparents, my parents and their children not only span the entire twentieth century, but illustrate the enormous social changes that took place, and the familiar theme of children getting on in ways largely denied to their parents' generation. While others would tread this upward path, thanks not least to the 1944 Education Act, there are still surprisingly few detailed accounts of what, for me at any rate, felt like something of a pilgrim's progress.

I had a university training as a historian, at Cambridge, at the beginning of the 1960s. The historical methods then employed were highly traditional, rooted for the most part in conventional documentary sources, and using an approach that focussed largely (apart from those pursuing political theory and the history of ideas) on constitutional, diplomatic, and political events and personalities. There have been significant shifts in the intervening half century. The urge towards a wider and deeper social learning has coincided with tendencies within professional historical practice to move away from top down, constitutional, diplomatic and military history, and towards the production of alternative, more richly elaborated, bottom up narratives intended to 'recover' large areas of historical social experience that the traditional approach all too often neglected. This change of emphasis has also redirected historians to a range of less traditional sources, including diaries, letters, film, photographs, and even oral histories. Recently there has been a spate of autobiographical accounts, not just by the big names, but by a wide range of people from all walks of life. These trajectories, the amateur and the professional, complement each other to produce historical accounts rooted in everyday social experiences, both past and present. The study of political and social elites and their doings still plays a major part in our historiography, but there are increasing efforts to retrieve and uncover the history of ordinary men and women.

I find this approach congenial, and use it myself, but it is both a problem and an opportunity so far as I am concerned. For example, in the account I will give (in Chapter 4) of 'a child's war' in the Yorkshire village of Appleton Roebuck, my own memories as a child who began the war as a toddler are necessarily scattered and dim. My consciousness of these times depends enormously on the stories and accounts handed down by my mother and father. Both had excellent memories, but my mother, Josephine, or Josie, was recognised in the family for her willingness to make a good story better in the telling. She would often cap a story by declaring 'it's the living truth', and if you heard that phrase you knew that her imagination had been working overtime. My father (also called Martin) was more prosaic, but less 'economical with the truth', and late in his life set out in a series of handwritten diaries an account of his own life as an agricultural labourer, itself something of a historical rarity.

Following fondly in my parents' footsteps, what I offer here is one version of reality, which derives from these family sources as well as my own limited memories, gives a flavour of the life and times of one family, and adds detail, colour and authenticity to broader, less partial accounts. Since memory is notoriously unreliable, it is quite possible that there is a little fiction mixed up with the fact. It may well be that others who lived in those times and places I describe would tell different stories, or have different recollections. There are many versions of the 'living truth', and all enliven and enrich our perceptions of the past which is, above all, a shared (though not a common) past. I hope that this particular story of one family and its extraordinary experiences over the whole twentieth century may resonate with more general themes of our social history, and help us to judge what has changed for the better over that century, as well as pointing to much that seems not to have changed at all.

# Chapter One

## Hard Times

*The lads in this place think you've nothing to do but to go across the sea and fill a bag with gold, but I tell you it is hard work, and in those countries the workhouses is full, and the prisons is full, and the crazyhouses is full, the same as in the city of Dublin*
J.M.Synge: *Travels in Wicklow, West Kerry and Connemara (1905:1911 edition)*

I firmly believe that the world we inhabit can best be examined and understood by looking at the life stories that for each one of us stretches both behind and before us. This is why I have embarked on this story of my family, both memoir and celebration. In large part it is the story, not of the good and the great who dominate most histories, but of the ordinary people without whom the leaders and elites of society could not have achieved what they did, whether for good or ill. Their stories are too seldom told, their innate heroism and sacrifices too often unrecognised. This family memoir is in large part about what it meant to be poor in twentieth century Britain, and about the ways in which it became possible to escape into a better world, a British version of the 'American dream' that, as we advance into the twenty-first century, already begins to have a sepia-tinted aspect.

In my early years I was oblivious to all this. But poverty was something my parents, and their parents before them, and many generations further back, had been obliged to live with permanently, with little means of escape. Theirs is a socially illuminating history, because it embraces rural poverty on my father's side, and urban poverty on my mother's side. It takes in the wrenching experience of Irish immigration through my paternal Irish grandfather, and the bitterness of industrial conflicts through my maternal coal-miner grandfather. Through both my father and mother, one working as a country estate farm labourer, the other as a maid in The Castle, it even demonstrates the almost mediaeval character of the curious intermingling of aristocracy and working class that could still be seen on aristocratic estates in the period between the two world wars, and which, in my parents' case, even lingered on into the 1950s. Yet their children's educational and material achievements blasted a path through this stifling social and economic system in ways simply not available to them. In short, the story of my immediate family is a notable illustration of the history of the working classes in twentieth century Britain, as well as demonstrating the ways in which social mobility would promise significant changes in the structure and effects of the British class system, though these promises have arguably, not ultimately been realised.

My father's origins were wholly Irish by birth right. His father Thomas, a large, raw boned country Irishman, had been born into a Catholic family on 30th December 1878, in the parish of Outrath, some two miles from the centre of the city of Kilkenny. His parents were John Minogue, born in 1846, and Kate Clear, born in 1851, both surviving the desperate years of the Great Famine. His grandfather, (my great-great-grandfather), born just before the end of the Napoleonic Wars, was also Thomas Minogue. My Grandad was the eldest of ten children, mostly bearing predictably Catholic names such as Patrick and Bridget, but including also the rather mystifying Anastasia. According to a family account by my cousin (another Tom Minogue) Grandad would wax nostalgic about his early days, recounting how he and his brothers would walk barefoot from the countryside into Kilkenny, their boots laced around their necks, stopping just outside town to put them on: boots were a precious commodity, not to be worn out too quickly, but they didn't wish either to be seen as country 'spalpeens', in Irish usage a derogatory label for a migratory farm worker, likely to be a rascal.

Grandad and his brother Patrick left their rural birthplace village for England in or about 1900 (and would soon be followed by their sister Nelly). All would marry and settle in Yorkshire in due course. There was little enough reason for Irish people to stay in rural Ireland. Land was scarce and unproductive; paid work on a regular basis was difficult to find; and Irish society was still in a state of shock after the traumatic experiences of the 'Great Hunger' years from 1845-52 that had seen the deaths of more than one million people (in a population of eight millions), while an equal number tried to escape by migrations to America and Britain: by 1900 the Irish population had halved its pre-Famine total. Small tenant farmers and rural labourers were the principal victims. Many reacted by taking the path of political resistance and violence, largely underground, and the Fenian movement, precursor of the IRA, attracted many recruits. But political rebellions were suppressed, many of the participants transported to Australia up to the middle of the nineteenth century. Power and control still rested with the property-owning class. For example, in Grandad's Kilkenny home, the principal landholder, the Butlers of Ormonde, in 1880 received £22,000 annually in rents, an enormous sum at that time, while large numbers of the surrounding rural population lived in abject poverty, without hope or prospects. A local newspaper report at this time describes how local gentry not far from Grandad's birthplace, would, while inebriated, fire guns from their drawing room at deer herded past by their employees, some of these men being occasionally winged. In this society, you either stayed to live a miserable, downtrodden existence, migrated overseas, or rebelled at risk of life and limb. Grandad was essentially uninterested in politics or dissent, a devout Roman Catholic who took to heart the stern remonstrances of the Irish Catholic hierarchy aimed at anyone who might threaten the social and political status quo. When he and Patrick decided to try their luck in England, travelling light (according to cousin Tom's account), Grandad's only possession was a bundle of clothes tied to a blackthorn stick, also doubling as a straight, smooth, heavy 'shillelagh' for protection: fifty years or so later it would lie in a suitcase under his English bed, fascinating Tom, his then small grandson.

Grandad, in my own experience of him in later life, almost never spoke of Ireland or his family there, but in these earlier years he would very occasionally return to the country of his birth, typically for a major Catholic gathering, such as the annual Eucharistic Congress in Phoenix Park, and probably for the funerals of his mother in 1913, and his father in 1920. He did once take his wife and first two children back to his home, but Granny was so seasick she refused any further invitations. He lived the greater part of his life in England, as did Patrick. They naturally turned to agricultural work, the only work with which they were familiar, initially joining a gang of casual labourers, all Irish, who stumped the North of England seeking contract work. Such Irish gangs, usually of seven or eight, were commonly used for seasonal work, mainly the harvesting of crops such as potatoes and hay, or corn in the later part of the year. The farmer could negotiate a low fixed price for a set piece of work, to be completed in a fixed period of days, while leaving his permanent labourers undisturbed in their normal routines. This system also meant that farmers could employ fewer permanent (and more costly) labourers. The essential requirement of this type of work was speed; get your potatoes or turnips or grain to market before everyone else did, when the price would sink downwards. Irish contract groups were notoriously and suspiciously speedy. They could pick clean a decent-sized field of potatoes in a couple of days, at a going rate in 1930 of around 50 shillings per acre. Their tricks were legion, the best known being to tread deep into the forgiving turned soil at least one potato for every half dozen picked up, but the farmer could never complain about how long it took to 'clean' a field. All this meant some free pickings of the leftovers, and even as late as the 1950s we kids would be sent out with baskets in the early evening to scuff aside the soil and claim the bright, hard pearls waiting to be rediscovered. When, as a young child, I helped my Grandad to pick his garden crop, he said to me with a stern face but a twinkling eye: "Young Martin, I have picked thousands of potatoes, but I have left millions". A farmer once said to Grandad: "Tom, if there were two potatoes in a field, you would leave one of the buggers".

While working in this way, Grandad Minogue frequently stayed in a boarding-house in York which specialised in providing cheap lodgings, owned and run by a family, Michael and Mary Harrison, who were themselves Irish, originating in County Mayo. It seems they may have been part of a migration of some 2,000 Irish people to York during and after the famine years of the 1840s. Life was almost certainly very hard for them: in 1901 a Seebohm Rowntree poverty survey showed that in the city of York, 20,000 people out of a total population of 46,000 were living in acute poverty. After some years of scraping a living, the Harrisons established their lodging house for itinerant Catholic workers in the Pocklington district of York. In this household, Grandad Tom met Agnes Harrison, who would soon become his wife and eventually my much-loved Granny Minogue. But before Tom could get Agnes, he had to surmount the formidable obstacle of her mother, who ran the Deans Lane Model Lodging House, and her whole family, with a very firm hand. She had little schooling and may have done her accounts on a primitive abacus, but she had been well educated in the harder school of life, not least in the matter of making a living out of unpromising materials. Most people then regarded itinerant Irish workers with hostility and suspicion. They would, in the popular stereotype, drink heavily, carouse the nights away, knock each other senseless at the slightest opportunity, and fail to pay their dues. And, of course, they were Catholics, adding in a deep-seated and traditional sense of difference. But Mary Harrison knew well enough that she was dealing with young men who would be as high-spirited as any, but with simple virtues to compensate for their simple vices. She made sure they knew and obeyed her rules, the principal ones being that rent was always delivered into her hands directly on pay-days, and that anyone who broke any of her house rules would be out on their ears forthwith. By the standards of the day, and at a time when in some places signs saying 'No Dogs and No Irish' could be seen, she provided accommodation that was cheap, clean and homely, and meals which were noted for their abundance (even if this often meant chiefly an abundance of potatoes: an astonishing fact gleaned from a book about the history of Irish cooking is that the average Irish consumption of potatoes was 14lbs a day per person). My great-grandmother must have thrived on this life as at her death she was celebrated in the local newspaper as Pocklington's first centenarian, (a claim that is somewhat uncertain judged by admittedly vague Irish birth records). The public newspaper description of her as 'the Mother of Thousands' testifies to the high regard in which she was held locally: there is no doubting a formidable tally of 16 children, 58 grandchildren, and 41 great grandchildren (of which, of course, I was one): a true matriarch.

One of my great-grandmother's unwritten rules was that her lodgers should keep their eyes and their hands off her daughters. But youthful ardour will always prevail. Agnes was one of five daughters, standing less than five feet, and with a sweet oval face and a deceptively gentle manner. Tom Minogue couldn't resist her, nor she him. They must have looked an odd couple, this tall, strong, broad-shouldered, fine-moustached man, and his tiny waif of a wife. They were a splendid match, her calm and steadfast temperament perfectly complementing his strong will and occasional stubborn passions. Their devout Catholic faith also united them, and must have made their marriage (on 13th January 1902) more acceptable to Granny's parents. One day, I would witness for myself her desolated courage in the face of Grandad's final illness and death. But that would be fifty-eight years later, years with that due mixture of joy and pain that seems to be the lot of any close family.

Marriage meant, of course, 'settling down': Grandad had to find a steady job and a house for his new wife, not to mention the large brood of children that any Catholic family at that time would take for granted. He secured, somewhat fortuitously, a position on the Catholic estate of Allerton Mauleverer, not far distant from York, the seat of Lord Mowbray, Segrave and Stourton, Premier Baron of England (I will use Mowbray hereafter, except where the family name of Stourton is more appropriate). The family story tells that, as the 24th Lord Mowbray was riding on horseback, he caught

*Minogue family in the 1920s. Back row: Martin, Peggy, Mary, Clara. Front row: Billy, Grandad with Bernard on his knee, Granny with Pat, Tommy, Frank. Eldest son John missing, and Agnes not yet born.*

sight of my grandfather directing operations in a field, and shouted to his Agent: "I want that man to work for me!". The Mowbrays were aristocrats of the oldest Norman vintage (scarcely a recommendation) with links, if somewhat vaguely defined, back to circa 1066. Their progress from that point was fairly typical of the times: according to a Times obituary of the 25th Baron on 14th April 1965, 'the name of Mowbray goes ringing down the Middle Ages from the Conquest...forfeit, imprisonment, capture in battle, the hangman's rope, and the headsman's axe came their way. But they survived and waxed fat on titles and estates'. The Mowbray family remained loyal to their Roman Catholic religion despite the problems this posed for them in the social and religious conflicts of the sixteenth and seventeenth centuries, and on into the nineteenth century: only then did the Catholic Emancipation Act of 1829 fully relieve such families of some of the penalties and exclusions visited on them, not least exclusion from political affairs and state office. The Allerton Park estate had for some 500 years been the seat of the Mauleverers (aptly meaning 'harrier of the poor') who claimed a lineage back to the Norman Conquest, but had in the Civil War of the seventeenth century embraced the Parliamentary cause: indeed, Sir Thomas Mauleverer had been a signatory to the death warrant of Charles 1, and only avoided certain execution by dying before the Restoration in 1660. In the mid eighteenth century, the estate passed to Richard Arundel, as Master of the Mint a prominent Royal official, and Member of Parliament for Knaresborough. Briefly acquired by the 'Grand Old Duke of York' in 1786, it was in due course bought by the Mowbray family and transformed in the middle of the nineteenth century into a large pseudo-Gothic pile with income partly derived from coal estates at Rothwell, near Leeds. When Grandad arrived, the 24th baron, Charles Botolph Joseph Stourton was in occupation, and the blood seemed to be running a bit thin judged by the bizarre behaviour of various members of the family. William Marmaduke, eldest son of the 24th Baron, would one day inherit the estate and become my father's employer (in the early 1950s), just as his father had been my grandfather's employer (from well before the Great War to the mid-1930s). Rural England could still seem fairly mediaeval in the middle of the twentieth century.

Relatively few public documents are available to trace the history of the Mowbray estate, and it is evident that this was not a particularly cultured family. Ampleforth was their public school of choice, a Catholic foundation under the Benedictine order of Ampleforth Abbey (though with annual fees currently at £33,000 a year you would now need rather more than spiritual purity to gain entry: and you might look askance at an institution whose reputation has been significantly dented recently by evidence of substantial sexual abuse of boys by some monks). As for university, until the early twentieth century devout aristocratic Catholic sons often disdained the ancient universities of Oxford and Cambridge through the antagonism of the Catholic hierarchy itself to these irreligious and sinful places. Daughters were expected to do little other than find an acceptable Catholic husband and produce future generations of Catholics. However, estate accounts for the period 1910 to 1936, which coincide more or less with my grandfather's employment there, throw some light on the finances and organisation of the Allerton estate, and the changes taking place in this crucial period in rural economy and society. In 1910 we are still in the Edwardian calm before the storms of the Great War; the estate will move through post-war economic decline and upheaval, and on into the depressed and problematic early 1930s. In 1914, though in the middle of a continuing agricultural depression, the record indicates a relatively prosperous estate. There is a large, directly managed Home Farm, (which also supplies food directly to the Castle), 12 tenanted farms, some 60 cottages, a blacksmith's, a pub (The

Mason's Arms), and extensive productive gardens; it also supports a school (and schoolmistress), and a Catholic chaplaincy. Eighteen of the 60 cottages are rent-free including those of the Head Gardener, Patrick Colohan; the schoolmistress, Miss Annie Murphy, succeeded in 1913 by Miss Teresa Byrne; the estate Carpenter, Wilfrid White; the Head Gamekeeper, Jesse Box; and the Chaplain, John Prendergast. Wage levels at this time varied according to status (permanent or casual), age and experience, and duties (and are denominated here in the pre-decimalisation period at the rate of 20 shillings to the pound, 12 pence to the shilling, 240 pence to the pound). Young casual labourers earned as little as £2 per month, while married workers would double this rate. In 1916, the head gamekeeper's wage for three months was £16/5 shillings, plus £1/19 shillings for the upkeep of two dogs. Meanwhile estate rents (in 1912) were worth £4500 and the accounts show regular transfers by Lord Mowbray to Coutts Bank in London (then as now the bank of aristocratic choice). Some of this would be given back: £8/2 shillings for the Annual Rent Dinner at the Crown Hotel in Knaresborough; £100 for estate worker pensions. In this early part of the century the aristocratic landowner is making steady profits to support a highly privileged lifestyle. But by the early 1930s, a time of severe economic depression, we see significant changes. Rents have stayed level in monetary terms but in real terms have declined substantially. The cheques sent to London get smaller and smaller, down from £1400 for a half year in 1916 to £975 in 1931. The estate, like many others, was struggling to stay afloat.

These accounts give glimpses of my own family connections. It's clear that Grandad began his regular employment on the estate in 1911, the year of my father's birth. In 1912-14 he is recorded as T. Minogue, Garden Labourer, then later T. Minogue, Labourer at Home Farm. From 1912 -1915 he has a rent-free cottage, but in 1919 his cottage is described as having a rental value of £3 18 shillings for the half year, which corresponds roughly to the rental value of 3 shillings per week accorded to tied cottages under wages legislation of 1924. This rental value stays the same in 1921 despite general increases of 8-10 percent (it is not clear whether this was rent deducted from wages, or is a notional rental value, which seems more likely). From this period, his wage is invariable at £7/4 shillings per month, about 33 shillings per week; by comparison the Coachman gets 8 guineas, the Home Farm Foreman 10 guineas per month, both with rent-free houses. Tom Minogue's eldest son, my Uncle Frank, appears as a casual employee in 1931, earning between £2 and £7 per month for mending ditches and drains. Other names appear that are familiar to me: William Harper, a local builder, is paid for building work; his son Mick would one day be my best school friend. A tenant farmer, Cawkwell, changes farms; he would still be there in the 1950s and his son William would also go to school with me.

Separate accounts give details of repairs carried out to estate cottages by the specialist carpenter and others employed for this purpose. For example, in 1930 there is an entry for 'new window and repairs to T. Minogue's cottage, valued at £12 9sh and 9d': some of these costs could be recovered by the owner as a subsidy under legislation governing tenanted properties in agriculture. The accounts include items which are clearly charitable, for example the free let of a cottage to a retired schoolmistress, and to former domestic servants (presumably, though the accounts do not clarify this, such concessions depended on staff having served a considerable number of years on the estate or in the Castle). Several pensions are listed, again, presumably, dependent on length of service: they are very small sums, generally £1 a month for men, and ten shillings a month for women. One item lists support for a farm worker who had been permanently incapacitated through illness or injury: in 1930 'John Poulter, sick' is paid £1 per month. What is noteworthy here is that such welfare was not generally available, the dreaded workhouse remaining a threat for the poorest of the poor through the nineteenth century Poor Law Amendment Act (not finally abolished until 1948). The Labour Book accounts for Allerton Estate in this period show, as noted earlier, about £100 per year paid as pensions and sick pay. It is worth recalling that on an estate owned by a Roman Catholic peer, and predominantly employing Roman Catholics as permanent workers and servants, the ties and felt obligations of a religious community were significant in producing this type of social support, small though it might have been. One consequence was that labour unions and disputes over wages and conditions were largely unheard of on such estates until after the 1939-45 war, despite the ravages of the economic slump and its aftermath in the 1920s and 1930s. Matters were rather different in regions such as East Anglia, where land owners had become more detached from their tenanted farms, and farm labour was beginning to be unionised, pressing for better wages and conditions.

The Allerton estate accounts from 1910 - 1936 let slip some fascinating glimpses of the effects of outside events. In 1916, it is recorded that one of the tenants had volunteered for military service and had been killed in action. Another note records the presence of German prisoners of war living in an estate cottage in the post 1918 period. An account in 1928 refers to a tenant farmer having emigrated to Canada without notice or warning: his tenancy is regarded as vacated and another tenant is installed. It would be fascinating to know what happened to this emigrant to Canada, a welcoming place for British farmers from as long ago as the time of the Tolpuddle Martyrs, several of whom settled on farms in Canada after being returned in the late 1830s from their transportation sentences in Australia.

The accounts provide an occasional insight into the increasingly desperate efforts of the estate to balance its books and ensure sufficient revenues to support the still highly privileged lifestyle of the Mowbray family in the turbulent economic times after the Great War. One measure was to ensure that the Home Farm made constant and consistent losses, which could then be written off against income and local authority taxes. Another was to take advantage of agricultural subsidies during the 1930s, particularly valuable in relation to wheat production. These arable farms in the Plain of York were ideal for growing corn. Usually the focus would have been on oats and barley, and root crops for cattle fodder, but strong international demand for wheat, and the need to satisfy a growing national population, meant that wheat crops were strongly encouraged both in the 1930s and in subsequent wartime, and in the immediate post-1945 period. The growth and harvesting of corn would give a special flavour to my rural childhood in the 1940s and 50s.

In the late Edwardian period Grandad settled down in his small cottage on Home Farm, the main estate farm. A narrow lane linked the Home Farm to Allerton Castle, a peculiar mix of architectural styles now regarded as a prime example of Victorian Gothic. It's all still there today, not much changed from 100 years ago, though long since sold off to commercial interests with the effective collapse of the whole family estate after the death of the 25th Baron in 1965. Various farm buildings straggle out from behind the handsome Georgian Home Farm house, which for a short time in the 1950s would be our family home. The road winds away towards the Castle on a slightly up-hill course. On the right-hand side stands an imposing detached house, set back inside an imprisoning wall of shrubbery. This is where the Butler used to live. Almost opposite is an old stone Anglican church, named (happily, I always thought) St Martin's, and originally founded in the early 13$^{th}$ century by the Mauleverer family. Badly neglected when I lived within view of it in the early 1950s, it is now a Grade 11 listed building, handsomely restored to its original Romanesque style, a remodelling in 1745 by Richard Arundell. Now redundant, it had served local Anglicans: until 1936, estate-employed Catholics were expected to worship in the Castle's Catholic chapel, served by the resident chaplain. If you didn't fear God enough to go to mass, you would certainly bring down on yourself the wrath of the Lord and Lady Mowbray, who reckoned themselves no less in charge of the souls than the bodies of their Catholic workers.

*The cottage on the right was the Minogue family home at Allerton in the 1920s and 1930s.*

Granny and Grandad were devout enough and needed no one to tell them what were their spiritual duties. Their beliefs were simple and straightforward, and total, and guided their lives. Indeed, they obeyed the Biblical injunction to go forth and multiply to such good effect that they rapidly established a family of twelve children, six girls and six boys, though an infant Theresa died of the Spanish flu (not many years ago my 90-year-old Aunt Peggy would look at a family photograph with me and point to the space where the missing child would have been in place.) Two of the girls became nuns, the said Aunt Peggy in a closed Carmelite Order, which in effect meant that she left home for ever at an early age. It was many years before her parents would see her again, and even then only at arm's length behind an iron grille. I'm glad to report that when in 2007 we visited Aunt Peggy, formally Sister Theresa, in her convent in Kirkcaldy, the nuns had decided to abandon the

*Meeting Aunt Peggy (Sister Theresa) age 90 at her convent in Dysart, Kirkcaldy, Scotland.*

less user-friendly aspects of their existence, including the grilles, which had been replaced by a sort of low counter; nevertheless, a beaming Aunt Peggy leaned over and almost hugged the breath out of me, saying how much like her dear brother Martin (i.e. my Dad) I was. Peggy was Grandad's favourite daughter and though they took an uncomplicated pride in this service to mother church, it almost broke her parents' hearts to lose her. Peggy didn't find it easy either, by her own account, saying of her eventual graduation into the closed order that 'the first forty years were the worst', but leaving no doubt of the strength and sincerity of her calling. None of her brothers showed any sign of such vocational fervour, though Irish families always talked fondly of such possibilities for their sons. Until the 1950s, for Catholic offspring in Ireland, much less so in Britain, to join the priesthood brought not only considerable spiritual merit, but no mean social status, and it represented a safe economic harbour when harsh economic winds were blowing. It was a social safety valve too, a way of keeping young men out of mischief, and intelligent spirits out of politics. In those earlier days, for many young men, it represented the only possibility of a career, the only channel by which young working class and lower middle-class men could move upwards. Still, you had to have a sense of religious vocation, and perhaps an ability to suppress your sexuality, a test, we now know, that many priests in Ireland in particular failed abysmally, resulting in many cases of sexual and physical abuse. It is no surprise that with new prosperity both in Ireland and Britain, the supply of both male and female candidates for the religious life has rapidly dried up. It's also no surprise to find that Dad and his brothers appear to have been regarded, even then, as unpromising material. Dad at least did some service as an altar boy, reporting that his morning altar service in the Catholic chapel regularly meant late arrivals at the village school. But he earned much moral credit, until one day the reverend Father found him and two other altar boys dipping holy wafers in the communion wine, and sucking them with every sign of exaltation, though not of the spiritual kind.

The old schoolhouse is now someone's ideal home: slick with white paint, roses around a trellis entrance to the front door, it glows with rustic virtue. I stand there and see my father, a young close-cropped boy such as I had once been at ten, trail (not unwillingly) down the road and into the stiff formality of the schoolroom. There was nothing complicated about the schooling dispensed here. The children of Allerton and Hopperton were taught to read, to count, to write, to recite poetry, to fear God, to keep a sharp lookout for the many manifestations of the devil, and to show respect at all times to Lord and Lady Mowbray. These lessons once absorbed, they would be expected at fourteen years (not long earlier it would have been thirteen) to leave school, and often enough home, and proceed to the aid of their families by finding paid employment, either on the estate, or on other farms in the district. There was little question of any of these children going on to secondary school, let alone any further than that. There was in those days a vanishingly small number of scholarships for boys (even fewer for girls) somewhere near the category of genius, but little encouragement for Dad to think of such possibilities (I find it telling that an otherwise fascinating booklet on early twentieth century Yorkshire rural life and labour produced by the Castle Museum, York, has sections on markets, religion and leisure, but no mention whatever of schools and education). Grandad Minogue, ever the traditionalist, could see no merit in education: get a job, that was the thing. Education was for other people. His aristocratic employers took much the same view of their staff and workers. I was astonished to read in Dad's memoir that, well regarded at school, he was given access to Lady Mowbray's personal library, and allowed to borrow one book each week: but she required this (almost) penniless son of one of her (pretty much) penniless estate labourers to pay her a penny fee each time. I have no doubt that, born thirty-five years later, my intelligent parents would have gone to grammar school and even on to University. Their children would enjoy these prospects, thanks to the 1944 Education Act, but they themselves had nothing to anticipate but a life of unremitting, badly paid labour. Not that this was so apparent to them at the time; only when they saw their own children grow and open out like flowers in the warm sun would they begin better to understand what they themselves had been denied.

But in the early 1920s, Dad was a happy go lucky schoolboy, living only for the moment. His favourite trick was to play truant on hunt meeting days. He had a pal called Maurice Hornsby, son of the Coachman. He and Maurice would leave home early, meet up behind the church, make sure that Grandad was nowhere in sight, then scurry off into the woods to catch up with the horses and hounds. Once found, they never lost the scent. On foot, their aim was to anticipate the Hunt's movements, which often as not meant second guessing or even sighting the fox, because they had to be fairly nippy to be at the right gate at the right time, opening it for the horses and their riders, and politely tugging their forelocks for the Master. There was usually the chance of a penny from some soft-hearted rider. Despite these truancies, this was the school where Dad learned by heart the poems mentioned later in this account, and which he would never forget. He would also never forget Maurice, whose life would in his early twenties be sadly cut short by a motorbike accident on the Great North Road: a simple wood and metal cross still stands in the Anglican St Martin's churchyard, marking his grave in a separate walled off section reserved for non-aristocratic Catholics, places for the aristocratic ones provided separately in family vaults in the Castle Chapel. Social class divided people even in death.

# Chapter Two

# ... and Hard Masters

*The people on these estates work and live in poverty in order that these men and their families may enjoy leisure and luxury...all of these people allow themselves to be overworked and bullied and starved and robbed by this little crowd*
Robert Tressell: *The Ragged Trousered Philanthropists*

In 1925 there had come an end to this semi-idyll of childhood. Dad reached the age of 14 and the end of his formal schooling. The Labour and Liberal elements in post First World War governments pressed for a broadening and deepening of the education system, so that it would provide new opportunities to the working-class heroes who had returned from war with the hope and expectation that the post war world would be a different place than it had been in 1914. But these hopes withered in the atmosphere of economic hardship and financial gloom in the 1920s and 1930s known as the Great Depression; it would take a second world conflagration to make social and educational changes unavoidable. Meantime, Dad found himself in Knaresborough marketplace one cold November morning, standing in line with a lot of other likely fourteen-year-old lads, in what was usually known as the Martinmas Hirings, a process by which master and man would strike an employment contract, usually for a calendar year. Dad stood there nervously, seeing handshakes on either side of him as contracts were made, wondering what might turn up for him. What turned up was someone Dad reports as 'a huge man with a big bullet head on which was a large homburg hat, and hanging on his huge frame was a large overcoat. I was frightened to death of him. He said he would give me £13 for the year and my food and lodgings but no overtime. This I accepted as I had no idea how much I should get but a good single man with experience would get £1 per week so I suppose 5sh a week was about right. He gave me my 'fastening penny', which was 2sh and 6d and I thought I was rich'. Dad later discovered this man to be Tom Morrell, a strong local Wesleyan. He was known to the other lads as Hungry Tom. The work contract for these young unmarried men meant 'living-in' with the farmer and his family and sharing in their meals. It seemed that Hungry Tom was mean with board as well as money, and a grumpy boss to boot. Those in the know avoided his eye, or refused his offer. Dad, wet behind the ears, was so glad to be made an offer that he grasped Hungry Tom's hand enthusiastically, along with the half crown. He would often recollect his year at Hungry Tom's farm in Scriven, a village close to Knaresborough. Almost every day they would eat cold fat pork for breakfast and hot fat pork for dinner, derived from the pigs kept and slaughtered on the farm. When pay day came at the end of the year, Tom turned away from Dad, holding the small enough amount of money in a hand extended behind him, and said: "here lad, tek it, tek it": he couldn't bear to see his precious money disappear into someone else's hand. Dad left this farm at the end of the contract, a lot wiser and more careful about who he committed himself to; but even the next farmer had his little ways. On the first time at the dinner table he said: "Dost want any more lad?" "Yes please," said Dad eagerly, starving after a long hard day's work. "What's that lad, what's that?" roared the farmer, scowling. "No thank you, sir" said Dad, seeing what was expected. "That's right, lad", said the farmer, "Speak up". At the last Hirings Dad attended, in 1929, he was employed by a Mr Goodwill, aptly named and known as 'a good meat shop' because although most meals during the week were the ubiquitous 'fat boiled bacon', on Saturdays there were 'warm cakes and fried eggs and lean bacon'. Dad's diary notes that the farmer typically killed a pig every seven weeks to supply the farm household with food.

Dad went his peripatetic way in this fashion, increasingly able to choose his own employer as the Hirings system petered out (it had not been helped by the practice some lads introduced of taking several 'fastening' pennies, leaving a false address in each case). He steadily acquired some basic farming skills. In those days, these skills were real and hard-learned. By the time he was twenty, Dad knew how to handle the whole range of farm animals, how to break in horses and plough with them, how to cut and lay hedges by hand with a billhook, how to cut corn and hay using a scythe; in 1930 he clipped his first sheep, 'and what a hard, hot greasy job it was' he writes. He was also learning how to build corn and haystacks, and thatch the tops of these. Elsewhere these arts were beginning to give way to the onset of more mechanised forms of agriculture, with the introduction of tractors, tractor-driven binders, and more efficient threshing machines, and he would learn to adapt to these too in the fullness of time. But in the inter-war period English farming was still backward in many respects, a situation only to be remedied by the onset of war in 1939, and the consequent pressures for the national economy to be self-sufficient in food, against the possibilities of blockade and food shortages (the dangers of this had been grimly illustrated during the First World War by the effectiveness of the economic blockades of Germany, which resulted in the deaths by starvation of many thousands of German people).

In the 1920s and early thirties the structure and habits of agriculture did not vary all that much from the accounts of farming practice 100 years earlier by William Cobbett, notably in his famous 1830 book, *Rural Rides,* or documented for the end of the nineteenth century by George Ewart Evans in Norfolk. In the Yorkshire Dales hill farms, donkeys were still used to carry milk churns down to the villages. In the 1930s times were only marginally better than they had been in the 1830s for working people, both in town and country: it is scarcely an exaggeration to say that the most visible difference between the two periods was that attempts by workers to organise themselves to improve hard conditions of work and life could no longer, in my parents' time, result in transportation to Australia. In this period of considerable hardship for the rural poor the 24th Baron Mowbray, Dad records, would go to the corn fields at harvest time to make sure that the men would not catch

*Grandad at harvest time with other workers and some of the children from the Castle.*

any of his rabbits to supplement their meagre diets. People dealt with need in different ways. There was, inevitably, some poaching of the reprieved rabbits, and something of a cat and mouse game played out between local poachers and the unloved gamekeepers. Poor families would also help each other out, often through borrowing of staple foods such as milk, flour and tea. My father's family had neighbours called the Robinsons, with ten children: when short of tea or flour one of these children would appear at the door with a large 'borrowing cup', but 'always repaid the debt in a much smaller cup'.

A different sense of community seems, at first glance, to be inscribed in evocative photos of the period which show smiling groups of harvest workers, my grandfather at their centre, mingled with charming aristocratic children and attendant nannies. But these apparent illustrations of a fetching rural idyll are deeply illusory. This whole decade from 1925-1935 was held fast in economic decline and depression, both in town and country. Wages were low, unemployment high, and by the mid-thirties the National Government was threatening to reduce unemployment benefit by 20 per cent (though farm workers did not qualify anyway). Poverty was endemic and ill health chronic. But people survived, as they must. Dad, a hard worker and a responsible and reliable man, always kept himself in work (except for short periods in the early 1930s, the height of the recession), though the pay was extremely low. In 1927, aged 16, he got £21 a year, or approximately 7sh and 6d a week. He bought his first bike for £4 and 5sh, an astonishing fifth of his annual wage: but this was a prized and necessary form of transport for an active rural worker. In 1931, now regarded no longer as a lad but as a skilled single man at the age of 20, he was paid 26sh for a 52-hour week, with 15sh knocked off for board and lodging and 9d for accident insurance, leaving him with 10sh and 3d for all other spending (his Irish father, married with seven children at this time, earned, as we saw earlier, not much more at 33sh a week). Extra money could be earned by overtime, often on 'piece work' i.e. pay according to the size or extent of a particular task. A typical kind of piece work involved the hoeing or gathering of root crops, particularly mangolds or turnips. From the age of 18 Dad was paid for this at the rate of 3d per 100 yards, rising at 4 am to begin the piece work, then doing his normal day's work from 7 am until 5:30 pm, then working 'on piece' again until 10pm: an 18-hour day. It would take 400 yards of hoeing to earn one shilling, the price of a bus fare to the nearest town of Knaresborough; entry to a village dance cost 600 yards of hard hoeing.

*My handsome Dad, Martin Minogue Senior, probably aged 18.*

As a carefree young man Dad could spend his spare shillings on visits to the cinema to see, say, Al Jolson in 'The Singing Fool', or live shows at the Harrogate Empire (clearly Dad had inherited his father's twinkling eye, as he writes 'we used to go there to see the chorus girls'). There would be village hall dances, for example at the Long Memorial Hall in Spofforth, near Wetherby, featuring, according to Dad, the unlikely sounding Babs Tappin and the Rhythm Boys: he would dance the whole of his life, still enjoying ballroom dancing in Harrogate at the age of 70. He was also, in his youth, something of a locally known athlete, once challenged by a leading amateur runner to a public race, with bets taken, around Ribston Park near Knaresborough: he trained for a whole week, a large crowd turned out to watch, and he records in his typically understated way 'I won fairly easily as I was quite a good runner'. Dad's employment was always in the neighbourhood of his family home, never more than a few miles cycle ride away. He often told of how, when ensconced with such as Hungry Tom, he would think nothing of cycling six miles home for a bit of home cooking, and back again after no more than an hour's break spent gossiping and teasing with his favourite sisters Peggy and Pat. His diary records at that time an industrious, close family life: typically, his father would be mending boots, his mother baking for the next day, the assembled children carrying out allotted tasks, including clipping old clothes for strips for home-made rugs. 'When all the jobs were finished my Dad would sit in his armchair with one of us children on either knee, and would sing us, with eyes closed, such patriotic songs as 'The Wearing of the Green', or 'Wrap the Flag Around me, Boys', lightened by 'The Stone outside Dan Murphy's Door', or 'Phil the Fluter's Ball'. Good thing for me and my sisters that Dad would later return as often as possible to this welcoming family hearth, for this is how he met our mother, Josephine. He records in his diary for 1931: 'this year affected my whole life as a young girl of 17 years came to work at Allerton Park as a kitchen maid. Her name was Josephine Simpson, a chubby girl full of life and confidence'. The description 'chubby' is a surprise, as we only ever knew Mum as small and slender. Dad was even more impressed by the fact that she smoked, considered daring for a young woman in this conservative rural world. Doubtless they were also brought together by their shared Roman Catholic heritage.

*My Mum, Josephine (Josie) Simpson aged 17.*

Josephine Simpson was born in Wallsend on 1st December 1914, the fifth of six children. Her father, Joseph Simpson, is recorded as a 'coal hewer'. Birth records show that his parents were both Irish Catholics, so replicating my paternal great grandparents exactly (an astonishing coincidence is that Joseph Simpson Snr is recorded as running a Lodging House, just like my great grandmother in York: it's conceivable that he too was addressing the housing needs of itinerant Irish workers). My Grandad Simpson's first wife, Mary Wannop, had tragically died of childbirth-related puerperal fever in 1898, the child dying too at a month old, and in 1903 he married Mary Wood, of Scottish stock, but living and working as a wire spinner in South Shields. My mother always claimed that a branch of the Wood family ran boxing booths, and there may be confirmation of this in the recorded description of her maternal grandfather, Thomas Wood, as a Travelling Showman. Her maternal grandmother (my great-grandmother) Margaret Campbell is recorded in the 1911 Census as having had 18 children, of whom 12 had died, six surviving. Before her marriage she had worked as a 'fish-wife', daily carrying fish, in a basket on her head, between home and the fish market in South Shields. I met her just once, as a very old lady, rather forbidding in head to toe black bombazine, and disgraced myself by rejecting her proffered embrace because, I whispered to my Mum, "she smells".

My mother was always proud of her 'Geordie' heritage, much more ambiguous about the religious one. She and her siblings grew up during a tough period, of international war, followed by economic recession and eventually the Great Depression. It was a particularly hard time for a coal-mining family in the North East of England, which was the scene of bitter industrial disputes, both in the mines and the shipyards that dominated the employment scene in those parts. These disputes culminated in the General Strike of 1926, in which all trade unions brought their men out of the workplace in protest at attempts by employers to protect their profits by reducing their workers' wages. While the General Strike was relatively short-lived, the miners defiantly stayed out for a further six months. This was a disastrous situation for such as Joseph Simpson and his family. Joseph, a fine-looking man, was employed at the Rising Sun colliery, largest and most profitable of the string of mines owned by the Wallsend and Hebburn Coal Company. Coal-mining was still a highly dangerous industry: in 1913, the year before my mother's birth, an underground gas explosion at Senghenydd pit in South Wales had killed 493 miners, the negligent owners being fined a derisory £10. The Wallsend company's workforce had known their share of the grim side of coal-mining, having suffered many deaths and injuries over the previous 100 years. The most recent accident, an explosion in 1925, had killed five people; but 102 men and boys (the youngest eight years old) had been killed on one day in June 1835, a disaster covered up by the owners to such an extent that these 'forgotten' miners, buried in an unmarked grave, were only officially commemorated in 1994: the plaque records that their ages ranged from 8 to 76. Happily for my family, the Rising Sun colliery was one of their relatively safe pits. Joseph and his family lived in Hopper Street

*Granny Mary Simpson and her children in Wallsend circa 1915. Left to right: Meg, Molly, Josephine on Granny's knee, Sadie, Tommy and Jimmy.*

(a row of miners' terraced houses) less than a mile away from the pithead. According to my mother he had been active in the mineworkers' union and all his sympathies lay with the ordinary miners. He was out of work for more than six months, with a wife and six children to support. Family lore has it that he once fought a public boxing match with a chained bear for money with which to feed his family (boxing ran in the family, and his son Jimmy would one day be an Army boxing champion, but never had to compete with bears). The privileged upper-class owners, most living on country estates well away from the urban grime, cared little about these privations. The list of directors shows that their selfish and uncaring treatment of their dissenting workers was rewarded for two of them by knighthoods from a grateful Conservative party. Curiously enough, one of these, the principal owner, was also a Simpson, Sir Frederick Robert Simpson; even more curiously I would, quite by chance, while researching for this account, stay in the Hedgefield House Hotel near Blaydon, which turned out to be Sir Frederick Robert Simpson's former country mansion: had she known this, my mother's glee would have been considerable at what she would have seen as a small victory in the always ongoing class war.

She had close enough experience of this, for her childhood took her through the short-lived General Strike of 1926, followed by the desperate and finally isolated and unsuccessful effort by the miners' unions to wrest concessions from the recalcitrant mine owners, who enjoyed the support of a Conservative government deeply hostile to industrial actions of this kind. Winston Churchill was a particularly aggressive player in this brutal confrontation, and my mother always recalled that he had relentlessly opposed the extension of universal suffrage that came finally in 1928. Mum often talked about the hardships of their life during this time, and these experiences gave her a hard edge quite absent from my father's political attitudes. Curiously, it also gave her a stronger sense of class difference, perhaps because urban politics at the time were more 'socialist' in content, and marked by a spirit of collective consciousness different in kind from the more personal and individualistic structure of rural social and political relations. Mum's bitterness centred in part on the iniquities of the economic system which gave so much to owners and managers, so little to the workers without whose labour neither owners nor managers would have profited as they did. It was Mum who directed me, when she thought me old enough to take an informed interest, to a heart-breaking account of these economic and social relations in *Jarrow: the Town that was Murdered* (murdered by the stony-hearted strategies of the shipping and mining interests who controlled the town's economy, creating by 1936 an unemployment level of 80% of the town's workforces). Published in 1939, and written by Ellen Wilkinson, Labour's first female MP (in 1929, but by 1936 MP for Jarrow), this book tells the story of the rise and fall of a local North Eastern community on the River Tyne. The town rises first as a coal-mining community in the early nineteenth century, then as a shipbuilding centre, but is riven by bitter disputes as miners and shipbuilding workers try to obtain a less inhumane and exploitative set of working conditions. Battles take place over the fight for a Nine Hours Day, and over the dreadful exploitation of child labour as young as seven. A subsidiary theme is the hellish living conditions and desperately bad health of working people: they, and most notably their children, die regularly of typhoid, and fevers occasioned by the complete absence of proper sanitation, as well as the weaknesses resulting from poor diets and, in the worst times, malnutrition and near starvation. It is a grim story and one that is better known than most such tales because of the famous Jarrow March of 1936, which is the central focus of Ellen Wilkinson's book. Protest marches to the nation's capital and centre of political power were by no means new, with antecedents going back to the times of the Tolpuddle Martyrs, and the Chartist marches of the 1840s. In 1932, with unemployment rising to nearly 3 million, a National Hunger March had been organised by the National Unemployed Workers Union, impelled to act by the failure of a now truncated and enfeebled Labour Party to do so on their behalf: Ramsay Macdonald, former Labour Prime Minister and now PM of the National Government coalition, refused to receive their petitions. These failures would arouse my mother's ire, as well as angering Nye Bevan, another of my mother's heroes. But it was the long trek from Jarrow to London by a ragged but determined and representative band of some two hundred local shipyard workers that both caught the national imagination and roused the pride of all workers everywhere. A feature of the March was the ways in which working class and other sympathisers would turn out in many towns along the way to provide support, sustenance, and somewhere to sleep, a hymn to working class solidarity. The Marchers actually passed through Harrogate on 10th October 1936 and were addressed there by Ellen Wilkinson. Since Harrogate was only some 7 miles from Allerton, I scoured my parents' diaries in the hope of finding some reference to this, but could find nothing and think that they may have been distracted by life-changing developments at that time on the Mowbray estate. Apparently, the Marchers got a warm welcome in this overwhelmingly Conservative town: Stuart Maconie, who has written entertainingly of retracing (in 2016) the entire route from Jarrow to London, tells that a 1936 Marcher recorded that 'they were shedding buckets of tears in their fur coats, I can tell you, down in Harrogate'.

My grandfather's colliery and the miners and shipyard workers of Wallsend were hit just as hard as the workers of Jarrow, including a great many who had served and often died for their country in the First World War. His family knew what it was to go hungry, and the petty humiliations attendant on the hated 'means test' applied to those seeking what little social relief was available. Mining families struggled to feed their children, and lived from hand to mouth, often on charity. Mum recalled how she and her favourite sister Sadie, mere schoolgirls, and half-starved, tagged on to the end of a queue for a soup kitchen set up by a local Anglican church. Joseph Simpson appeared out of the blue, dragged them away and threatened dire punishment should they ever do such a thing again: for him, they were risking their souls to satisfy their stomachs. A Catholic God would provide. He never did, Mum typically snorted, he was too busy attending to the prayers of the faithful wanting a better world after this one. In any case, she thought that her father was angered less by the religious issue than by his inability to feed his own children. This attachment to Mother Church would pay off, though, for one of the ways in which she looked after her own was by ensuring that girls from respectable Catholic working-class families would be put in touch with the many aristocratic members of the church who required domestic servants, so creating a mutually beneficial employment network. According to the 1931 Census, a million women worked in domestic service; and it was in 1931 that my mother, at the age of 17, travelled all the way from urban Tyneside to the Mowbray estate in Yorkshire, where she would meet and marry my father, combining in one family both the urban and rural strands of the British working class.

Josephine (or Josie as she was always known), the kitchen maid from the Castle, and Martin, the farm labourer born on the aristocratic estate, were destined for each other, given their above average intelligence and shared political and social attitudes. But it was a tempestuous relationship because they both had strong personalities. Moreover, Lady Mowbray took an active interest in the social friendships and relationships of her staff, doubtless acting *in loco parentis*. She soon detected Dad's interest in her attractive new maid, for he constantly lingered at the back doors of the kitchen, seeking a few shared minutes. With Mum working a six-and-a-half-day week, and Dad an occasional weekend visitor, as he was working away from home, they could only meet formally on her half day off. Lady Mowbray warned her about the handsome young man who, said Her Ladyship, was known for whispering sweet nothings in *all* the maids' ears. Once, she forbade her charge from going to a village dance if Dad was going to be there: Dad went anyway, without asking permission from anyone. Their friendship developed and strengthened, but Dad records that 'our relationship was quite stormy as we parted for a short time more than once'. This was almost certainly down to Mum's fiery temper, something we children would often fall foul of later on. But with her, the sun usually quickly emerged from the clouds and Dad, knowing that he had met his soulmate, had the equable and calm temperament required to win over this proud, edgy, clever woman who had parachuted into his life. There was a slight hiccup. In 1933, with Lady Mowbray at last won over, they had travelled by Pullman train back to Hopper Street in Wallsend, to meet and get the approval of her stern but affectionate father, who in character she so much resembled. He stipulated only that they should wait for formal approval when she came of age; he wanted her to be sure she was doing the right thing. And so, on 1st December 1935, my mother's twenty-first birthday, she and Dad became engaged. The following Saturday they set out for York to buy an engagement ring. Dad was late meeting up, so that they missed the bus; Josie promptly struck him over the head with her umbrella. Once she had the prized gold ring (cost: £2 and 10 shillings, more than a week's wages), she kissed and made up. Though hardly a promising portent, this incident summed up their lifelong relationship pretty well.

*Martin and Josie are engaged to be married, Wallsend, 1935.*

Stormy relationships, though without much in the way of kissing and making up, now characterised the life of the Allerton estate. In

July 1936 the 24th baron died and was succeeded by his eldest son. Captain William Stourton, a choleric, authoritarian bully, who many thought more than a little unhinged, fell out instantly with his whole family and most of his staff and tenants. Dad records this: 'the new Lord chopped down some of his father's favourite trees, and sacked many men. His mother and sister had to leave what had been their home for many years. He closed the Catholic chapel (a social meeting point for the whole estate work-force) and closed the Priest's House. All the maids were dismissed (this of course included Josie)'. Dad describes how his Irish father, after some 28 years of service on the estate as gardener and farmworker, got peremptory notice early in 1937 to quit his job and house. The mediaeval powers enjoyed by the Mowbrays for centuries were still continuing on their oppressive way.

We will encounter Lord Mowbray and further appalling behaviour by the Premier Baron of England (and, laughably, local Justice of the Peace) in a later chapter. For the time being, the Minogue family were relatively unconcerned by the treatment meted out to them. Grandad Minogue, experienced and popular locally, quickly got another job and house. Mum, looking ahead to marriage, was glad to be free from the increasingly intolerable constraints of personal service. She and Dad duly married, at the Catholic Church of Our Lady and St. Columba in Wallsend, on Easter Monday, 29th March 1937. Mum's brother Jimmy, a handsome, fierce-looking soldier in a Scottish regiment, the Gordon Highlanders, was best man; the bridesmaid was Molly, dark, pretty, early teenage daughter of Mum's eldest sister, Mary. They celebrated with beer and sandwiches in the small dark house in Hopper Street, and

*Wedding of Martin and Josie at Wallsend, Easter 1937.*

like true Geordies, danced and sang into the wee. small hours. After the wedding, Dad and Mum had three shillings and sixpence between them, wages of 34 shillings a week, and a hire purchase debt of £50 for their furniture, to be paid off at 5 shillings a week (the 'instalment plan' becoming increasingly popular at this time), so it would take four years to pay off. They were, to coin a phrase, poor but happy. Another happy chance was that their first house was the other half of the cottage now inhabited by Grandad and Granny, known as Halfway House because it was half way between Knaresborough and the outlying village of Goldsborough. The stage was now set for my arrival.

# Chapter Three

## First Footsteps

*The bird sings sweetest where it was born* Gaelic proverb

Perhaps the first question you ask yourself as you look back on your own life is: what do I first remember? This is by no means a straightforward question, because our direct memories are so overlaid by the variety of accounts, from parents, grandparents, aunts and uncles, brothers and sisters, cousins, that tell us who we were and what befell us in our earlier years, and even thereafter. Separating our own memories from these second-hand ones isn't easy, and the mix of accounts coalesces into a family history we may lay claim to, but can never be entirely confident about. So I am full of admiration for those many writers of autobiography who seem to be blessed with instant and voluminous recall. Vladimir Nabokov, in *Speak, Memory,* maintains that he can remember the very hour of his birth, and *even before that.* My memory is absolutely blank on this score. It isn't even established beyond a reasonable doubt just when exactly I did arrive. My mother's recollections of my past, and of much else besides, are sometimes unreliable as to the facts, while by my father's own account he spent much of the crucial 48-hour period from $22^{nd}$-$23^{rd}$ December 1937 tending to the beasts of the field on the farm where he worked as a labourer. He himself only received confirmation of my eventual arrival by word of mouth from his Irish father, whose laconic, twinkling comment to Dad was "sure now, they didn't say anything on the news about Martin being born".

It turned out that for some time there had been considerable doubt whether I had survived early pregnancy, when Mum was deemed to have had a miscarriage. But when she was suddenly taken ill again and rushed to hospital it was discovered that I was still present and correct. My actual birth was some 4 weeks premature. For a short time, it was again thought that I would not survive, and the priest was summoned to Mum's bedside, in case we might require the final rites (without which you would be consigned to Limbo: my mother's expression when telling this story made clear that Limbo was not a place in which you would want to find yourself). This was all by Mum's account. Until well into my adult years I assumed that this included me, that the prospect of being launched into eternity after so short a stay had given me a second wind, and inspired my first rejection of the claims of mother Church. I would later learn that the final rites cannot be administered to children below the age of seven: another case of my mother never letting a good story be spoiled by inconvenient facts. There is, however, some speculation that I might have hastily been christened on the spot, my mother choosing my father's name for me because she could not immediately think of any other.

At this point my parents embarked on a sort of rural progress around bits of Yorkshire where we never stayed for very long before moving on. This was often down to my mother's restlessness and her resolute unwillingness to tolerate the more demeaning aspects of owner-worker relationships under the tied farm cottage system. But it was also due in part to my father's determination to get the best wages he could: on a wage of some 35 shillings a week, in 1938, money was very tight, and an increase of only 5 shillings very desirable: after all, it would meet the hire purchase debt payment for the few sticks of furniture bought when they married . The average worker's wage at this time was about £3 a week, or 60 shillings, which indicates how far below the norm were farm workers. Trying to improve this position must have been a strong motivation, despite the great difficulties moving around with a sickly baby.

In March 1939, we moved away from our cottage next door to Granny and Grandad in the Vale of York, to a farm at Badsworth, near Pontefract, on the edge of the South Yorkshire coalfields, for a wage of 40 shillings a week and 3 days holiday a year (quite a perk, as there was no holiday entitlement for farm workers at this point, unlike most urban workers). Perhaps it reminded Mum too much of the gloomier aspects of her native urban Tyneside life, or perhaps she was unsettled by the early death, on 23rd March 1940, of her coal miner father, Joseph, someone who did see me at the age of one but of whom, unhappily, I have no recollection. Mum told Dad what he must do, i.e., obtain a job nearer home territory in Nidderdale and Wharfedale. On his first venture, at the end of the day's work, he cycled some thirty miles in the wartime blackout to seek a job, got lost several times, found the job had gone anyway, and cycled back to arrive at 6am just in time to feed the cows. Then later in 1940 he obtained a job in Poole-in-

Wharfedale, but Mum immediately fell out with the farmer, who wanted her to do his housework for no extra income: she had not, she declared, not a little proudly, left aristocratic service as a lady's maid to become a farm servant. Off we went again, after only a couple of weeks, taking our much prized, not yet fully paid for furniture with us on a horse-drawn open farm wagon to Nun Appleton, where Dad had landed a job as horseman on the estate of Sir Benjamin Dawson, near to Appleton Roebuck, and again close to the comfortingly familiar city of York.

*Me aged about 2 or 3, with Dad and one of the farm horses.*

Since I was barely two and a half years old at this point, my memories are necessarily a bit dim. But I do remember with awful clarity the tremendous shock I received at the unheralded appearance of a sister, Maureen. I believe my parents did make some attempt to communicate what was in store, but I was incapable of the feat of imagination needed to translate their puzzling hints and coy smiles. After all, I rarely had met any other children of any kind, because of our isolation on rural Yorkshire farms. My parents, acting no doubt from the best of intentions, packed me off at the eleventh hour to Auntie Sadie, in Wallsend-on Tyne. I was thrilled to bits. To start with it meant my very first journey on a train, and not just any old train, but the fabled *Flying Scotsman.* This was in early 1941, and the train was stuffed to the roof with soldiers, sailors and airmen going home on leave. People were packed shoulder to shoulder in every compartment and corridor. My father somehow got into a compartment, hoisted me high in the air, and packed me neatly into the netting luggage rack, with my head on a sailor's navy-blue kitbag. It was rather like being in a hammock, except that hammocks rarely move along at 100 miles per hour. But I still recall the strangeness and the excitement, the overwhelming air of urgency and expectation as the majestic express cleaved through the dark night air. I was exactly three years old, and

*Mum with me and baby sister Maureen 1941.*

this was an unforgettable birthday present. The revered old train, once famously derailed by striking Geordie miners in the 1920s, has now retired to the National Railway Museum in York.

I remember nothing of our arrival and my father's immediate departure, nor of my first of many stays in Geordieland. What I do recall is the shattering homecoming when, on reaching the safe haven of home, a tiny, red-faced, crying object was wheeled in: my new sister, Maureen. I had a tremendous sense of grievance. No-one had consulted me on the question of another child in the family. I didn't want one, and said so in plain English. I think I knew at once that the good times were over, an impression reinforced by the sickening behaviour of my parents, cooing and sighing over the pram, while ignoring me, and making frequent references to the infant's resemblances to both the Minogue

*The granary steps from which Maureen and I jumped when we were small children.*

and Simpson families. "It doesn't look like *me*", I declared. Maureen was "it" for some time after this. I refused to credit her with any relationship to humanity, gender, or indeed my own family. I even tried to sell this unwanted object to the grinning postman. 'You can have her for sixpence' I told him. In truth, he could have had her for nothing as far as I was concerned. This was a genuinely traumatic event for me, in that I had been perfectly cocooned and secure, but came now to an awareness that I was neither the centre of my known universe, nor master of my own destiny. I had the clear presentiment that life, in all its varied and unpredictable incident, was already getting out of control.

But I wasn't one to give in easily: if Maureen was not a marketable commodity, I'd have to get rid of her by other means. A feature of the farm architecture was a long flight of stone steps—fifteen in all—leading to the granary where the seed corn and apples were stored. At the tender age of two, my little sister had a deep and innocent trust in me. So I led her to the topmost step, held fast to her dimpled little hand, and said that we should jump off when I said 'jump'. And that's exactly what we did. Down we bounced, gently at first, then with gathering momentum. On the twelfth bounce, my chin made contact with a hard stone rim, and I lost (temporarily) any further interest in the proceedings. Maureen, smaller, rounder and bouncier, continued to the bottom, unscathed, only then to meet an inconvenient brick head on. We lay there twitching gently, both with profusely bleeding chins. We still carry small identical scars on our chins, mementos of the day my sister's innocent trustfulness died. Thereafter it was open war, and I never really stood a chance. After sundry skirmishes, I reached my Waterloo in early 1945 when I was seven and my sister only four. One night, as we sat in our pyjamas on the springy bed in our parents' bedroom, I pinched her rag doll and wouldn't give it up. Mum didn't have much in the way of make-up on her dresser: a lipstick, a powder compact, and a jar of cold cream saw her through her few social occasions. But the cold cream came in a jar constructed of thick brown glass, a solid and heavy object. Infuriated, my sister took the jar and threw it at me from quite close range, hitting me smack on the temple. I was carried off to hospital for a fortnight, thoroughly concussed. Both somewhat shocked, and after the reading of a less than motherly riot act, we declared a truce. Nearly eight decades on, we have long been the best of friends.

I carry many bodily scars, not exclusively the result of sisterly attentions, but of an early passion for exploration of the unknown. For me, the unknown had very precise boundaries at this early age. They were set by the Nun Appleton estate, the centre of which was a stretch of parkland with a neat wooden white painted fence running around it. On the far edge, a narrow tarmac lane entered the park from the direction of the village of Bolton Percy, with the town of Tadcaster (where in 1941 my sister had been christened at the local Roman Catholic church) and the city of York some miles beyond that. A pretty lodge guarded the entrance, inhabited by the jovial Hoyle family, and several lodgers who were conscientious objectors working on the estate. The road circled round into a hollow at the end of the park where stood Nun Appleton Hall, once famously the country seat of Cromwell's leading general during the 17$^{th}$ century Civil War, Sir Thomas Fairfax, who after the regicide of Charles1 'spent the rest of the war out of politics raising horses and collecting books at his house Nun Appleton' writes Diana Purkiss in her history of the English civil war. The poet Andrew Marvell, who resided there for a time as tutor to Fairfax's daughter, Mary, immortalised the fine gardens and riverside meadows there in his poems *Upon Appleton House*, and *The Garden*: since I wandered these sylvan settings as a child, I like now to fancy that I trod in the poet's footsteps, living 'a green thought in a green shade'. Some two centuries later the estate was bought by the Milner family, from the Leeds merchant class, then in the 1920s was sold to Sir Benjamin Dawson, scion of a Bradford mill-owning family, and my father's new employer.

When I recently returned to Home Farm (ignoring the efforts by the present owner, a former chairman of Samuel Smith's Breweries of Tadcaster, to keep members of the public at bay by several threatening notices) I had that experience remarked on in most memoirs; it appeared to have shrunk almost to nothing. My memory replays a huge, rather frightening place with an inexhaustible series of buildings and passageways, small dark corners and vast open spaces, all fronted by a large, menacing lake (a lake described in more alluring terms by Marvell). I suppose that comes partly from being about thirty inches high: things are bound to look big. A farm, more than almost anywhere else is, for a child, a paradise to be endlessly explored, but a paradise full of pitfalls. The perils came in three shapes: animal, mechanical and architectural (there was also the farm manager, George Mallinson, an unsmiling and taciturn man, always accompanied by his dog Rap, who wore a similarly unsmiling and taciturn look).

My closest animal encounter was with a runaway Scottish terrier which belonged to Ted Fish, our next-door neighbour, someone I already shrank from because he had a most disconcerting wall-eye which made him seem to look off at a tangent while talking to you. There were three farm cottages, including ours, built in a terrace along one side of the farm buildings. They had small gardens, and the communal lake, at the front. The back doors let out into a narrow passage which traversed the whole length of the terraced cottages. On its other side, it was bounded by an iron railing which made up one side of the rather smelly fold-yard, an internal fenced and roofed square in which cattle were kept and fed during the winter months. I often squatted happily in this ginnel for hours, oblivious to the redolent smells of cooking and cow-clap which assailed me from different angles. On this occasion, my childish daydreaming was disturbed by what used to be described as a hue and cry. The commotion was so loud as to have apparently rendered insane its object, Ted Fish's Scotty, which was running helter-skelter, frothing prodigiously at the mouth. He was, I instantly perceived, on a collision course with me. Scotty leapt, and I did an undignified backward tumble, throwing up a weak arm in self-defence. Scotty, maddened further by even this feeble resistance, bit my arm hard. I was only slightly less wounded by the inevitable injection that duly followed. I have no recollection of the doctor: he was probably a vet.

Naturally, Maureen just had to go one better than a dog. She placed herself in the path of a berserk cow. You may think that cows are dull, placid creatures, given to nothing more threatening than a moody swish of the tail, a quiet, plaintive moo. In my experience that's all pure pretence. Anyone who has ever entered a field full of cows will have noticed that they instantly get together, look at each other meaningfully, then collectively begin to follow you in a quite sinister way. If you stop, they stop. When you start again, walking a bit more quickly, they walk a bit more quickly too. Very soon you find yourself running flat out, bellowing mindlessly, followed by a herd of galloping cows, also bellowing mindlessly. It may have surprised Dad and Ted Fish when this cow suddenly ran amok, but it didn't surprise me. I can safely say it surprised Maureen, over whose prostrate body the cow lumbered. No one shot the cow afterwards, though they did for the unfortunate Scotty. I still wonder at the difference in response. Perhaps mad cows were rare in those more fortunate days, or perhaps a live cow was simply more valuable than a live dog. I noticed recently that each year a surprisingly large number of people in England are killed by cows: no surprise to me or to Maureen, who remains terrified of cows to this day.

Then there were the horses. I admire the elegant way some people sit on a horse, and I'm very happy for them to do so. Dad had been appointed as a skilled horseman on the Nun Appleton estate, under Head Horseman Dick Thirkill. In the 1930s and early 1940s estate farms still employed all sorts of specialised labour: horsemen, cowmen, shepherds, woodmen, waggoners, gardeners, even joiners and bricklayers. The horsemen eventually would turn into tractor drivers and the horses would disappear, but mechanisation was slow to establish itself, especially on relatively small farms, until after the war: in 1939 heavy horses outnumbered tractors by 30 to 1, and according to Ronald Blythe's *Akenfield,* the horsemen were always the 'big men' on the farm. Back then, Dad would plough with two huge Suffolk Punches, splendid glossy backed creatures with proud necks, thick manes, and enormous feet clad in iron. These shod hooves would have crushed any child who might have inadvertently got in their way. When I was four years old I was allowed, if Dad was working near to the house, to take him his mid-morning 'drinkings': a billy-can of hot sweet yellow tea, and a piece of caraway seed cake, or jam tarts. Mum would make up this basket and point me in Dad's general direction. I was all too easily distracted. I might arrive with a billy-can of cold tea, having progressed via butterfly chases, raids on hazel nut trees, and prolonged investigations of the denizens of watery ditches. I would sometimes turn up with the billy-can empty, having spilled the contents; there were occasions when, overtaken by a consuming hunger, I would duly consume the cake or tarts *en route*. Yet I never ever remember Dad scolding me. Farm work is often a solitary task, and I think he was glad to see my shining little face and enjoy my piping company for a while. We would sit companionably on a tussock; away from Mum's apron–strings I felt grown up and important, admitted to the wider and mysterious world of man's work. On the days when I arrived with everything intact Dad would crumble a piece of cake for me, tip some hot tea into the billy-can top and blow on it so that it would not burn my tender young mouth. The horses would graze quietly in the hedgerow, their harnesses creaking and clinking gently as they moved. I suspect that I was happier at four than at any time before or since. Sometimes I would stay with him as he worked, rooting about in the rich black-brown furrows of earth turned by the bright steel ploughshare, getting satisfactorily dirty and cooking gently in what I only ever remember the weather to be, hot sun beating down from a cloudless blue sky. At midday, Dad would unhitch the horses from the plough and head for home and dinner (in those days Yorkshire folk didn't do lunch). This was the nasty bit, for he would lift me up and set me on the back of one of the great shires. I was always petrified. A shire horse's back is a vast, flat expanse of smooth, slippery hide. My legs were much too short to get any kind of grip, my fingers not strong enough to keep a purchase in the flowing mane. Meanwhile, the whole platform would move about in all directions, bumping me upwards, downwards and sideways in a most disconcerting way. When I began to slide, there was simply no stopping until I hit the ground, occasionally head first. My father's pet theory was that this treatment did much to account for my later educational successes.

My relationship with machines was scarcely less fraught than that with animals. I was fascinated by things mechanical as are all small boys, but unlike most small boys I never really came to terms with them. The only mechanical object I was ever really attached to, and that literally, was an electrified fence. The fence surrounded a field of ripening corn and sent out regular electrical impulses to administer shock treatment to any animals that might try to invade the corn field. Cows, for instance. But as we have seen, cows are cunning creatures who quickly learned to avoid the fence, whereas I unthinkingly became addicted to the shocks. I can recall holding on to the fence for minutes at a time, jerking occasionally; perhaps another clue to later educational success.

Another mechanical object that plagued my childish life was a bicycle, my first two-wheeler. My initial pride in this possession was such that I insisted it had a good night's sleep in my bed, and would awake each morning in a tangle of sheets and sprockets. But to my mortification, I just could not get the hang of riding the thing. When I first went to school, which was at the end of a one-mile long lane, I would solemnly walk the full distance, wheeling my bike alongside. If anyone met me on the road, (the postman, or farmworkers), I would hastily lift up the bike and carry it. When questioned about this curious behaviour, I would explain "My bike's tired". At some point I must have triumphantly learned to ride it, but the moment has vanished from memory.

I had begun school quite early, at four and a half years old. No doubt Mum was glad to get some peace, while the problem of preventing my premature demise was transferred to other hands for at least part of the day. I think she also hoped I would have some of the rough edges knocked off me, that in the most fundamental sense my behaviour would be civilised by contact with other children. But she also feared that I might not find it easy to adapt to a whole village-load of children, considering my difficulty in adapting to a single girl. She need not have worried on any of these counts. I took to school—indeed to the whole educational system—like a duck to water. I swam happily about in my first little ponds of knowledge, at least, in some parts of the pond, for I had by the age of five established what would be the dominant educational pattern in my life, graphically displayed in my very first school report:

~

| | |
|---|---|
| English | 10/10 |
| Spelling | 10/10 |
| Physical Education | 10/10 |
| Arithmetic | 1/10 |

~

It was early established that the world of numbers, of maths and physics and chemistry and engineering was not for me; the world of the imagination, of poetry, of literature and history was a different matter altogether. That first report has other pointers to the habits I would develop, (or fall victim to) later in life. For example, *Position in Class:1,* a proud statistic only slightly tarnished by the additional information: *Number in Class:3*. As I rose up the system and through a variety of schools (as you'll see, my parents remained pretty peripatetic) the 'numbers in class' steadily increased, but I was usually to be found at the top of the mark lists, except of course in subjects which depended on scientific understanding, or substituted numbers for words. C. P. Snow would at the end of the 1950s write a whole book about this problem, based on his experiences in those Cambridge colleges which were stuffed full of people like me, brilliantly knowledgeable in some areas of our culture, practically illiterate in others. One day I would join them, but for now that was far off, and would have seemed as remote a possibility to my labouring class parents as landing a man on the moon then also seemed to be.

They were probably more concerned about the remaining statistic to be found in that first school report:

~

| | |
|---|---|
| Possible attendances | 180 |
| Absences | 35 |
| Late attendances | 123 |

~

That last, mind-boggling figure conceals a veritable rake's progress. The problem was this long, winding lane, the kind G. K. Chesterton must have had in mind in his poem *'The Rolling English Road'.* After half a mile or so my legs and my patience were invariably exhausted, especially if I happened to be carrying my tired bicycle as well, along with the irritating gas mask box we were supposed to carry at all times, though I rarely did. Posted along the route were insidious attractions: Ma Wright, for example (she was never known as anything else), the exceedingly ample wife of the cowman, Jack Wright, and famed for her bakery. A warm, motherly woman, she wooed me from my prospective studies with brown scones, thick with yellow butter and rich red jam. She reputedly baked a tasty rook pie but I'm glad to say this was a treat never offered to me. Joan Coulthard, the daughter of Sir Benjamin Dawson's chauffeur David Arrand, tells that Ma Wright once fell heavily through a hedge while brambling and had to be extricated by two grinning farm lads: roaring with laughter she cried: "My word, this licks hen racing!", a story which reminded me of my Granny Minogue's fabled hen racing exploits. It was in the 1920s still a country custom on feast days to release a hen which would be pursued by the women of the village, the hen being the prize for whoever caught it. Sharp elbows and determination were required, and Granny Minogue evidently had both.

If Ma Wright missed me, a neighbour further along the way didn't. I don't recall her name, but she was a middle-aged spinster with no family of her own. A kindly woman, her speciality was home-made ginger biscuits which she kept for me, hot at the oven door, on Tuesdays and Fridays. She and Ma Wright did their best between them seriously to limit my early education and were mainly responsible, with my enthusiastic cooperation, for those 123 late attendances. I also made my own unique contribution to 'Absences' when, one day, seduced by the pleasures of exploring the nearby woods, I spent the whole day in them and reported home in mid-afternoon, while school was still in full swing. I couldn't understand how Mum divined what I had been up to. It may have had something to do with the fact that I had been caught short at some point and soiled my short trousers, which I was carrying nonchalantly over one shoulder. 'A cow kicked me' I explained when questioned. I might add here that the woods were in fact a well-known place, not a likely source of Grimm-like perils. This was because at weekends, as a family, we would repair there to gather wood from fallen trees as fuel for our domestic fires: this was a hangover from the old common rights long enjoyed by rural labouring people, and much reduced by enclosures and other forms of property exclusion. Diane Purkiss, writing about 17th century food riots 'occasioned in part by the loss of common and woodland rights' is 'reminded of farm labourers even in the 1930s who trawled the wood for waste wood for their domestic fire grates'. Well, we were still claiming this ancient right in the 1940s, every Sunday morning, the sticks stacked on Maureen's pram.

I can't recall how I was received at school on the many occasions that I turned up late, with or without trousers. Perhaps my teachers became resigned to my habit of arriving in mid-morning. I don't recall ever being scolded or punished. Indeed, my memories of this first school are rather dim, perhaps because it was only one of four primary schools I attended, or occasionally looked in on, in my first five years of schooling. But I do remember that my first teacher had the ideal name for a teacher of infants: Miss Love. I also remember being teased by the bigger boys who sent me, glowing with innocent helpfulness, to the little village shop and post office across from the school playground. "A pint of pigeon's milk, Miss Silversides," I would warble. Miss Silversides would peer over her spectacles at me, well below the top of the counter. "Go on with you, young Martin". "Yes, honestly, Miss Silversides", I would plead, anxious to acquit myself well with the bigger boys, "and a glass hammer as well, Miss Silversides".

*Me at 4½, the age I went to school.*

# Chapter Four

## A Child's War

*Please, Mr Hitler, please drop a bomb on our school!*
Billy, schoolboy in John Boorman's 1987 film *Hope and Glory*

While I was pursuing these minor skirmishes, a larger conflict was raging around me and in some cases above me. World War II scarcely touched me directly and brought only novelty and excitement in its wake. It stirred up our sleepy little rural community no end. Britain, partly dependent on imported food (some 70% of cheese and sugar, 80% of fruit, 90% of cereals and fats and 50% of meat), strove to increase farm production. According to Gardiner's study of wartime Britain in 1939-45, this brought many changes on the farms, and an increase in food production of 91% by 1944. One happy consequence was that farm labour was designated a reserved occupation, so

*Walking in our favourite woods, Dad in his Home Guard uniform.*

Dad didn't have to go to war, which was good news for his family, and an extraordinary piece of luck for our fighting forces, if rather less fortunate for the Home Guard. As every watcher of *Dad's Army* knows, the Home Guard was Britain's reserve army, the one which would throw the German Panzer divisions back into the sea when they crossed the Channel.

When family or friends a generation younger than I am watch *Dad's Army*, they weep with laughter and admire the rich comic invention of the man who created the series, Jimmy Perry. I have tried to explain to them that none of it is invented. The whole thing, in its extravagant comic opera, comes under the heading of factual reporting. The real Home Guard was just as funny as the screen version. I know, because I saw it in action (if that is the right phrase) and even at the age of five I could see that a splendid farce was being played out. The Appleton Roebuck Unit was initially the LDV or Local Defence Volunteers, a precursor of the later Home Guard, (also known affectionately as Look, Duck and Vanish). It was a motley collection of farm workers like Dad, several other reservists, and assorted middle-aged men too old for active service. The commanding officer was, naturally, the senior social member of our community, Dad's boss, Sir Benjamin Dawson, always known behind his back as 'Benny'. Though the owner of the fine Appleton Hall with its significant historical connections, Sir Benjamin, knighted in 1929 (essentially for political services to the Conservative Party in Bradford) wasn't a real local squire with all that might have brought along with it in terms of local roots and custom; he was an incomer, son of a mill owner who had made money from the Bradford sweatshops known as textile mills, in this case the Joseph Dawson Cashmere Works. But in Appleton Roebuck, the only thing that mattered was that Benny was both the CO *and* the principal employer. If he said jump, which he much liked to do, people jumped, usually to attention. Mind you, even coming to attention took the Appleton unit approximately five minutes. Dad records in his diary 'When it first started there were only a few rifles so some of us had to drill with broomsticks. Sir B Dawson was made the commander though he knew nothing about military matters and he also had his uniform made out of special material because ours was too rough for him: they were also very poor fits....one man used to chop sticks with his bayonet.' Guard duties were two nights a week, with a parade on Sundays. He records also that they held local manoeuvres (I can remember watching these once, with Dad and others trying to move a field gun and getting it and its camouflage snagged up in an uncooperative tree, and I recall the firing of white lines of dummy tracer bullets, which was very exciting). Dad tells that the Drill Sergeant, a farmworker who had been a regular Army sergeant, said to them "That's the second time I've drilled turnips this week," and that on one parade when Sir Benjamin mistakenly gave the order 'left turn' the men ignored him and turned right, as they knew perfectly well in which direction they should be headed. Dad's diary also records that when once they made a family visit to York and we sat next to two soldiers in a café, I said to them proudly, and much to their amusement "My Daddy is a REAL soldier, he's in the Home Guard." Later, in 1944, he comments that 'we had to take the Home Guard more seriously, and Sir Benjamin lost his position and was very put out'. All this is probably a bit unfair to poor Sir Benjamin, who after all took on a significant administrative and financial burden in running the Appleton Unit, and had to make his own sacrifices in giving up a large part of his beautiful home as a Maternity Hospital.

Generally, the local Home Guard kept a low profile, and Dad had very little to do. But every so often he had to undertake a guard duty at Appleton House, their CO's headquarters and an official Observation Point. One night came when, reporting for duty, Dad and Ted Fish were electrified to hear that there were German aircraft in the area, and that they should keep a sharp look-out for German paratroops. German paratroops were the last thing Dad and Ted were inclined to look out for, and they spent a few nervous hours peering anxiously into the night skies. Happily, the guard duty ended without incident. Dad cycled home quietly down the dark track to Home Farm. As he drew level with a small spinney, a sharp report suddenly cracked the night silence. Dad immediately fell off his bike, then gathered himself up and ran the remaining 200 yards to the safety of the farmyard. He fell into the house with a great shout of "Josie! Josie!" My mother rushed downstairs in her nightdress. Dad was white-faced and shaking. "Ah've been shot, Ah've been shot," he gasped "German paratroopers". Mum was transfixed but kept her head and bolted both front and back doors. Dad was groaning piteously, stretched out now on the sofa. "Where is it then, where have you been shot?" demanded Mum. "It's ...it's ...er... Ah'm not right sure." said Dad, feeling his ribs feebly. Mum stripped off his clothes: no wound met her eyes, no trace of blood, though there was a small bruise on Dad's hip. Dad stopped groaning and began to look sheepish. Only when they crept out suspiciously in the light of day was the full truth revealed: Dad's back tyre had burst. The bruise sustained in falling off his bike was the nearest Dad got to a war wound: the bruise to his military reputation was rather harder to bear.

The Home Guard was a home-grown, homespun affair, and distinctly unmilitary. It was difficult to make any connection between this and the real World War. But the war touched our lives in myriad ways, nonetheless. Appleton Roebuck village lay uncomfortably near to RAF Church Fenton, the base for a fighter squadron that provided defensive protection against enemy aircraft flying in over the East coast, while Bomber Command Groups were also on the fringes of York, notably at Pocklington and Fulford. York became a specific Luftwaffe target in the so called Baedeker raids of late April 1942, but air raids on Leeds and Sheffield also had a local impact. Dad records that coming back from village dances late at night they often saw returning German bombers overhead, and once saw a plane crash while taking off from one of the local air stations. There is no doubt that the night raids made local people feel uneasy as they hunched behind blacked-out windows, and listened to occasional distant explosions from the nearby city, while searchlights (at that tender age pronounced by me to be 'lurchsights') could be seen flickering across the sky. We could also hear the scream of fighter engines as the Spitfires scrambled from Church Fenton to meet incoming bombers over the North Sea coast. As Mum and Dad anxiously searched the sky from a bedroom window I would hang out of the window, craning to see the planes, and in my childish excitement cried out "I like German bombers" and "PLEASE drop a bomb on us!" Several decades later I would absolutely recognise the similar plea of the urban schoolboy in John Boorman's autobiographical film *Hope and Glory,* for Hitler please to drop a bomb on his school.

We were relatively immune from the perils that urban families nightly encountered but we had our own small incidents, discounting Dad's burst tyre. Just outside the farm gate, alongside the park road, stood a large metal windmill, which pumped water to a galvanised iron tank, and so supplied the various animal inhabitants of the park with their drinking water. One night in 1942, we were taking our usual after-dinner walk. At this stage, my sister Maureen qualified for push-chair treatment, while I spent most of the walk pestering Dad to carry me on his shoulders, something I loved. Suddenly, we were startled by several loud bangs; then a strange drumming noise made itself heard, rapidly growing in volume. At the same time, the ground under our feet began to shudder. Dad cried out "the horses, they're running wild". And they were, they streaked out of the night, right past us, eyes staring and manes flowing. They brought up short at the gate, milled about, then pounded off down the line of the fence and back into the blackness. We had begun to run too, Maureen jostled half out of the pushchair, me grabbing Dad's hair to hold on as I bounced around on his shoulders, all of us scared out of our wits. We were made more so by a terrible groaning, rending sound from the windmill. We had barely got past it when it crashed to the ground, right where we had just scurried pell-mell. It was thought later that a German bomber had got into difficulties and had been forced to jettison its bombs, which had landed somewhere nearby, frightening the horses and bringing down the windmill. It was a narrow escape from what could easily have been death or injury.

Our quiet backwater was certainly livening up, from everyone's point of view. Our social isolation was breached by several varieties of outsider, or what in other parts of the country are called incomers. The first category was 'war workers': land girls, and conscientious objectors, always known as 'conchies'. Both were viewed with some suspicion by our conservative little community. The land girls, providing additional voluntary labour on the farms (some 80,000 were eventually recruited nationally), included at least three local women, but also some 'town' girls. The land girls didn't get much help from me. I used to wait to open the farm gate at Home Farm for Sir Benjamin when he turned up in his 2-seater Rolls Royce, known as the White Knight. "Morning young Martin" Benny would say as I opened the gate for his gleaming car; "mornin', Sir Benjamin Dawsonum," I would say brightly back, "if you want to know where them land girls are, they're lakin' in't barn". Sir Benjamin would make off, looking angry, while I would retire to a safe distance with the threepenny bit he used to give me. The poor land

*Sir Benjamin Dawson's 'White Knight' Rolls Royce.*

girls never understood how Sir Benjamin so often caught them having an illicit smoking break.

The land girls were soon well enough accepted locally, some being local girls anyway, but life was no easier for conscientious objectors in Appleton Roebuck than it was elsewhere. In the early stages of the war, many farmers throughout the country refused to employ them: initially more than 2,000 who had been instructed by tribunals to find work on the land could not do so. But the imperatives of increased food production and reduced labour supply meant that by 1941 more than 8,000 were working in agriculture, mostly on private farms, and were recognised as hard and willing workers. The Appleton Estate had ten such men, received locally with reluctance and some hostility. Why should *they* get out of the fighting, was the general feeling, when our lads *have* to go and fight; no apparent recognition of the fact that these 'conchies' were contributing just as much to the war effort as farmers and farm workers designated, like my Dad, as having reserved occupations. Of course, some local sons did go to war. Dad mentions that Mr Raper, two of whose daughters were land girls, had a son, Sgt Pilot Geoffrey Raper, who had flown from a local station, RAF Dishforth, in May 1940, was shot down over Hanover in 1942, and became a prisoner of war. Ironically, his father, Oliver Raper, was for a time put in charge of the prisoners of war working at Appleton. Perhaps it was not surprising that, as Dad puts it in an understated way, 'some of the other men were not very nice to the conscientious objectors'.

Many of these outsiders might have suffered a permanent quarantine had it not been for Mum and Dad and a very small handful of like-minded people. My parents were remarkably tolerant, given their social background and lack of formal education. They always treated people as they found them, without preconceptions or evident prejudice, their attitudes formed too by their socialist politics. Indeed, they positively welcomed the influx of life into the narrow social system of the village and the farm estate. My mother was herself an immigrant in these terms, a town girl by up-bringing, and had already experienced how hurtful to outsiders rural narrow-mindedness could be. Dad, for his part, found in the men who had made a clear moral and principled stand about the war, people who were as passionate about politics as he was himself. So all strangers were welcomed into our house, and rarely a night went by without a visitor or two to share a smoke, a cup of tea, and a good old-fashioned barney about life, death, and politics. I learned the pleasures of free and open argument literally at my father's knee, though as the words grew hot and the tea cold, I would usually end up asleep on my mother's lap.

*The Appleton Estate Land Girls, including Auntie Sheila, third from right.*

Some firm family friendships were forged during these war years. One of the land girls, Sheila, became Maureen's godmother, and remained (to us children, Auntie Sheila) a close family friend for life. Mum and Dad would go to her wedding in Leeds to George Tann, an airman. Sheila and George adopted Chris, the only child of her sister, killed in one of the bombings of Leeds, a reminder that living in the countryside was much safer than life in the towns. Another family friend made during the war was Kenneth Binks from Bradford, a conscientious objector who had eventually landed up at Nun Appleton, and lived together with other COs in Red Lodge, on the estate. Kenneth Binks never ceased to look us up each and every year after the war, cycling from Bradford to wherever we might be found. A convinced pacifist and stubborn libertarian, Kenneth had probably suffered as much hardship and indignity as the average combatant. He had stoutly refused to wear the King's uniform, had been imprisoned for a short spell for these offences, and had embarked on a hunger strike before the authorities could be persuaded to accept his good faith. He was short and spring-heeled, with ginger hair above bright blue eyes, and always struck people as remarkably fierce for a pacifist. When he was waxing passionate about some iniquity or other, which was pretty frequently, his blue eyes blazed, and his eyebrows shot rapidly up and down. He was, in these later postwar years, selling newspaper advertisement space. I think he was disappointed that all the youthful passion and sacrifice should have led only to this. "I sell nothing," he'd say, eyebrows working overtime, "just empty space", and he'd give a short, sad bark of a laugh. But he never lost his twinkling brightness of eye, and we were always warmed by his presence. I recall a faded sepia wartime photograph (now lost) which shows a tractor and trailer: on it sit the land girls, conchies, and farm workers, all mixed up together. They look happy, grinning amiably and striking comic poses for the camera as was so often the rather self-conscious response to being photographed in those days. You could see at once what a different place the village must have been with all these foreign bodies introduced to it.

Altogether different foreign bodies were the prisoners of war who supplied Sir Benjamin with a cheap source of labour. They were Germans and Italians mainly, but we had a wide assortment of nationalities and religions to contend with over the war years. Dad records that the Germans never gave any trouble, and that they were good workers. This could not be said of the other groups who worked on the farm. One very ragged and sorry group were evidently Muslims from Central Asia. They were displaced persons, and had been slave labourers for the Germans, first captured in the Soviet Union, then left behind in France and captured again in France by the advancing Allied forces. They kept disrupting the working routines by periodically throwing themselves to the floor in accordance with their prescribed religious practices. Dad's diary comments that this considerably annoyed Albert Marsh, who was in charge of them. But no-one ever tried to stop them, though it meant halting the binder, or muck-spreader, or potato-picking in mid operation. To our English country men, accustomed in line with sound Protestant ethics to keeping religious practices firmly outside working hours, this must have seemed to be carrying religion altogether too far.

There were no such problems with our most permanent group of POWs, who were Italians. Good Catholics all,

*Me aged about 3 in Dad's Home Guard cap.*

they knew that God's place was in Church and should not interfere with the serious business of making a profit, or a living. At the same time, they took the view that hard daily work was not something with which any self-respecting prisoner of war should be unduly burdened. Dad was in charge of them for a period after an accident he had, and his diary entry reads 'they were very funny but clever as well. As they used a distant wood for a toilet they would walk very slowly there and very slowly back, and as the first one arrived back, a second one would leave, and so it would go on. If it came even a drop of rain they would immediately down tools and cry "No work! No work! Geneva Convention!" The Italians, who came every day from a camp near Tadcaster, were never happier than when they could break off, have a smoke, and talk volubly about life in general and Italy in particular. Maureen and I were constantly at their heels, like little dogs who knew that our bright-eyed fidelity would be rewarded in the natural course of things. These particular Italians, desperately missing their own beloved children in many cases, were infinitely generous and affectionate to us. They would sit us on their knees and sing Italian lullabies, often, in the process, bringing themselves to tears. One of them, Rosario Pistritto, was a downed sergeant pilot (just like our own Geoffrey Raper), but an artist in civilian life, and drew splendid pencil portraits of Maureen (Morin) and also of my mother, signed in my mother's case 'in grateful remembrance of a friendship which

*The pencil portrait of Josie, by Sergeant Pilot Rosario Pistritto, Italian PoW.*

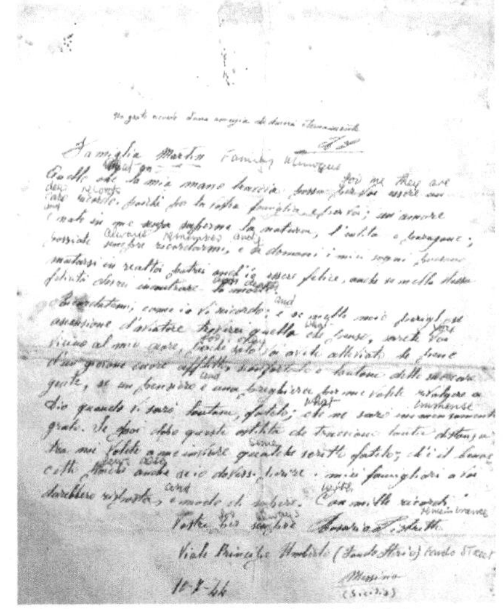

*The letter from Rosario on the back of the portrait, sent from Naples in 1944.*

will last eternalli: RIA Piloto Rosario Pistritto 10-7-44'; below he has written 'Con amore a chi Josie'. On the reverse side of the portrait of Mum, drawn we think from a photograph which we still have, is a letter in Italian, sent from Messina in Sicily in July 1944 (presumably these prisoners had been returned home after the fall of Mussolini in 1943 and the subsequent 'co-belligerence' agreement between the Allies and the Royal Italian forces in the South of Italy). The letter, articulate and in a fine script, is full of declarations of undying friendship and gratitude. Perhaps he was a little in love with her, I now think. At the very least here is evidence of how eagerly these warm, generous spirited Italians responded to the easy friendliness and human kindness offered by my parents. In turn, their own natural gregariousness disarmed and drew in all but the most hardened of xenophobes.

That there were some of these around is testified to by an entry in Dad's diary which reads: 'One woman who had lived on the estate a long time was known as Dr Goebbels or the Ministry of Information, as she told Benny everything she saw'. This eventually produced an enormous row. Both prisoners and farm workers were drawn up in front of Sir Benjamin and the prison camp commander, and lectured sternly on the evils of so called 'fraternisation'. The ostensible complaint was the exchanges of tea and cigarettes between locals and prisoners, but really what the authorities didn't like was the unpatriotic good fellowship that was being shown to the enemy. It was decreed that this must stop (much the same thing famously happened in the First World War trenches at Christmas in 1914, with orders firmly enforced in the following Christmas of 1915 to shoot at the enemy rather than acknowledge, dangerously, that they might actually be human beings.) Henceforth, the Italians were carefully restricted and their opportunities for contacts with local civilians kept to a minimum. My mother was unrepentant, and defiantly continued to stop and talk to particular friends like Rosario and smuggle a handful of Woodbines to him. Fortunately, no-one had thought to include children in the rules about fraternisation, so we still from time to time drank from our small beaker full of the warm South, and, I believe and hope, gave a little solace to men whose only fault lay in fighting on the losing side in a war most of them did not want, and for a dictatorial leader who most of them didn't support. Joan Coulthard, daughter of Sir Benjamin's chauffeur, gave me a copy of a letter from a German POW who worked at Appleton Hall after the war until 1948, thanking her parents for their 'goodness and kindness'. So here is more evidence of the ability of some local people to transcend the hatreds and conflicts of war.

The war turned up quite a different kind of refugee, and one almost as alien, in the shape of my urban cousins. Children in the towns, vulnerable to bombing and related hazards, were often 'evacuated' to the countryside, supposedly for their greater safety. Whether this was always so is a matter of opinion. Many such children were temporarily adopted by complete strangers, and there were precious few checks on such arrangements. We now have many accounts which show that evacuation was by no means the romantic experience that we so often assume it to have been, with stories of ill treatment and abuse not uncommon. Apparently the few from Leeds who initially arrived in Appleton Roebuck left within the week because there were not enough shops. My cousins at least had the good sense to lodge themselves with relatives (and my parents may have received some sort of allowance for their upkeep) but they found it a strange experience for all that, and must often have wondered if they might not have been safer back in Newcastle upon Tyne, bombs or no bombs. Registration records show that in September 1939 four of my Tyneside cousins were lodged with us, though they also came at other intervals, and my cousin Joe recalls being with us on VE Day in May 1945. These visits must have made it very crowded in our two-up, two-down cottage. They came in two batches: first Russell and Joe, the two sons of Aunt Meg and Uncle Tommy Burns, from Gateshead. Aunt Meg was one of my mother's elder sisters. Russell and Joe, about 10 and 9 respectively (15 and 14 by the end of the war) flaunted their urban sophistication, and treated me in the lordly manner appropriate to green younger country cousins. I longed for their approval and acceptance, and got it only on the most grudging terms, ever the way between older and younger boys. I was secretly delighted when Dad took them down a peg. One day he emerged from the cow byre and, producing two tins of condensed milk, told the two town lads that these had just come straight from the bull. They were open-mouthed and utterly believing. They watched the bulls for hours after that, hoping to see them drop a few tins of milk, and speculating in whispers and giggles about the precise point from which these might emerge. I missed them when they left, and Joe would later be a very kindly and life-long friend.

The second batch of cousins were Molly and Billy, from Byker, the children of Mum's eldest sister Aunt Mary, married to Uncle Billy Whelan. Billy Jnr. was about 8, but Molly the eldest of all our evacuees at 12, and by the war's end 17. All I remember about Billy later in the war period was his obsession with football, a true Geordie in this respect. He used me as a permanent goalkeeper. He would stand me up against a wall, draw chalk marks a few feet to either side of me, and proceed to boot all manner of objects at me, over me, past me, and sometimes it felt like through me. Footballs were in very short supply so he had to make do with substitutes: tin cans, bundles of rags, crumpled up wads of newspaper, old hats, and even, unforgettably, lumps of hardened cow-clap, which often exploded messily when saved. Fielding these assorted objects was a trying business, and nurtured in me a determination that when I got older, I would do the booting while some other hapless victim did the goal-keeping. This wish was only to be fully realised several years later with the advent of my younger sister Sally. Meanwhile, it was no surprise to me that in due course, cousin Billy became a demon centre-forward (now called strikers), and (I believe) played at some level for Newcastle United. Kicking an actual football must have been child's play after his early training in Yorkshire, and he'd have probably reached the first team if they had been obliged to play with balls made from hardened cow dung.

As for Molly, I was moonstruck when old enough to register her presence. She was a lovely girl, slim, petite and dark haired, with creamy skin and smiling eyes. I worshipped her unconditionally and with total innocence across the immense gap between six and sixteen years: I was completely in love with her. So was everybody else. Molly caused a great stir in village circles and reduced our local youths to quite dumb devotion: even the land-girls had their noses put out of joint. All this was then above my head. I remember my extreme puzzlement when I missed Molly's presence one evening, and was told that she was 'going out' with a pilot from nearby Church Fenton. What possible interest, I thought, could a girl have in aeroplanes? And didn't they mean 'going up' rather than going out? How could she leave me bereft at home in favour of some bloke she wasn't even related to? Then I fell to hoping that she would bring the pilot home; perhaps they would land in the stack-yard and I could have a go at the wheel (as I thought it would be). When he arrived, a handsome French-Canadian pilot, he gave me a smart salute; after that I worshipped him unconditionally too.

Not that pilots were entirely unknown quantities: they were yet another group of outsiders to enliven our local scene. They turned up in droves to the shows and dances that were held in the village hall, and to the annual garden fete run by the parish church. These activities were devoted to raising funds for what was always known as the 'war effort', and the whole village joined in. The women spent most of their spare time knitting for victory, the men digging for victory. We sent an unlikely number of socks to the front. Mum's knitting was more likely to cripple than comfort, so she threw her considerable creative energies into the shows and the fete. She had always suffered from writer's itch, and often scribbled poems on little bits of paper, this to be a lifetime habit. The shows beckoned to her small but vigorous talent and she scripted whole chunks: playlets, one man acts, songs, and what would now be called the continuity material. She refused to go on stage herself, but contrived to get me on the boards. I made my stage debut, in what would be an enthusiastic but undistinguished theatrical career, at the age of five. Predictably, it was a personal disaster for me, but huge entertainment for the audience. I had carefully rehearsed my two songs, *The Little Nut Tree* and *Little Sir Echo* and was word-perfect. I still am, nearly eight decades later. But when the curtain went up, and I opened my mouth to respond to the first notes from the piano (off stage, right) I suddenly saw this sea of upturned and expectant faces, some on the front row perched on top of heavily decorated uniforms. My mouth stayed open. I stared at the audience. They stared back. A hoarse croaking voice suddenly made itself heard "there was a little nut tree, nothing would it bear..." the pianist thought that I had forgotten the words. But I hadn't, rather, I felt entirely undisposed to utter them. For a start, I couldn't get my mouth to close, or my jaws to move. I could not tear my hypnotised gaze from the audience. I couldn't even turn and run, for it appeared that someone had nailed my feet to the boards. It was a classic and severe case of stage-fright. The audience began to whisper and giggle. Ted Fish, who had secreted several bottles of beer beneath his seat, and was well into them, shouted "Now then, young Martin, where's your bike?" Laughter broke out in several places. The pianist desperately moved on to my second number and croaked "Little Sir Echo how do you do, hello..." Ted Fish jumped up, bottle in hand and sang out "Hello' then obligingly rendered the next line, since my mouth was still wide open: "Little Sir Echo I'm feeling blue, Hello..." "HELLO" roared back several young pilots. The whole audience now performed the song for my benefit, conducted by Ted Fish and his beer bottle. My open mouth transposed itself into a huge, embarrassed grin, which became jammed in position. As the song ended, my mother appeared on stage and uprooted me. She appeared to be crying helplessly, overwhelmed, I then thought, by my tragic failure. As she led me away, the audience stamped and cheered: it was easily the biggest reception any act got that night. Never had one performer done so little to earn so much applause. I was hooked on the stage ever after.

The annual garden fete involved my mother in a performance of her own. She was fascinated by the art of 'telling the future'. She would tell anyone's fortune, using playing cards and tea-leaves, as well as the reading of palms. I loved to watch her 'read' a tea-cup. Strong tea, brimming with tea-leaves, was an essential ingredient and, I suppose, an inefficient tea-pot. Once you had drunk your tea, leaving a little drop at the bottom, you had to swirl the tea-leaves around, then quickly drain off the remaining liquid. The black tea-leaves would form patterns around the sides and bottom of the cup. Mum could project quite amazing possibilities into these patterns: dark strangers, marriages, fortunate meetings, fateful letters - all would be persuasively offered up to the credulous ears of our neighbours and friends. But the annual fete was an altogether more serious business. Mum would dress up as a gypsy, and sit in a tent marked 'Madame Josephine: hear your fortune from her incredible crystal ball'. Mum was dark-haired and green-eyed anyway, and with her hair in ringlets, a dishcloth round her head, and bare feet in open-work rope sandals, she really *did* look like a gypsy. I found the transformation a bit unnerving. When I was older, she told of the difficulties she met with. One after the other, in came boyish, fresh-faced young pilots, sometimes hesitant, sometimes full of bravado and jokiness, but in all cases, what they wanted was some reassurance that they still *had* a future. What could she tell them except what they really wanted to hear? She would invent stories of pretty strangers, marriage, children, a cheery, above all *distant* future. As she spoke, and they listened intently, half believing, both she and they were thinking of the grim present reality, which was that some of them would have no future to speak of at all. The casualty rate for operational air crew was around 50% in the war years, at an average age of 22 years, and Bomber Command alone suffered more than 55,000 deaths in total. The younger and greener the pilot, the less likely was he to survive unscathed, simply because the most reliable planes were kept by the longer-serving pilots. 18,000 men died flying from Yorkshire airfields alone. For some of the young men who anxiously crossed 'Madame Josephine's' palm with silver, the future might stretch no further than the end of the week ahead.

Of course, I had no conception of this sort of reality. With one thing and another, it was something of a disappointment to me when the war finally came to an end on 8$^{th}$ May 1945, when I was seven. Our village celebrated VE day with joy and relief. Sir Benjamin gave a great party in the grounds of Appleton Hall, and everyone was there: of our expanded war-time community only the POWs were missing, and doubtless in their different ways they too were celebrating the end of their involuntary exiles. We ate and drank our fill at trestle tables which groaned under the weight of sandwiches, pies, cakes, jellies, puddings, bottles of pop and crates of beer. The austerities of the Home Front were temporarily suspended. A huge bonfire was heaped at the end of the garden, and perched on top was a guy made up to resemble Adolf Hitler. I had, by some inscrutable process, been chosen to light the bonfire, perhaps an expression of the greater hopes that lay ahead for young people. Determined not to muff my second public performance, I shyly but firmly stepped forward with a large taper, and touched the glowing end to screws of paper bedded into the heart of the bonfire. The wood crackled fiercely, and tongues of flame soon rose up to lick Hitler's unsmiling countenance. He smouldered, then crumbled, and the war seemed truly over.

As the night grew colder, we went indoors and danced along the narrow passageways of the long glass greenhouses. Phyllis Raper, plump and motherly, led me on to the impromptu dance floor and smiled as I whirled excitedly round, almost falling over in my exuberance. Everyone was singing an enchanting song:

~

*Neath the spreading chestnut tree*
*I loved you and you loved me*
*Oh, how happy we shall be*
*Neath the spreading chestnut tree.*

~

If ever I hear that song now, it brings back the ripe, heady smells of compost and victory.

# Chapter Five

## The Taste of Victory

*Seeing them casually in their heavy and uncleanly clothes, no one would have dreamed of the great qualities in them - the kindliness and courage and humour, the readiness to help, the self-control, the patience. It was all there, but they took no pains to look the part: they did not show off.*
George Bourne: *Change in the Village, 1912*

Not many around that celebratory bonfire realised that things would never be the same again as they had been when the Second World War started in 1939. This was supposed to have been the case after the Great War of 1914-18 too, but life had been grim in the 1920s and early 1930s, when the iron of economic decline and depression had eaten deep into the souls of working people. The very recurrence of the experience of war and economic hardships seemed to give rise to a new resolve in the younger generation like my parents, a heightened sense of their true worth. They did not intend to let post-war Britain fall again into the cold hands that had held the reins and the whip before and between the wars. A different kind of war was about to break out, with toffs like Sir Benjamin on one side, and their natural adversaries, like my father and mother, on the other. This class war (for that is what it was and always had been in British society) was a curious affair, in which a thousand small skirmishes were fought out at the level of the workplace - mines, docks, factories, even farms - while at a higher remove a battle raged for the control of the state and the 'commanding heights' of the economy. Harold Nicolson commented in 1945: 'Class feeling and class resentment are still very strong'. The ruling class posture then was notoriously made explicit by the wealthy socialite Sir Henry 'Chips' Channon, who reportedly looked round the room with champagne flowing at a celebratory victory party in the Dorchester Hotel, and said: "After all, this is what we have been fighting for." Dad might have been consoled had he known that one distant day his son would sit together in a Whitehall meeting with Chips Channon's son,

Conservative MP and Old Etonian Paul Channon: for that, after all, was part of what the working class had been fighting for.

David Kynaston in his *Austerity Britain 1945-51* quotes a survey of 200 families suggesting that in the immediate post-war period only 21 out of 200 male workers had any interest in politics, in a working class that was estimated to be about 75% of the population; for their wives, the proportion was even lower at 7 out of 200. My parents were something of a phenomenon in our part of rural Yorkshire, where overtly partisan political activities of any kind were thin on the ground, and leftish political activists non-existent: except, that is, for Dad. How this son of a cautious, conservative, apolitical Irish immigrant came to be such an eager and committed supporter of the Labour Party is something of a mystery, not least because he was himself by temperament a naturally cautious and conservative man. His formative years had been spent in surroundings - an aristocratic country estate - where forelocks were expected to be tugged with unfailing regularity, and were. The answer lies in Dad's primary personal characteristic, which was a stubborn independence of mind: right or wrong, he would cleave whole heartedly to his own opinions, and was ever ready to put those opinions to the test of public debate. Though possessed of a quick intelligence (as was my mother, though hers was of a hazier, more imaginative kind) he had little schooling. In the 1920s, the sons of farm labourers had no chance of escaping, by the educational ladder, from a bleak future of grindingly hard work, long hours, and the lowest of wages, well below the national average for manual workers. In 1939 the average wage for an agricultural worker was still, at around 35 shillings a week, no better than it had been two decades before, and only around a third of the average urban labourer's wage. While wages everywhere began to rise in these early war years, food prices increased by 17% and the price of clothes by 25%, so there was not really much improvement in standards of living. During my first decade, with my father on low wages and a growing family to support, feeding the family was a constant preoccupation. Much is made in accounts of the war of the hardships caused by rationing, and in later years I asked my mother about the shortages created by food rationing. She gave her familiar dismissive snort: the chance of being able to afford what was allowed under food rations would have been a fine thing, and even the cheapest cuts of meat were a rarity for them. Rationing was not in itself a hardship, for such as she had been surviving on the tightest of budgets for years, rationing enforced by poverty rather than some bureaucratic edict. Her response is confirmed in Juliet Gardiner's excellent chapter on 'The Kitchen Front' during the war years, which quotes a government survey finding that 'very large numbers of people cannot afford to take up their full ration... the poorer people... do not regard their food position as materially altered', and stories of women who went without food in order to ensure that their menfolk and children could eat properly. Class privilege asserted itself, as 'chauffeur-driven cars pulled up outside grocers' shops and stripped their shelves bare'. It was the middle classes who most disliked rationing, and who were best able to benefit from black market purchases, while the wealthy still drank copious quantities of champagne. As a land girl reported in her post-war autobiography, 'the upper middle class remained more equal than the working class. Food was the most obvious case in point'. As far as my own family were concerned, only in the early post-war years, as real living standards rose for farm workers, did rationing have any real impact on our circumstances. By the end of the war the cost of living had risen by 35%, though subsidies on bread, meat and potatoes mitigated the impact of this. The social and economic system had in the past assumed that working class children would neither need nor want any other than the most basic literacy; more to the point, perhaps, their parents could scarcely wait for them to reach the age where they could earn a wage, however small, with which to swell the meagre resources of inevitably large families (very much the case for my parents, both children of Catholic families).

Dad's education was a brief and inessential interruption to the serious business of growing up to get a job. Yet, amazingly, this man who left school on the stroke of fourteen years, could later in life recall, word for word, long poems, and extracts from Shakespeare, which at some point he had swallowed whole, and which were evidently thought to improve the minds of the rural poor. Given his nature, it is perhaps significant that the two poems he could recite in full were Gray's *Elegy Written in a Country Churchyard* and Goldsmith's *The Deserted Village*. Dad was always, at family parties, liable to jump up and declaim, without any advance warning, such passages as "Old John of Gaunt, time-honoured Lancaster", and whatever the extract, usually took all the parts himself, since his University-educated children were quite incapable of following him for very long; though there was an unforgettable occasion when he and my sister Sally, by then an Oxford graduate in English Literature, recited the whole of Keats' *Ode to a Nightingale*, with Dad filling in the bits Sally couldn't remember. And when in my early teens I was wrestling mightily with what were (to me anyway) intractable mathematical problems, he would take a quick look and tell me the answer. I could never explain to the Maths master how I had worked out such answers, and unfortunately for me, neither could Dad: but he was rarely wrong.

Perhaps this intelligence, allied to his independent cast of mind, made him a natural rebel against the economic and social structures in which his life and work were inexorably set. At the same time, his calm and phlegmatic temperament gave him a considerable resilience in the face of adversity. He did not attempt, as many others did, to abandon farm labour and the countryside for more promising urban alternatives, not least because he loved working in the open air and could still in the 1930s and 40s deploy the wide range of agricultural skills he had learned since he was 14: horse-breaking, ploughing with horses, hedging and ditching, making and thatching stacks of corn, cutting hay by scythe, hand sowing crops. He had the same pride in his skills as any artisan. But both he and our equally political Mum knew that social and working conditions should be improved, and that they had to be wrested from the employing class, workers coming together and fighting as best they could to improve their existing situation through political activity. This was not inherently promising in our particular bit of Yorkshire, given the conservatism of rural life and its domination by the owning class, who did not easily tolerate trade unionism or take kindly to anyone who tried to promote it among their workers.

In 1945, the national euphoria of victory would soon be eroded by the bitter acid of political conflict. Dad established his position early on, presenting himself to the local branch of the Labour Party and offering his services. These were readily embraced, and it was not long before he was asked to be a local political organiser for the Labour candidate at the forthcoming general election, in the constituency of Barkston Ash. Dad threw all his energies into the campaign. The Labour candidate was Bert Hazell, by origin a farm worker from Norfolk, but then a local organiser in the East Riding of Yorkshire for the National Union of Agricultural Workers, strong, as it happened, in Norfolk, but weak and poorly supported in most other parts of the country. Bert and Dad had something in common: both had started their young farming lives as crow-scarers (as had Joseph Arch, the grand old man of nineteenth century agricultural unionism). The Conservative candidate, a true blue High Tory who had held the seat comfortably since 1931, was Colonel Sir Leonard Ropner, Harrow and Cambridge educated, whose money came from shipping. He was altogether a more socially established part of the local gentry, and Sir Benjamin Dawson had to be content with lesser Conservative Party office. He was infuriated to find Dad, one of his own labourers, taking an active role against him. Moreover, Bert and Dad and others, in their well-attended and passionate public meetings, repeatedly drew attention to the long working hours, low pay, and poor living conditions of farm workers, a theme contemptuously ignored by the other side, employers to a man of overworked, badly paid, and poorly housed farm labour. Above all, though, what Benny couldn't stomach was Dad's clear defiance. Labourers, he believed, should know their place and accord deference and respect to their employers. But none of this could deflect the democratic political process from taking its course. Benny even came to a Labour meeting, and tried to catch Dad and Bert out by raising obscure issues such as Labour's policies on the gold reserves, or the future of Singapore. In this extraordinary confrontation between elementary school man and independently educated master, Dad was well able to hold his own. "Never you mind about Singapore" he cried "let's get a bit nearer home. And it's *your* gold reserves we've got our eyes on. It's about time we all shared in the benefits of the labour that lets you and your lot ride about in Rolls Royces". Dad scored a palpable class hit here: a Rolls Royce at this time could cost £2,500, unimaginable riches for ordinary farm labourers earning at best £250 in an entire year, and Benny had at least two of them, as well as two small yachts. "I must protest, through the Chairman" spluttered Benny indignantly "at the personal nature of these remarks". "I *am* the Chairman," replied Dad implacably, "and I don't intend to rule myself out of order." Benny pounced, his voice rising squeakily "Ah yes, that's what we can expect from a Labour government, dictatorial behaviour". Dad feigned surprise: "Well now, Sir Benjamin, that's a practice you are better acquainted with than me." The old boys in The Roebuck Inn chortled over that one almost as much as Mum did when telling me this story in later years, for Benny was notoriously bossy. He would often steal up on people when they were not looking and try to catch them not working in his time. Once, when Dad and a gang of men were picking and bagging potatoes, they spotted Benny hiding behind a tree, at eight o'clock in the morning, making sure that his men didn't make off with the odd bag of potatoes.

The results of the 1945 General Election must have done little to improve his temper. The crushing parliamentary majority for the Labour Party over the baffled Churchill-led Conservative Party was a severe shock to traditional Tories, who now imagined themselves, mistakenly as it turned out, in real danger of being on the losing side in an actual class war. Even in the supposedly safe rural seat of Barkston Ash, Bert Hazell had nearly pulled off a miracle, reducing a large traditional majority to just 116 votes, a mere 0.24% of the vote. As it happened, his share of the vote at 49.88% almost replicated Labour's national average. Though Sir Leonard Ropner defeated Bert again in 1950 by a much larger margin, and kept hold of his parliamentary position until his retirement in 1964, he must have had a bit of a fright. Coincidentally, dear old Bert (Bertie to his friends) entered the House of Commons in that same year as Member for North Norfolk. From 1966 to 1978 he would become President of the NUAW, so able to model himself on his union's former President George Edwards, who in the 1920s had become the first farm-worker MP to sit in the House of Commons: crow-scaring must have been good for Bert, for he died at the ripe old age of 101, in York, in the same place and at the same age as my great grandmother.

The response of Tories like Sir Benjamin to electoral humiliation was to hit out in any direction they could. He couldn't hope to land a blow on the people Dad had helped to vote into power, but by Mum's account Dad was for a while removed from his skilled job as a horseman and put to menial work that involved no dangerous contacts with the rest of the farm labour force. Day after day he was set to the solitary, back-breaking, and humiliating task of breaking stones in the park, as if he were a kind of one-man prison gang. It was a classic case of victimisation, an employer meting out punishment to one of his workers for daring to practise the democratic freedoms for which the war had supposedly been fought. Weak existing legislation (and a weak union) offered no real protection unless you were prepared to risk a considerable amount of money in legal costs and the like. How could Dad, with two small children, now on around £3 12 shillings a week, take such a risk? Moreover, like most farm workers who were married, he was a prisoner of the iniquitous 'tied cottage' system, by which the very roof over your head depended on holding down your job, and holding down your job often meant doing nothing that might offend your employer. Bill Holmes, General Secretary of the NUAW from 1928-44, is reported to have told a meeting with American farming trade unionists: 'in many of our villages, a man who joins a trade union is worthy of the Victoria Cross: but to be a branch secretary! That is to risk one's livelihood every day'. How difficult it is, now, to recall just how recently farm labourers were at a severe disadvantage in their relations with their bosses, and how much more personalised the employer–employee relationship was in rural areas than in an urban, more unionised context. A hard boss meant a hard life. According to Dad, Benny wasn't necessarily much worse than other farmers: a bit more modern minded, a bit more idiosyncratic, a lot more lofty and snobbish, yet he paid above average wages and generally valued good workers, despite his hostile treatment of Dad. He and his wife were kind to their domestic staff, and worthy local patrons of music (notably in their support and encouragement of the promising Yorkshire composer William Baines, who died very young of consumption). But the inexorable pursuit of profit was the ultimate arbiter of the behaviour of him and his kind, Thatcherites before the word existed. Farm workers had few weapons with which to resist, given their own innate conservatism and inability or reluctance to organise themselves in some collective way. They were particularly vulnerable at times of illness. For example, when temporary workers such as land girls fell sick, some farmers would give them the sack, so that they need not be paid while off work. When the land girl recovered, she would get her job, and her pay back. Working people just could not afford to be ill or have accidents.

Unhappily, Dad had earlier suffered a quite appalling accident in the winter of 1942. One of the winter tasks was to saw up the considerable amounts of timber cut down around the heavily wooded estate during the summer months, and left for several months to season. The farm had its own rudimentary sawmill. The centre-piece was a bright, saw-toothed circular saw, driven by a conveyor belt attached to a little electric generator. It sliced through thick tree trunks with terrifying ease and a high whining noise. All the men were roped in to help, for there was a good market for sawn timber, and a speedy supplier could make a handsome profit. Logs were also supplied to the Hall and cottages, after a special 'sawing day' at Home Farm. On just such a day, Dad was given the task of directing the long pieces of timber along a metal platform up to the edge of the rotating saw, giving the end of each piece a hefty shove to add final impetus and ensure a clean finish. Because it was very cold, with snow on the ground, Dad was wearing woollen mittens. As he pushed a piece of timber up towards the saw, his foot slipped on the icy ground. The whirring circular blade caught the edge of a mitten and dragged his hand forward. The jagged steel teeth sliced his forefinger clean off, cutting deep into the next two fingers and knucklebones. Blood gouted from his shattered hand and splashed vividly on the white snow. Dad slipped quietly to the floor in a dead faint. We lived a long, long way from the nearest hospital. It took twenty minutes just to get to a telephone; there was no such thing at the farm, and one of Dad's fellow workers had to career madly on his bicycle up to Appleton Hall. David Arrand, Sir Benjamin's chauffeur, drove Dad to the nearest hospital in the city of York, but it was three hours in all before they got Dad - and his severed finger - on to an operating table. Because of this time delay, the surgeon was barely able to save Dad's life, let alone his finger. The forefinger was lost for good, the two fingers next to it remained throughout his life bent into a gnarled and inflexible position. He was seriously ill for weeks, but a naturally strong constitution, and his stubborn will, prevented a more disastrous outcome. He comments that he suffered most pain where the nurses had to scrub the oil and dirt from the raw and bleeding wound. He also hated having to miss a much-loved Christmas at home with his wife and children; he tried to persuade Matron to discharge him on the grounds that he had two children awaiting him at home. "I don't care if you have 22 children," declared Matron implacably, "you are staying here". Amusingly, his principal fear was that he might be in greater danger of losing his life from any bombing of York. Eventually he was allowed to return home, pale and thin, to a warm and tearful welcome. He didn't have a proper hand, but he was Dad, and he was ours once more.

*Dad on the farm, a picture which shows his damaged hand, minus a finger.*

The welcome from Sir Benjamin demonstrated what a weak position in law existed for workmen suffering disabling injuries at work. Dad's wages had continued to be paid in full, but Sir Benjamin curtly informed Dad that his lawyers had advised him that there could be no question of obligatory compensation for the loss of limb occasioned by the sawmill accident, since it was understood that the machinery had been incorrectly operated without a guard. In these circumstances Sir Benjamin's insurers were prepared to make a once-for-all settlement of £50 as a measure of compensation. He advised Dad to take it. Dad discovered from the farm workers union that he *was* entitled to compensation under Workmen's Compensation legislation and that his employer had broken the regulations by not posting warning notices, and by not ensuring that a guard *was* in use. George Mallinson, courageously, was ready to testify to these errors, perhaps feeling some sense of guilt for his own lack of foresight as the responsible foreman. But Dad, shaken by his illness, and in a weak position, in his damaged state, if it came to looking for another job, had no stomach for a one-sided fight with his employer. He took the £50, woefully inadequate compensation for the loss of a crucial part of his body, at work, despite his employer in all probability being legally negligent. It's interesting that Nye Bevan was deeply angered by the shortcomings of the Workmen's Compensation legislation because it did not recognise as an industrial disease pneumoconiosis, the lung disease caused by inhaling coal dust, from which his miner father died; revision of this legislation would be one of the first reforms of the post 1945 Labour government.

Dad's £50 was good news for me, at least, for I got a pair of new shoes and trousers out of it. This was a considerable relief to me, because children at school frequently teased me on account of the numerous patches to be seen on my behind, a place about which I could become very sensitive. My main recollection of the undoubted poverty in which we lived for most of my childhood is not hunger, or cold, or damp, or illness: I had my fair share of all of these things save hunger, though I suspect I avoided that only at the expense of my parents' suffering it instead. No, my main recollection is of shame, and pain. Pain for my parents, who quarrelled over money and spending, though they rarely fell out over anything else; shame for myself, the patches on my trousers and the holes in my shoes, the ignominy of being taunted by other, more fortunate children. Much later, shame when I had to bring school friends home to what by comparison with their own middle-class homes must, it always seemed to me, have looked rough and uninviting and somehow reprehensible. I suppose I should now feel ashamed of my own embarrassment, but I don't. I see it clearly for what it was, a painful part of the harrowing experience of moving between different social worlds, something that would increasingly become a feature of my life the more successful I became. I regret the callowness of youth that made me embarrassed by and for my parents and their relative poverty, but in truth I don't think my parents really noticed: no one was much hurt except myself, but the hurt was real, and strongly felt, and as I moved onwards and upwards it took me a very long time before I was mature enough to honour and proclaim my roots openly. These feelings are brilliantly anatomised by Richard Hoggart in The *Uses of Literacy,* to which I turn in my final chapter.

Once peace was declared, Dad (or more likely Mum, who was mightily displeased at the ways in which Dad had been treated by his unfeeling boss), decided to move on. This was the beginning of another little peripatetic progress across Yorkshire, my parents in search of improvement in our lives, better wages, and often because of the poor state of the tied cottages in which we perforce had to live. This entrenched condition of the farm labourer's life was essentially a product of the eighteenth-century Enclosure Acts which restricted rural dwellers' access to common land and pushed them into paid agricultural labour. The development of the tied cottage system could in one sense be seen as a benefit, since it meant that a job brought with it a roof over one's head, often (though not always) rent free. But the disadvantages were considerable. Most farmer-owners felt no obligation to act as good landlords, so that repairs and improvements were few and far between, even though post First World War legislation, strengthened after the Second World War, provided financial incentives for the landlord/owner to improve their workers' houses. Another effect was to keep wages at a low level: the labourer and his wife seldom dared to get on the wrong side of the boss, since dismissal meant being out on the road and in search of another job and house with only two weeks' notice of eviction and no real protection against this, so that whatever the conditions of work and house, complaints were rarely made. This had a political dimension too, as we have already seen with Sir Benjamin's petty punishment of Dad for his open political activity on behalf of the Labour Party. As late as 1965, while helping the county council election campaign of a friend who was a Labour candidate in rural Hampshire, we were puzzled by the ostentatious rash of Conservative posters in the houses of workers on a local landed estate. Closer enquiry revealed that while many of these estate workers were Labour supporters, they were terrified that if they betrayed this, they would be kicked out of their tied houses by the local, hard-nosed Tory squire. I'm glad to be able to report that many of them rode to the polling station in cars thoughtfully provided for them by the said squire, then used the secrecy of the ballot box to vote as they really wanted to. For me, one of the most irritating failures of post-war Labour governments was their unwillingness to take on this particular special rural interest. The Labour Governments of 1945-51 took no action whatever on tied cottages, despite the pleas of the NUAW, because they were more concerned to win the acceptance of the National Farmers Union for the 1947 Agriculture Act and a new system of state support for farmers. I can tell you that the name of Tom Williams, Labour's Minister of

Agriculture at that time, produced spitting invective from Mum and much resigned head-shaking from Dad.

Not that any of this ever deterred our formidable mother, constantly taking up the cudgels, especially when trying to bring up babies in poky cottages without electricity, running water, bathrooms or inside toilets, often damp and unhealthy. In 1944 some 30% of rural dwellings in England had no mains water supply, and in 1947 almost 50% had no bathroom: we ourselves would not enjoy electricity, hot running water, a fixed bath, or an inside lavatory until 1950 (and I recently discovered at The People's Museum in Edinburgh that a whole decade later than this, a quarter of the households in that city still had no fixed bath). Mum's rather one-sided battle meant that we were often 'on the road' again.

In 1945, leaving Appleton behind, we found ourselves back at Poole in Wharfedale, attracted there by the presence of Dad's favourite brother Billy. This didn't last long, particularly as one day I returned home and fell in a dead faint straight down a hole in the kitchen floor, where the drains were being repaired. This was too much for my mother, already impatient with the state of the cottage. So off we went again, to the Yorkshire Dales proper, with six months or so in a village called Thornton Steward. This I recall as some sort of nightmare. I was, at the age of seven, still a somewhat sickly child, not yet thriving after my premature birth. During a very wet autumn I would watch water running down the inside walls of the poor cramped cottage that came with Dad's job: this didn't do much to improve my already delicate chest. We were well off our usual beaten track, and in these still close-knit Dales communities, were regarded with suspicion and distrust as outsiders. The price I personally paid for this was to be regularly beaten up by the local lads on my way home after school. This was quite a rude shock after the kindly ways in which I

*Dad and I revisit what was our grim old tied cottage in Thornton Steward.*

had been treated in Appleton Roebuck. To add to the enormity of it all, the village was cut off from what was now to our yearning gaze civilisation, that is, anywhere that was not Wensleydale, by immoderate downfalls of snow. My mother told us later that things were so bad that supplies, including coal for heating, had to be dropped from aircraft. Once we (and the Dales) had even partially unfrozen, Mum and Dad decided they would like to get back to what was for them something like home, the Vale of York, fetching up in a little hamlet called Ellenthorpe, two miles from Boroughbridge, an old coaching stage post on the Great North Road. At the age of eight I settled into my fourth school.

# Chapter Six

# Country Life: Happiness and Miseries

*If you carry your childhood with you, you never become older*
Abraham Sutzkever, Yiddish poet

Our new house was a big improvement in some ways, being a former Lodge House at the gates to a long drive that led to Ellenthorpe Hall. There was a decent-sized garden with Victoria plum trees and gooseberry bushes, and fields all around for me to explore. We still had no electricity (in 1946-49) and were lit by smoky paraffin lamps: I twice contrived dramatic explosions lighting their paraffin-suffused wicks, once burning off my eyebrows. We also had no bathroom as there was no mains water, which had to be carried in pails from a hand-pump in the small, dark back yard, which also housed a crude outdoor lavatory. The house could be very cold in winter, and a lasting memory is that Mum warmed our cold beds with house bricks heated in the wood and coal-fired oven and wrapped in a piece of blanket. But the house, known as Ivy Nook because of the walls wreathed in ivy, was pretty on the outside, and Dad soon had vegetables and flowers on the go (almost always wallflowers, lupins, and sweet williams, to this day special flowers for me). We also had chickens, great fun to chase, while keeping a beady eye out for the equally beady-eyed rooster; and after a year, in 1947, we suddenly acquired a pig and two ducks, to which sister Maureen and I were devoted. We were even more devoted to the other surprising acquisition at the time: another sister, Sally. Sally arrived in the most trying circumstances. The winter of 1947 was the severest in most people's memories, with sixteen degrees of frost, and snow blizzards creating a soft, deep white carpet which persisted for weeks, while the frozen ground became so unyielding that in many places root crops had to be harvested by pickaxes and pneumatic drills. In February, in the middle of all this, my mother went into labour. The midwife was called, but got stuck in a snowdrift; Dad and a couple of local farmhands rushed forth with spades and matting and dug her out, only to find a happily smiling and relaxed Mum when they reached our house: Sally had already made an entrance. I missed all this excitement, for I had once more been removed to stay with my Auntie Sadie in Wallsend. The harsh winter prevented me from travelling back for some weeks, and I was temporarily placed in the local town school. This was a culture shock even greater than that I had suffered in the Dales. The school was large and bleak, and I was again bullied as an outsider, while my treatment by authoritarian and uncaring teachers was no better. Maureen had been similarly exiled, with George Mallinson and his kindly wife, but at last we were reunited and able to welcome our new sister, who thankfully had survived and prospered. She became our third pet alongside the pig, and one of the ducks that had adopted us and often sat on the back doorstep waiting to be fed titbits.

*We are reunited with Granny Simpson in Wallsend, 1947.*

Little did we know that these pet animals were intended for our dinner table. I still recall vividly the day when our dear old pig was killed. Gruff, burly men arrived and set about their deadly business. We children had been warned to stay out of sight of the pigsty, but it was impossible to be out of earshot. The pig, not deceived by the noises of encouragement emanating from the gruff, burly men, set up a deeply distressing squealing: I pushed my fingers deep into my ears and hid in the outside lavatory, aware that something terrible and unknowable was happening. All I recall after that is the appearance in our scullery of steaming buckets of blood and disembodied lumps of pig. Dad teased me with an equally disembodied curly pig's tail. I refused to be won over, and if looks could have killed he would have been laid out right there next to the curiously bleached looking pieces of pork. Thereafter our kitchen ceiling was host to some choice smoked sides of bacon, enough for breakfasts non-stop for a year. But not for me: I rejected every offer of pig put on my plate, and indeed was unable to eat red meat of any kind until my late teenage years. Sister Sally had her own personal issue over the pet duck, which soon became our special Christmas Day meal. Sally, by then just over two years old, determinedly forked bits of roast duck into

*Mum and Dad at Ellenthorpe.*

her mouth, bitter tears rolling down her cheeks, saying repeatedly: 'Pore duck! Pore duck!'

Meanwhile, for me, the three post-war years or so in this small rural hamlet were the best part of my rural upbringing and education. I was old enough to be allowed to roam free across the fields and along the hedgerows and copses of the two or three surrounding farms. Houses were sparse and remote, yet more open and welcoming than those in the Dales had been. I wandered happily in this magical playground, discovering nature at first hand, curious enough now to engage with the variety of creatures I came across, to begin to know and understand the ways in which this rural world worked. I investigated the habitats of birds, taking particular delight in finding the ground based nests of the many peewits. The hedges were full of tits and sparrows, thrushes and blackbirds, wagtails and yellow hammers. I knew, but never took *all* their eggs. The house eaves were home to delightful swooping house martins, for which I felt some affinity through our common name. Exploring the nearby River Ure, I watched for hours as sand martins sped in and out of their nesting holes deep in the sandy banks. One practical result of all this birdwatching was an essay on the chaffinch, complete with drawings (no cameras affordable to us then) and detailed observations of the chaffinch's home life. This won me, at the age of 10, my first ever public prize, a copper Medal struck by the Royal Society for the Protection of Birds. I have to confess that this acquisition gave me even more satisfaction than the chaffinches which had made it possible; but the chaffinch remains deeply engrained in my affections, and I still thrill to its wonderful bright colours and perky demeanour. Only recently have I discovered that the grounds by the river which I so happily inhabited had once been graced, and drawn, by the great painter J. W. M. Turner, who in 1815-17 walked through this and other parts of Yorkshire and made sketches and drawings. A collection of these may be seen at Tate Britain, and include a pencil drawing, now extremely faint, of the original Ellenthorpe Hall (Yorkshire Sketchbooks 1, 1816) later replaced by the farmhouse owned by Dad's employer, Joe Holmes. An eighteenth century History of Knaresborough suggests that 'Ellingthorp' derived from an ancient Saxon word implying nobility, 'which seems to point out this place as having once been the residence of a Saxon prince'. I was still making a habit of walking in famous footsteps: first Marvell, now Turner, possibly even a Saxon prince.

The other abiding memory is harvest time. This would be a common trope as the years moved by, but my first memories seem so framed as to be almost sepia coloured and clouded with age. I am still entranced by those black and white farming photographs to be seen in many rural histories: they are vivid, and speak to me, but can they really be my memories? They are separated from later harvest experiences by the changes which were now taking place in the agricultural landscape. At this point, in 1948 or thereabouts, the fields of wheat and oats and barley were typical of arable farms in the Vale of York. In our case, the corn was still harvested by horse-drawn binders, Dad still working for a farmer not yet able to afford tractors. Binders were an odd-looking contraption, with a sort of wooden sail at one end attached by wheels and pulleys to a flatbed edged by nasty sharp metal teeth. Dad sat on an iron seat in the middle of all this and directed the horse into the swathe of standing corn. The wheels and pulleys would turn a wooden wheel, whose flaps would push the cornstalks down to be reaped by the row of chattering metal teeth. The stalks of corn would collapse gracefully into neat rows on the flat-bed, from where they would be carried up into a sort of dark maw, and disappear into the binding mechanism at the back of the binder. At set intervals the maw would spit out a sheaf neatly (or often not so neatly) bound with yellow twine. Men and women, even older children, all were gathered in to this process, so central to the ancient rhythms of country life, and would gather up the sheaves and stack them, corn pointing skywards, into what were known as stooks, neat little self-contained heaps, set to dry out in the sun. Often enough the women would have to make straw bands to bind the sheaves when the binding mechanism misfired, as it often did.

What I remember best of this time was the rabbits. The cornfields were full of these soft, furry little creatures, but this was not the world of Beatrix Potter (not yet known to me, so rabbits were not as yet anthropomorphised). From our point of view, they were ripe for the cooking pot, and one of the few sources of a free dinner. If painted, the scene would have been a Brueghel: a triangle of uncut corn waving in a slight breeze on a perpetually sunny day with blue skies overhead; the horse-drawn binder methodically slicing through the remaining and ever dwindling patch of golden ears; an assortment of men and women in clearly defined tasks, men catching the sheaves spat out from the binder and pitching them together in stooks, cursing occasionally as errant thistles in the sheaves fought back; women setting out at the edge of the field under a shady tree the makings of a veritable picnic: hot tea in billy cans, rough-cut cheese and pickle sandwiches fondly known as door-stoppers, and if the farmer's wife was feeling particularly generous (and it was baking day) round tins filled with cakes and buns. Then suddenly, a great commotion: some half dozen rabbits shoot out from their hiding places in the corn triangle, immediately the two farm sheep dogs race excitedly after them, followed by us children, a little gaggle of boys and girls armed with sticks. For a few minutes the field is alive with animals and children in a frenzy of running, leaping over stooks, colliding, aiming largely ineffectual blows at the rabbits and often enough landing indiscriminately on dogs and each other. As if by some ancient ritual, Dad and the other men would enter this maelstrom and quietly but devastatingly fetch telling blows on the actual quarry. Dad once told me that you could paralyse a rabbit by running around it in a tight but decreasing circle, and then simply pick it up. I never actually saw him do this, and don't know to this day whether he was pulling my leg, something he much liked to do. Whatever the method, we would triumphantly bear still warm furry corpses off to our mothers, who would welcome this excellent addition to the family larder. We knew there would be tasty rabbit pie ahead.

My mother's poem, written at this time, catches some of the atmosphere:

~

*The Last Load*

*I see the last load of sheaves swaying down the field,*
*Wisps fly from the top as men riding, chiding each, reach for forks,*
*Corks fly from bottles as dry throats are eased.*
*Greased with oil by first light, axles groan and creak.*
*Weakening like the weary men, moiling mares,*
*Sweat on the belly band, move with slower gait,*
*I wait for Roger, Violet, Charlie drinking now*
*Hooves shifting, mouths deep in the trough.*
*One mare coughs, moves against the carter's calls,*

*Whoa there! Stan' offer! Stand I say!*
*They shamble, stumbling still, into the warm stable*
*Then, fed and watered, one final pat.*
*The carter and his wife walk down the yard,*
*His arm, tired from bearing the saddles and traces,*
*Heavy on her neck.*
*They come to the cottage and the table*
*Forgotten the harvest, the weary legs,*
*Rest: tomorrow is another day.*

~

This was a time when I was given some free rein, abetted by a bicycle I finally had been able to master (though it had a tendency to shed chains, burst tyres, and be a source of great irritation). The small town of Boroughbridge lay some two miles distant and contained the nearest shops. Mum would regularly send me off on an expedition to get, say, a packet of flour, and receive me back some considerable time later, bearing half a pound of margarine. The first distraction for a small but curious boy was the Milby Level Crossing and the rather frightening Crossing Keeper, Mrs Burgess. The crossing may have been on a narrow little country lane but it served a connection to the East Coast York to Newcastle main line, with steam trains a regular feature. It was Mrs Burgess' task to ensure the manual opening and closing of the gates. She was a forbidding looking, rather blowsy, dark haired woman who had an inbred dislike of children such as me, and assumed the worst of us, however politely we conducted ourselves, admittedly under pain of instant retribution from Mum if she heard of any other behaviour. But Mrs Burgess was immune to good behaviour, her own included. She would start to shout at me as soon as I appeared on her horizon, haranguing me incomprehensibly as I shot at speed across her railway line. Sometimes, after dark, I would hear laughter and singing from the creepy looking brick crossing keepers' house, and I would make off home as if pursued by demons, little knowing that by this time of day Mrs Burgess was usually the worse for wear from drink: a harmless old bag lady really. However, not so harmless as all that: not once, but twice, a train slammed clean through the crossing gates which Mrs Burgess had been either too drunk or too forgetful to open at the scheduled time. The whole family walked the half mile from our house to inspect the thrilling sight of bits of white wooden gate strewn for at least a hundred yards down the northbound track. Mum became worried about us using the crossing and for a while under her vigilant eye I had to stagger across an intervening field and haul my bike across the rail track through a hole in the hedge. Evidently Mum thought this was a safer procedure than trusting my fate to the unpredictable Mrs Burgess. At any rate, this poor old lady was soon relieved of her job, doubtless to the relief of many a train driver. I was astonished to discover recently that her once scary, forbidding dwelling was designated a Grade II Listed Building.

Another flirtation with disaster came from a different form of transport. The Great North Road - later the A1 and nowadays the A1(M) - had since early Roman times been the main route from London to the North, Ermine Street running via Lincoln to Isurium Brigantum (later Aldborough) and Eboracum (later York). Isurium Brigantum was then in effect Britain's northern capital, the Brigantes being the most populous British tribe under Roman rule. The Romans established their own Northern headquarters at York, home to the 6$^{th}$ and 9$^{th}$ Legions, from where they could control this fractious region, or reach further north to Hadrian's Wall. Aldborough, once home to the British Queen Cartimandua, though now a very small village, still has an interesting little Roman museum. Later, a crucial conjuncture of the River Ure crossing with the main road was moved from Aldborough to nearby Boroughbridge, then continued north to Newcastle and Edinburgh. Boroughbridge therefore came to enjoy a strategic importance in the Middle Ages, something of a battleground between English and Scottish forces. In 1322 the Battle of Boroughbridge between Edward II and a group of rebellious barons led by Thomas, Earl of Lancaster, ended particularly badly for the rebels, their leaders killed or executed. Much later, in the Civil War battle of 1644, the Royalists were famously defeated at Marston Moor, between York and Boroughbridge (many of the local aristocracy and gentry were Catholic Royalists: indeed, Guy Fawkes of 1605 Gunpowder Plot fame was a local man, born in York, and with a home in nearby Knaresborough). With more peaceful times, Boroughbridge prospered as a staging post for the mail coaches that ran from London to Edinburgh along the Great North Road. I like to think that I might have crossed paths not only with Marvell and Turner, but Dr Johnson and James Boswell, not to mention assorted Romans, as well as the Saxon prince.

At the age of 10, I was trusted to ride freely abroad on my beloved bike, frequently required to speed along the two miles of country road (watchfully negotiating the infamous level crossing) to what seemed then an exciting and busy town, a world away from our little rural hamlet. I had two regular ports of call. One was the barber's shop, not for a haircut, but to deliver the little slip of paper on which my father, a horse-racing fanatic, had carefully inscribed his bets, never more than a shilling in value. 'Street-gambling' had been made illegal in 1906 despite, or perhaps because of, its widespread popularity among the working class, and would not be made legal again until 1960: but illicit book-making was, in the late 1940s, an open secret. The barber ran the local 'book' and my go-between role was never questioned, nor was cash involved. Dad would settle up at the end of each week, and such was his close knowledge of riders and runners that he rarely lost or won much: his pleasure all lay in pitting his wits and expertise against the bookmakers. His interest in horse racing derived from his Irish father. A rare excitement for us a few years later (rare because we never ever had enough money for holidays) was to go as a family to the local race meetings at Ripon or Wetherby. My grandfather could be seen there too, but never watched the actual races, preferring to stay next to the bookmakers, since he didn't trust them not to make off with his winnings (this happened often enough in those days) and could check the results on the public tannoy. He had once backed a horse called Schubert which won; he then told Dad that it was not a good bet, as he had backed a horse called Scuthbert, and had heard no more about it.

My other usual cycling destination was Mr Gill's grocery shop, my task to get groceries for my mother. The shop was situated at the side of the Great North Road, and for a rather daunting 300 yards I would join the busy stream of cars and lorries rumbling northwards. One day, as I navigated the roundabout at which my country road joined the A1, a large lorry swung past me, perilously close; as it swung again to leave the bend, the open tail-end of the lorry whipped back at me and knocked me clean off my bike. I think the lorry driver didn't even know what had happened: at any rate, he didn't stop. I realised my right hand was gashed and bleeding. I limped to the Gills' shop, fell through the door, said: "half a pound of tea, please, Mrs Gill", and promptly fainted. The local doctor (Dr Rust, of whom more later) was summoned, and stitched my wounded hand, then Mr Gill delivered me home in his car, which was also our daily school taxi. Weakly, I asked my white-faced mother if she had got the tea; "It wasn't even tea I sent you for, it was sugar!" she responded, then burst into tears.

My next encounter with Dr Rust was not long delayed. I was helping Dad to dig in the garden as he prepared long fascinating furrows, into which he would bestow the horribly wrinkled and sad looking seed potatoes which miraculously would several weeks later transmute into a wealth of round white offspring. I was wearing my beloved first pair of football boots, a Christmas present: Mum and Dad were more or less forced into this by my propensity otherwise to kick to pieces any shoes provided to me. I was brandishing a garden fork, and as the ground was frozen, I had to jab down pretty hard to stick the tines into the earth. The next thing I knew I had jabbed the fork straight through the leather boot, through my instep, and out again at the bottom of my foot. More fainting. Since no telephone was remotely available to him, Dad had to cycle to Boroughbridge to get Dr Rust, who was just about to go horse riding and would have readily agreed with the characterisation by many of his colleagues of the proposed National Health Service as 'a dastardly socialist plot'. "Oh, bloody hell!" was his initial response to Dad's plea to come quick; but he knew Dad better than to refuse. My foot was cleaned and bandaged, medicines were administered, and now I just had to survive the fairly nasty pain I was in for some time. But worse was still to come. As my foot recovered, I was allowed out of bed, and on a particularly cold day sat close to the coal fire to keep warm, my bare foot stretched out to the heat. On an iron grid across the frame of the fire stood a kettle of water, boiling up to make tea or for washing the dirty dishes. Mum leaned over me to hook off the kettle, slipped, and dropped scalding hot water over my wounded foot. I got Mum's preferred all-purpose treatment, a coat of Vaseline, which promptly produced a mass of blisters, and another visit from the increasingly irritated doctor. Poor Mum was distraught: the medical costs of any doctoring were crippling for them, and would mean

*Family group outside Granny and Grandad Minogue's Knaresborough council house, looking somewhat down-at-heel in 1947.*

*Portrait of me and my sisters, dressed up for the camera, about the same time.*

more overtime labour in the fields for Dad. This was the hardest time of their married life. But they were rescued to a considerable degree by the great reforms of the 1945-50 Labour government. And so was I, as I was about to enter the brave new world accessible to anyone able to climb the post-war educational ladder.

# Chapter Seven

## Going to the Grammar

*Today the grammar school cap is a more potent emblem of privilege than the old school tie.*
New Statesman editorial 1953

An abiding concern and ambition for my parents was that their children should never suffer from the deprivations, poverty, and lack of opportunities that had blighted their own lives to such a considerable degree. Perhaps 'blighted' is too strong a description, given the ways in which, like many other working-class people, they so often rose above the economic conditions with which they constantly struggled, and contrived to create closeness, love and security in their social and family lives. Growing up, we three children lived a cliché: poor but happy. Nonetheless, I quite quickly began to understand the limits that might constrain our futures. We had always lived in a political atmosphere, and at seven years old I had shared (if somewhat uncomprehendingly) the wild joy of the 1945 Labour election victory, sitting on my father's shoulders among huge celebratory crowds in my mother's home town of Wallsend on Tyne. This victory (a mind-boggling parliamentary majority of 146, and a 47.9% share of the people's vote compared with 36.9% for the Tories) would take some considerable time to translate into the changes in class structures and relationships that would eventually underwrite some (albeit limited) social mobility, and real improvements in the material lives of workers. The shock experienced by the well-to-do classes was illustrated by novelist Elizabeth Bowen, who felt that war had created a more democratic society but was horrified by the Labour victory: 'I felt sick, and shortly afterwards was'. According to Rosemary Hill, in a London Review of Books piece in February 2013, Evelyn Waugh apparently contemplated buying a castle in Ireland to 'shelter from the Attlee terror'. They need not have worried. Clem Attlee would have more Old Etonians on his front bench than Harold Macmillan in the early 1960s, and it was the clearly middle class voice of middle class lawyer Hartley Shawcross that cried out from the back-benches, "We are the masters now!": while the new Prime Minister was self-evidently proud of his Haileybury schooling. Moreover, only 38% of Labour MPs were from working class backgrounds. In any event, class war was alive and well in myriad ways, which I would soon be able to experience at first hand, more obviously in the quasi-feudal setting of Allerton Park, but in countless small ways in the general social and economic life of the bit of rural Yorkshire we inhabited. In the post-war period people were 'class-conscious' to a degree that would now astonish and baffle; you were meant to know your place, and if you showed signs of not doing so there would be someone ready to remind you. This could come from both sides of the class divide, with middle-class people (and more especially lower middle-class people) ready to look down on those regarded as their social inferiors, and working-class people quick, often, to pour scorn on any of their number who appeared to be getting above themselves (a set of relationships to be wonderfully pinned down in the Sixties in a satirical sketch from John Cleese and colleagues).

Getting to 'the grammar' was, in the late 1940s and 1950s, practically a blood sport. No other form of social competition was so laden with hope, expectation, fear, and bitterness. The last year or so of primary school lead up to the eleven plus examination, and this sword of Damocles would divide the social flock into winners and losers, the winners going to the grammar school, the losers largely consigned to the dumping ground of the secondary modern school. There were so-called 'technical schools' as a notional in-between, but as Peter Hennessy shows in *Having It So Good,* his captivating mix of reminiscence and analysis of the Fifties, the Labour Government dismally failed to follow through on this supposed third leg of the tripartite system. What was being 'won' and 'lost' was opportunity, the chance to climb an educational ladder which would ultimately lead a favoured minority to the sunlit uplands of the university: only some 4% of the relevant age group in the 1950s, rising to 10-14% over succeeding decades (the proportion in 2018 was around 50%). Those just below that level would occupy minor positions in a variety of professions: teaching, banking, commerce, accountancy, social work, local government, the health services, and so on. Those with university degrees would still expect to be at the top of these professional heaps, comfortably leap-frogging their erstwhile schoolmates, though there were many examples of the latter making good. If you lost out in this competition, you got what was left: usually manual, unskilled labouring jobs, though later (and with the creation of better provision of technical training) many would be trained in trades and would become plumbers, electricians, joiners, mechanics, chefs. At the bottom of the pile, you might be dogged by constant unemployment, or at worst drift into those shadowy social peripheries where crime, drink, and drugs might be the tenuous means to a miserable survival.

At the age of ten I had no inkling of all this. I had settled into the local village primary school at Kirby Hill, just outside Boroughbridge, two country miles from my home in Ellenthorpe. Each day, some half dozen children were transported from this hamlet, and neighbouring farms, by Mr Gill's taxi. It was then a small school with few pretensions (now, the obsessive regime of measuring and ranking our educational institutions tells us that it was, in 2014, in the top 20% of such schools nationally). I remember best my pleasure in lessons in the school garden, where I was able proudly to demonstrate the planting and sowing skills already imparted by my father. I recall with less pleasure the extremely bad-tempered headmaster, Mr Thompson, who unbent once to my surprise by joining us boys in a game of cricket in the school yard, and displayed an unsuspected and crafty leg-break. My other strong memory is of the school races when, now finally (and to me, mysteriously) freed from the restrictions of ill health and faintheartedness, I competed doughtily all the way to the finish of the 100 yards (run on the tarmac road outside the school) with one Eddie Thirkill, who pipped me on the line.

I have dim but happy enough memories of this little village school, the first I had been able to settle into for any length of time. My mother was more exercised by the fact that it was utterly impracticable at this stage for her children to get a Catholic education, something which made the occasional *deus ex machina* visits from her somewhat distant nearest priest a bit of an ordeal. She managed to conform to his stern remonstrances by taking me and Maureen to Sunday Mass in a private house in Ripon. A small crisis arose when I was required to sing in the school choir in a Christmas service at the village Anglican church. This caused so much anxiety in the collective Catholic hierarchy that the priest tried to forbid this dangerous wandering of one of his flock. But Mum, so strongly committed to my educational future, fought the good fight and persuaded the priest to obtain a papal dispensation via the even more distant Bishop in Leeds; so I had in my short but eventful Catholic life been in on my mother only narrowly avoiding extreme unction, and had now actually scored a papal dispensation. I recall the wonder of singing my heart out, (I can still sing every word of 'The Holly and The Ivy') with my school friends, in the candle-lit and Christmassy church, while Mum and Dad watched proudly, Mum with moist eyes, perhaps contemplating the possibility that I was taking my first steps on the road to damnation. Perhaps I was, for my next steps took me off (with further lofty dispensations) to decidedly Anglican grammar schools.

Kirby Hill school had not, I think, sent anyone to grammar school in the years immediately after the war, but in 1949 two of us succeeded in passing the new eleven-plus examination, myself and Thelma Whittle. Thelma was a rare bird in the school, a middle-class child whose father was a Squadron Leader at the local RAF Dishforth station (a son would almost certainly have been sent to a public school). She was, I think, my first girlfriend, in that fantasy manner of most eleven-year olds. We shyly said our goodbyes outside the school gates, and I never saw her again. Then I ran for the school taxi, clutching the bit of paper that heralded my new dawn. Mum burst into tears again, Dad beamed a gruff and wordless happiness. I could not then know what an extraordinary event this was for people of their background and history, nor could I guess how the pride would be mingled with anxiety, for it meant a whole new set of financial demands on their very scant purses. Dad was at this point (1948-9) earning about £4 and 10 shillings a week, approximately two thirds of the average urban worker's wage, but now supplemented by the Labour Government's new child allowances, which for our family meant an additional 10 shillings a week. This still meant that a married family with three children had only some £5 a week to meet all their costs of living. It simply was not enough, and I well knew that Mum and Dad were struggling badly. We were so short of money that Mum cleaned our teeth with soot from the chimney back, wiping them with a wet cloth; when said teeth, perhaps unsurprisingly, protested, I would receive the traditional folk treatment of vinegar and brown paper (the use of charcoal for tooth-cleaning was attested by a Guardian correspondence in 2017). Not much later, I would suffer the first of several notably agricultural interventions by the local dentist.

Meanwhile, each and every day, in what amounted to a seven day week, my father would do hard manual labour from dawn to dusk. My mother would endure what must have been equally hard labour meeting the needs of three young children: washing nappies and clothes without the benefit of a washing machine, not even of piped water; pressing those cleaned clothes by putting them through a mangle, a contrivance of rollers that pressed water out of the wet clothes, then ironing them with a flat-iron heated (as was everything else) on the domestic range; keeping a house clean without the benefit of vacuum cleaners; providing daily meals for us all (Dad included) without the benefit of a cooker or any other labour saving appliances. This was drudgery of the most exhausting kind. On other occasions, I would be sent into Boroughbridge on my bicycle to the local hardware store to buy this or that: often, paraffin oil for our crude oil lamps, our only source of light other than the wood-fed fire. The Squeers-like shopkeeper would rub his hands and implore me beseechingly to tell my mother that he could not give her more oil if she could not pay something off her existing small debt: cruelty glistened in his eye as he observed my red-faced shame on my mother's behalf. So, it was not by any means an unmitigated blessing, my passing the eleven plus, and I wonder to this day how they managed: almost certainly more 10-hour days for Dad, more turnips hoed to get me a school uniform and a pair of shorts and gym shoes. It was against this domestic backdrop that I recall vividly my parents having bitter arguments about debts run up by Mum at local shops, for no more than the bare necessities. During these rows I would lie in bed with my hands over my ears, desperately upset to hear my beloved mother and father falling out with each other. As Flaubert writes in *Madame Bovary,* 'of all the icy blasts that blow on love, a request for money is the most chilling'.

On an autumnal day in 1949 my trusty if rusty bicycle delivered me, bright faced, colourfully uniformed, and proud possessor of my first ever school satchel, to the bus stop in Kirby Hill (dumping my bike in the yard of a friendly local farmer), from where I took a bus to the cathedral city of Ripon, what would be a daily 12 miles round trip. From the city square I walked about half a mile up to Ripon Grammar School and into an environment so alien to me that it took me a good week to pluck up the courage to speak to anyone ( Lorna Sage in her memoir *Bad Blood,* writes of a similar situation as feeling 'like an evacuee or a displaced person' and that she lacked the courage to put up her hand in class to volunteer comments). Ripon Grammar School was an ancient foundation dating back to 1555, originally set up to teach Latin to the sons of the well-to-do. Not only was my new setting still solidly middle class: it also was partly a boarding school with fee paying students, in effect what would become known as a direct grant school, largely privately funded but receiving a state grant in return for taking in free day boys like myself who had passed the eleven plus. I did not realise at this point that even so, as the son of a farm labourer, I was quite a rarity. The school motto, originating unusually in an Old English tag, translated as 'eager to learn and seek after righteousness': I'm not sure that I ever tried very hard to seek after righteousness, but eager to learn I certainly was.

Despite my initial shyness I soon settled in, not least because a clear enmity between boarders and day boys pushed me into a group which embraced me simply because of my dayboy-ness. But more than that, I was even able to cross this social divide (pretty much a class divide with which I would become all too familiar in the range of institutions I entered over the next decade) by virtue of my unsuspected prowess on the sports field. I discovered that compared with other boys I could run pretty fast, having had much practice outstripping my stick-wielding mother; and I was an excellent catcher of a ball, thanks to my cricket-mad father. The combination on the rugby field was devastating, despite the odd shaped ball with which I had no prior acquaintance, and I was soon moved up into the third-year class for rugby games, while also running the last leg for the school relay team in the annual district schools sports meeting. I had made my mark.

Unhappily, the art teacher soon made his mark on me. Enraged by an unruly class, and doubtless by life in general, he hurled a wooden chalk eraser in the general direction of the front row and hit me square in the eye. Bleeding and unable to see, I was led to the school matron who bathed my eye and returned my sight to me but anxiously warned me not to tell anyone how this accident had happened; no doubt the school had its reputation, and its fee-earning capacity, to protect. When I got home, I told Mum and Dad that I had fallen off my bicycle, an explanation so plausible that it was never questioned. The bruises soon vanished, but my relationship with art never really recovered, as my school record for that first year demonstrated. But in 6 out of 7 subjects I was top of the class, rewarded by my proud parents with a brand-new pair of football boots, the original pair still suffering from fork-damage. For some time I took them to bed with me, only dimly aware that they came at the cost of more extra labour by Dad.

This was a particularly apt present because I was about to change schools, from the rugby-playing Ripon Grammar School to the soccer-playing King James's Grammar School at Knaresborough, located in a different local education authority. The reason for this was that Mum and Dad were on the road again, seeking a little more income to cope with their increasingly costly children. Astonishingly, this search took them back to the place where they had met, and in Dad's case had been born, on the Allerton estate of Lord Mowbray and Stourton, now the eccentric and bad-tempered 25th

Baron. I described earlier the small estate hamlet of Allerton Mauleverer, based on recent visits, but when there as a child it was not much different, nor had it greatly changed, according to my father, from the mid-1920s. Both before and after the Second World War many such aristocratic estates were struggling to stay afloat, and Allerton Park was no exception, with working staff both on the farms and in the Castle much reduced. The notion of 'struggle' here is a relative one: it meant that upper class families like this had difficulty in meeting the costs of a privileged and taken-for-granted life style, which involved public school fees for their children, regular stays in London to accommodate visits to the House of Lords, participation in 'the London season', club memberships, regimental activities and so on. The Allerton farms were hard pressed to produce the income required for such a lifestyle, for they had been badly managed by their idiosyncratic owners, with poor choices of incompetent tenant farmers and managing agents. Dad arrived at a time when the chickens were coming home to roost, and for a while it seemed as though he would be able to play a part in making the farming operations more successful. He was first put into Gatehill Farm, with a pretty rural setting on the edge of woods, and where he had been employed for a time when a 12-year-old boy, tenting (scaring off) crows. Recent research has suggested that just outside Gatehill Farm lies the site of an ancient Priory, so what with this and the prestigious Catholicity of the Mowbrays, even Mum's yearning for a proper Catholic setting should have been satisfied. I was happy to have new fields and pastures to explore, despite a long walk, about a mile or so, to reach the ubiquitous Great North Road and the bus to my new school in Knaresborough. Mum was much less happy with the unmodernised, down at heel house, though we were allowed our very own cow for the provision of milk and cream. She was further mortified when the grim-visaged and bossy Head Gamekeeper shot her beloved pet dog Queenie, for no greater offence than excitedly chasing a few squawking pheasants around the nearby field, though never catching any. This gamekeeper was an unpleasant bully, and fell further in my estimation when I came across several animal carcases he had trapped or shot and pinned up on a sort of dreadful warning noticeboard, whether to us or the other birds and animals I was never quite sure. For some weeks Queenie wandered around swathed in head bandages, but sadly she never recovered.

Mum was bursting with anger, but we were all transfixed when Dad was asked to be manager of the Home Farm, the centrepiece of the estate. He was delighted to be given such responsibilities. As for the rest of us, it was the first time (this now 1950) that we had ever lived in a house with electricity, a bathroom, and an inside lavatory. Best of all, we had a very posh-looking white telephone: Mum thought she had died and gone to heaven. We now settled down to a happy little period and it seemed as though returning to this scene of their younger selves would be a turning point in my parents' lives. I don't know what Dad earned at this point but know that they were much less harassed financially, especially as Mum also received payment for running the dairy produce side of the farm, churning butter and cream, washing and packing eggs, and so on. I earned a little pocket money by helping out with these tasks, and also by taking a Sunday paper round on my bike to the local hamlets and farms and the nearby village of Hopperton. This way I not only got to know all the locals, many of whom gave me tips of threepenny bits and the occasional sixpence, but also established a first acquaintance with the whole range of the national press. I would collect the bundle of papers from the York bus bound for Knaresborough, then sit in the hedge-back for a quick read. I have to confess that the *News of the World* unerringly drew my attention with its vicarious gaze into the murky world of sex, violence, fraudulent commercial travellers and defrocked vicars, followed closely by the *Sunday Express*, and my favourite Giles 'Grandma' cartoons. 'Bit late today, young Martin' my customers would comment, eager for their Sunday read: they never knew that I had spent a good hour of free reading at their expense. These were precisely the papers held by such as Richard Hoggart to be responsible for the corruption of young minds like mine. I couldn't wait to get at them, and their doubtless misleading picture of the exciting world outside our rural environs.

In 1951, I would get a brief glimpse of this outside world when Mum and Dad took me with them on a union-sponsored trip to the Festival of Britain, on London's South Bank. Dad woke me up in the small hours: we had to walk in a pale dawn across fields and by country tracks to the nearby village of Whixley, and a coach to York railway station. Once in London, we were to travel by underground tube to Embankment station, then cross the Thames by bridge to the Festival. This was all too much for some of our party, who managed to get separated from the rest by failing to get out of the underground tube train. One elderly man looked thunderstruck as his wife disappeared into the tunnel. He clearly thought he might never see her again. The organiser speculated that since it was the Circle Line, she could safely travel right round the system without having to get off. I have no idea how this was all resolved. But I do remember the huge excitement of the dazzling Festival, and the famous Skylon, while the highlight for many was the excitement of seeing themselves captured on new-fangled television. Exhausted and exhilarated we returned to Yorkshire, led back by my father across midnight black fields. My sisters had stayed with friends and it was several weeks before Maureen discovered where we had gone, after reading a piece I wrote about it in the school magazine: she was furious.

I was opening out shyly to the human contacts in the village, and profited from them. There was Bill, like my mother a Geordie exile. He had made a living 'tinkling the ivories', as he put it, in Tyneside bars. As a favour to Mum, he would occasionally give me an impromptu lesson in his front room, but was so in love with his own musicianship that he always took over from my stumbling efforts to show how it should be done, so I didn't make much progress, not least because there seemed no prospect of me ever having a piano to practice on. Indeed, I was better served in this respect by Mum herself, who possessed and could play a battered old piano accordion she had picked up during the war. Across the road from Bill was Adolf Lelch, a Pole left behind by the retreating post-war tides of migration. Adolf played football for Knaresborough Town football team, and had some local notoriety because he was the first footballer there ever to execute an overhead bicycle kick, and spectators would come from miles around just to see him do this. He would often practice a quick bit of ball juggling with me. The best stop of all was at the village (and estate) blacksmith's, where the Raw family had been installed since the 1930s and knew Mum and Dad from those days. They held a sort of Sunday open house, and 'Mother' Raw would ply me with tea and cakes while their adult children, Norman and Denis, and Norman's girlfriend Jean, would tease me about the girls at school as I blushed deeply.

Cricket was something of a social cement at this time. The Raw lads formed a Hopperton village team with its headquarters at the local pub, The Mason's Arms. Dad was an enthusiastic member and I was just old enough at 12 plus to take part in real matches. These were played on the unforgiving surfaces of the cow meadow behind the pub, with a grass strip mowed down for a wicket, but the rest of the field left in its natural state. We played other village teams in similarly rustic conditions. By now I was playing and being coached at school too, so was relatively expert compared with our assortment of locals. I generally opened the batting. Denis Raw was a fiery bowler on our bumpy field strip; Norman, the budding blacksmith, satisfied a well-established bucolic tradition by disdaining any form of batsman-ship other than heaves out of the ground for six, a sound tactic since my careful off drives invariably got stuck in the long grass, though if these got lost (as they often did) it was quite common to take an all-run six, then down bats and go to help in the search. Our secret weapon was Old Jack (forty-odd perhaps but weather-beaten and gnarled) who bowled looping and tricky off breaks in his best suit trousers and braces. My memory of my Dad is rather a sad one; he had no little difficulty batting because of his damaged hand, with only two properly flexible fingers, and I would watch with my heart in my mouth, longing for him to do heroic things and win the day. He never did, but he was second to none in his grasp of the Laws of the Game, and probably won some matches by his magisterial interpretations, often hotly contested afterwards in the pub.

I have a memento of these days in the form of a photograph where I crouch companionably next to my father, (he playing in a flat cap, as always) squinting up at the camera. This was the occasion of a riveting visit to play against the local mental hospital, who put out a team made up of warders and inmates. They had a real cricket ground with grass beautifully mown, and boundary ropes, and a neat little white painted pavilion. This itself was sufficient to overawe us village yokels, but the large congregation of watching patients strewn in various poses around the boundary was even more distracting. One little group had a large gramophone on which they played music, very loudly, throughout the match. Others would shout incoherently and run up and down when the batsmen were running. From time to time, one of the spectators would run on to the field and try to claim the ball. The chief warder, who (naturally) was captain and also (naturally) opened the batting, dealt with all distractions calmly while swatting the odd ball for four. But even he had trouble with his opening batting partner, a patient, who very clearly knew how to bat, but who after hitting the ball always refused point blank to move from his position at the crease, so that many runs were lost to his team. When finally scuppered by one of Old Jack's devilish spinners, it was some time before he could be persuaded to leave the field of play. It all had an unreal, hallucinatory quality, yet in my mind's eye I see those scenes now, some seventy years on, with tremendous clarity, and recognise the confused, half frightened sadness I felt, experiencing mentally damaged people for the first time.

Class differences began to insert themselves into my barely formed social and personal consciousness around this time. They were difficult to avoid on an aristocratic estate, even one so down at heel as this one was.

For example, when Ian Milroy, the son of the estate's Agent, returned home from his public school for the summer holidays, he took my place as opening batsman as of right. Though I got to know him and his sister a little, I still burned with resentment. When I turned 14, it seemed that I qualified as cannon fodder, or at least membership of the poor bloody infantry, in the estate's weekly waging of war on the substantial population of game birds: pheasants, partridges, and a few woodcock. Lord Mowbray organised these regular shooting parties ostensibly as a celebration of that version of the sporting life venerated by his class, along with fox-hunting. In reality, financial motives played the main part, for these events brought in much needed income to the hard-pressed estate. The primary targets were well heeled local bigwigs who might be dominant in commerce and industry, and exceedingly wealthy, but who otherwise would find it no easy matter to rub shoulders with high born aristocrats. One of the practical problems here, as I would soon discover, was that such people could not always be relied on for a close acquaintance with the etiquette of shooting.

My initiation into these bizarre social rites was as a beater (my father's diary terms this 'bush beating'). A motley collection of farm workers, gardeners, retired estate workers, and local lads like myself would form a line at the behest of the presiding gamekeeper, the much-hated persecutor of Queenie. We would be directed across a field towards a distant wood. On the other side of this wood another, rather better dressed line of shooters would be formed up, waiting for us to flush out the game birds towards their positions. At first this seemed to be fun, as we marched forward, beating the farm crops with our sticks, and bellowing to scare up the birds. Once up, the poor birds had very little chance of escape from anyone who was even a moderate marksman, given the wide spread of shot from the modern gun, more of a blunderbuss than a sniper's rifle. But your average Leeds or Bradford businessman was not used to this stuff, he had simply not been born to it, unlike his hosts. On my third foray as a beater, we had already had quite an unpleasant time of it ploughing our way through a field of sopping wet, icy cold kale. Soaked and chilled, we reached the edge of the woods with some relief, and marched more happily forward, shouting at the tops of our voices. We were astonished to hear what turned out to be lead shot ripping through branches and leaves just above our heads. Two of the older hands flung themselves to the floor. I crouched uncertainly, absurdly thinking that I must not make a fool of myself. Another volley crashed through the trees, splinters of wood raining down on us. Then we heard loud roars from the head gamekeeper, who came running through the trees to where we had frozen still. It seems that that one of the shooting party, on his first shoot, had excitedly loosed off head high at the first emerging birds, and this had caused another of the party involuntarily to follow suit. The ensuing lead barrage could easily have done for a hapless beater or two (watching Edward Fox accidentally kill a beater in the 1985 film *The Shooting Party* brought a shudder of recognition). I never learned whether the culprit was taken away to the Tower, or simply not invited again. Perhaps worried by the thought of actual casualties among the children of the estate workers, the organisers re-allocated me to Lord Mowbray's son and heir, the Hon. Charles Stourton. I was surprised to find how well he shot, (he would one day captain the House of Lords shooting team) given that he wore a rather piratical black patch over an eye lost during the Second World War. The story goes that as he lay wounded, and being a devout Catholic, he sought to have a priest rather than a doctor. My designation was assistant gun loader and bag handler, handing out cartridges and taking in sadly dead and disarranged pheasants. It was not to my taste, and Dad readily accepted my plea to be allowed to pursue school games on a Saturday rather than real game. A decade and a half later the Hon Charles would tread the same Whitehall corridors that I did. I'm sorry to say that we never met, though I doubt if he would then have recognised his one-time bedraggled and incompetent lackey.

# Chapter Eight
# Changing Places

*And yet what else is there, to catch in any shape at all the fragile pattern of particular acts and hours long ago, before oblivion blows them to the winds*
Francis Spufford: *Golden Hill*

Meanwhile, we had not yet finished our progress around rural Yorkshire. In a cruel blow to my parents' renewed hopes and expectations, in late 1952 Dad was suddenly and unceremoniously sacked from his farm manager job. The unstable Lord Mowbray was, to put it mildly, a difficult and unpredictable employer. Our new house enjoyed a splendid apple orchard but Dad records 'Lord M sent a man to chop all the trees down, and chopped down all the orchards on the other farms too...he did not even wait for the apples to get ripe so it would appear he could not bear his men to have them. He was always spying on the men and would only let them have half an hour for their dinner: he said that if they had an hour they would eat too much and would not be able to work'. But worse was in store, through some sort of dubious practice by the Agent who, writes Dad, 'was a shady character and I found out afterwards that he was bankrupt. He had introduced a shady man called Danny Reed and they were doing some fiddling. Cattle were being taken away at night and being sold. Because I would not turn a blind eye, they wanted to be rid of me. Lord Mowbray was given to believe that I was behind these mysterious losses'. After a stand-up row Dad, never one to back down, was given the sack despite the complete absence of any evidence of wrongdoing. This meant two weeks' notice to find another job and house, with a wife and three young children, and we may recall that this notably upright man was the son of another notably upright man who had earlier given 28 years of unblemished service to the same Mowbray estate. No one locally believed for a moment that Dad had been implicated in any wrongdoing, and he immediately found a job, six miles away in the village of Roecliffe, again near to Boroughbridge, but now demoted once more to being a humble farm labourer, a bitter blow for both my parents. According to my mother, when the dust settled, the true story emerged, and Lord Mowbray sent the Hon. Charles to ask my father to return to Allerton and his old farm manager job. But Dad was too proud to do so, and records only that 'I was not sorry and it was a bad thing I ever went back there'. Lord Mowbray would soon enough demonstrate his volatile and ungovernable temperament, mistreating his wife so badly in a much-publicised scandal that she fled into the night, was rescued by a passing lorry driver on the Great North Road, and later won a divorce settlement on the grounds of cruelty. This appalling peer would later fight a bitter legal battle with his own son Charles over the succession to the estate, land and inheritance: a true aristocrat and gentleman.

I was somewhat baffled by all this, and sorry to leave the Hopperton cricket team and paper round behind. But we children, used to trotting around in our parental footsteps (this was the eighth time we had moved house during my brief existence) soon adapted to a new setting. Happily, it did not mean a change of school this time, as Knaresborough Grammar School was still accessible, and in due course both Maureen and Sally would go there too. King James's Grammar School was in many respects quite different from Ripon Grammar School, though it enjoyed a similarly ancient history, having been founded as a free grammar school in 1616 by Dr Robert Chaloner, under the consent of King James 1. Chaloner decreed a syllabus that focussed on Latin and religious knowledge: 'every scholar should be taught to say the Ten Commandments... and none above the First Form should speak English in the school or at play'. The Master was to see that his pupils 'come not uncombed, unwashed, ragged or slovenly'. I fear that I must often have fallen into any or all of these categories, constantly more preoccupied with getting down the long road to catch my school bus than with appearances. Many a time, while still at Allerton Park, I would fly across the busy Great North Road, dodging cars and lorries, hand held up to intercept the moving bus which had already departed from the stop further along. Most of the bus drivers came to know me, and mostly pulled up: "C'mon young Martin, jump in quick!" I soon had plenty of practice at Roecliffe too, always late after running the whole mile and a bit, encumbered by boots and satchel: same Great North Road, different bus drivers. On dark winter evenings, returning, I would run the whole way home again, terrified by swooping bats. No wonder no one could catch me in shorts and gym shoes.

King James's Grammar School had left behind its earlier foundation, and was housed in an unlovely brick Edwardian building which had been opened in 1901 by the Earl of Harewood (at the school's 350th anniversary in 1966 his successor would unveil a new Coat of Arms, and I would, as a representative old boy, give a Vote of Thanks to him at the formal ceremony). After an initial experiment with a form of rural secondary education meant to cater for the needs of an agrarian and market community (Latin had long been left behind, as had boarders), the school had gradually moved back to a more academic curriculum by the 1920s, and from 1922 had been strongly led by Mr A.S (Sam) Robinson. During the 1930s, he recruited well qualified teachers, and academic performance slowly improved to a level commensurate with the 'grammar school' title. Even Latin was restored, though children were no longer obliged to repeat their catechisms. A school history suggests that the most famous old pupil was a poor boy whose mother 'in her widowhood had to take in washing and scrub gravestones to earn sufficient money to keep the family from the workhouse'. Her son would rise to some distinction as Lord Privy Seal and Chairman of the BBC, rewarded by the title Lord Inman of Knaresborough, an example we were constantly exhorted to follow.

I arrived in early 1950, in the fabled Sam Robinson's final year before retirement. I immediately was struck by the differences from the Ripon

*Knaresborough Grammar School Football 1st XI, me and Mick on the left of the front row.*

school. First, there were girls, a species then not acknowledged at Ripon. Secondly, the whole atmosphere was more welcoming. On the first day, as I stood shyly on the edge of the playground, not knowing anyone, a tall handsome lad hailed me. What was my name? Which form was I in? Where did I live? Satisfied with my answers, he hauled me into the playground to meet his pals. His name was Billy Balsdon. I have never forgotten his kindness, and stayed friends, even when he for a time (and to my incomprehension) courted my by then very pretty dark haired, blue eyed sister Maureen. Later that morning, ensconced in my new Form 11a, I was grasped by another tall, dark haired boy: "What's your name?" "Martin". "Right, I'll call you Mart. Do you play football Mart?" Michael Harper, (Mick) was delighted to hear that I did, and we would become inseparable friends for many years (indeed, for life), both on and off the football field.

The third big difference between these two Grammar Schools was the attitude and demeanour of the King James's staff, at once less formal (no academic gowns apart from the Headmaster) and more approachable. Mr Fairclough, now Deputy Head and temporary replacement for the retiring Sam Robinson, would give us what purported to be a Geography lesson, but consisted mainly of him regaling us with accounts of how many German prisoners he had single-handedly captured during the First World War. We youngsters were awestruck and totally believing of what might have been thought of as 'tall stories', save that he had been wounded in action, had been awarded the Military Cross, and rose to the rank of Captain. Mr Street, (always nicknamed Strata) a bluff craggy character with unfeasible amounts of gingerish hair sprouting from ears and nostrils, gave extraordinarily rambling but thrilling accounts of what rural life would have been like around Knaresborough in mediaeval times, and before that under the Romans. I acquired a lifelong interest in history which I believe I owe at least in part to this very down to earth and compelling approach: one day I would be drawn to studies both in ancient history and in mediaeval history at university.

But above all, I came under the influence, even spell, of two teachers who would become lifelong and much-loved friends. Molly Sawdon, soon to become the Senior Mistress, and largely responsible for all to do with the girls' side of the school, taught English Literature. At this early stage I scarcely knew what this meant as a subject of study; but I did know that I had an all-consuming passion for reading. This meant everything in print, initially comics from *The Beano* and *The Dandy* (born in 1937, same as me), through *The Wizard* and *Hotspur* to the new-fangled *Eagle* (1950) with its space hero Dan Dare, sometimes known as 'Biggles in Space'. I thrilled to the tales of Wilson, the homespun hero who excelled at every sport and won Wimbledon with a racket with broken strings; I ran every step with Alf Tupper, a backstreet athlete who trained on fish and chips but invariably burst first past the tape to confound the posh favourite; I hoovered up the tales of Baldy Hogan, whose unlikely lads always won the Cup in the last minute; and the Blind Bowler, who bowled to where the wicketkeeper had clapped his gloves together, and spun the ball fiendishly past despairing Australian bats. From here I progressed, in no particular order, assisted by my mother's guidance and borrowings from the local library in Boroughbridge (a truly wonderful resource throughout my school career), through G.A Henty, Jeffrey Farnol, Baroness Orczy (*The Scarlet Pimpernel*), the American dentist who wrote wonderful 'Westerns', Zane Grey (*Riders of the Purple Sage),* Conan Doyle (*The Sign of Four* being Dad's particular favourite,) on to Edgar Allan Poe and Charles Dickens (I had read *Great Expectations* by the age of 10, and it was the first film I ever saw, in David Lean's compelling 1946 version whose opening scenes scared me half to death). I was constantly in trouble from Mum for swapping whatever meagre possessions I had for secondhand comics and books. In earlier years my Auntie Sadie had sent me, as a Christmas present, three perfect little metal military jeeps, and I immediately traded in these unwanted objects for a battered but large and wholly satisfying copy of *Boys Own Annual.* When I had to confess that the Dinky Toy armour was no longer in my possession, Mum was incredibly angry, in part because Auntie Sadie was about to visit and would expect to see me proudly playing with my military hardware. Mum contradictorily, while a great source of encouragement to my reading, would also get quite cross with me for always having my head buried in a book, hence as hopelessly uncommunicative as today's children are when in front of a TV screen or i-pad. I would withdraw from the scene early, to my plain but private little bedroom, my sisters keeping each other amused in their shared bedroom across the landing. In winter, the bedroom would get so cold that frosting would form on the insides of the panes. So I would get into bed, draw the blankets over my head, and read my latest book or comic by the dim and wavering flame of a sputtering live candle. Mum rumbled this tactic, perhaps alerted by the liberal droppings of melted wax on the bedclothes. Angry all over again, she read the riot act, over my weak protests about the cold. Doubtless her crossness flowed from the perception that I might well have set fire not only to *Boys Own Annual* but myself and possibly the whole

*Molly Sawdon, Head of English at Knaresborough Grammar School, later Headmistress.*

house. But she evidently had a word with Dad, who quietly appeared with sticks and coal and lit a fire in the small grate. From now on, I was allowed to have a proper fire in my bedroom grate and to read by it before going to bed. I loved plumping myself and my latest book down in front of the warm blaze, and I still like best to read in front of an open fire: it's in the blood.

So Molly Sawdon found in me someone who responded like a thirsty plant to water as she opened up the wider world of literature to me: over the next few years she would guide me (and many others of course) through all the classic authors, poetry as well as novels and plays. Molly had a special love of the theatre, and we read under her tutelage large swathes of Shakespeare (but also Ben Jonson, Webster, and Middleton); much Restoration drama (though this was never a favourite of mine, since many of the aristocratic characters seemed all too similar to the ones I knew in real life); Ibsen and Shaw. We often read plays aloud, taking parts: I fondly remember a scene from, I think, Shaw's *Geneva* in which a rare (in our school) Scottish boy called Ian Sampson had to refer excitedly to 'the Bolshies' (or Bolsheviks). Ian, in a broad Scots accent, yelled 'the Bloshies are comin'! The Bloshies are comin'! It took even Molly some time to restore order. Ian would a little later introduce the first skiffle band to the school, and for several weeks we could all be heard offering bad imitations of Lonnie Donegan.

As I progressed through the various levels of school, I was exposed at one time or another to detailed analysis and discussion of Milton's *Paradise Lost, Books 1 and 11* (an absolute revelation to me, since I knew nothing either of the Old Testament or of the classical texts that underpinned Milton's work); Elizabethan and seventeenth century poetry (another revelation to me then being that Andrew Marvell had lived for a time under Thomas Fairfax's patronage at Appleton House, and had, as we have seen, trod the very woods and paths I had scurried along myself as a five year old only a few years earlier); to the satires of Pope and Dryden; to later poets led by Wordsworth, Byron, Shelley and Keats; and to the novels of Jane Austen, the Brontes, Thomas Hardy and D. H. Lawrence. By some quirk of a West Riding educational experiment (a brainwave of the great educationalist Sir Alec Clegg) I was never initially examined in many of these works, the idea being that potential University candidates should have a more free-flowing set of studies, unconstrained by the new GCE curricula. In my case this applied to my main interests, English Literature and History, so my formal examinations were confined to subjects of less attractiveness i.e. Maths, Sciences and Languages. I stumbled through these without much interest or conviction. Mr Norman, the lugubrious Physics teacher had given up on me around Form III. I was later allowed to drop Maths, something inconceivable these days. My principal contact with the Biology teacher, Frank Hodgson, had been entirely physical; surging out of a classroom one day I was pushed from behind and crashed into the teacher, who dropped a set of glass slides prepared for his lesson, smashing several. Furious, he slapped me heavily around the head and face several times. He was notoriously bad tempered (though a good biology teacher) and today would probably have been hauled up for physical assault. Instead, he was soon promoted to the Headmastership of Boroughbridge Secondary Modern School, his bullying tendencies probably seen as a considerable advantage in this basement of the education system. Some years later, now an adult, I met him at a private dinner. He regarded me cautiously, and I knew intuitively that he remembered the incident, and that he knew that I too had not forgotten or forgiven. But I got my highest GCE 'O' level examination score in Biology, so perhaps his rough treatment galvanised me. In these exams I suffered only one failure, in Art. The gentle Mr Jenkinson had done his best to prepare me for the big set piece, which was to do a drawing from life of a flower. The flower 'set' for this test was meant to be revealed only in the examination hall, but for the past four years the subject had been the daffodil. Week after week, 'Jenks' would patiently help me to trace out a daffodil until I could draw one blindfolded. Unhappily, the flower set for my year turned out to be the humble pansy. My pansy was a dead ringer for a daffodil, to the evident bafflement of the examiners.

My experience with Mr Hodgson was pretty untypical. Most of the teachers were amiable, especially those who were engaged with me on the sports fields, where I now excelled, whether at cricket, football or athletics. Molly Sawdon was to become a huge influence. A stickler for high standards of decorum and deportment, her severity terrified many pupils, and not a few of the male staff. She had been at the school since 1935 and during the war had done sterling work organising evacuated children. She lived with a close friend, Paddy Wansbrough, who did not have an official position, but came in at times to make up for teaching shortages, notably in sports. A small, wiry, handsome woman with keen blue eyes, she came from an upper crust sort of background, had (typically) been a driver for a General during the war, and behaved not unlike a senior member of the military herself. She taught cricket and was the first person to show me how to keep a straight bat and play correct strokes. She also organised a senior girls X1, and when we callow second years played a match against them, I was absolutely mortified to be clean bowled for a duck by a pig-tailed sixth former. In my world, girls didn't play cricket, and had no business humiliating me in this way.

Despite having two sisters I was extremely shy with the girls. I would at this age, around 14, admire from a safe distance; any closer, and to my utmost chagrin, I would turn bright red and find myself struck dumb. Indeed, had I had the misfortune to be at a boys' school I sometimes think I might have entered a monastery, which would, at least, have much cheered my mother, constantly under pressure from her local church, now St Mary's at Knaresborough, to ensure a safe Catholic upbringing for her dangerously educated children. Poor Maureen paid a high price, Mum having while at Allerton given way to the priest's insistence that she should be taught at the primary school attached to St Mary's. We soon came to hear that this school was notorious for all the wrong reasons. It was run by two sisters, devout lay Catholics who were more interested in the safeguarding of the bodies of their charges than the maturing of their minds. Sally, who very briefly also attended St Mary's during our last few weeks in Allerton, told Mum that every morning the girls had to endure an embarrassing 'clean knickers' inspection. Much of the teaching time was devoted to rehearsals of the religious catechism. Unsurprisingly, it was extremely rare for these pupils to pass the eleven-plus. This was a prime example of how poor schools and bad or inappropriate teaching could hold children back and deny them opportunities. It was to my sister Maureen's everlasting credit that she was able in these conditions to pass her eleven plus (in 1951) and join me at Knaresborough Grammar School, against odds greater than any Sally and I faced. In 1953, now in Roecliffe, Mum resisted priestly pressures and insisted that Sally should transfer to Roecliffe's primary school, on the grounds that Sally was too young to make the long journeys to the Knaresborough school and back by herself. Sally flourished under the intelligent, firm and kindly headmistress at the Roecliffe School, Edith Farnsworth, who would become a close friend to my mother, and who, according to a centenary school history, 'will always be remembered with affection'.

My friend Mick Harper, son of a well-to-do local builder, was one of those at St Mary's who failed the eleven plus, and was sent to Knaresborough Secondary Modern, despite being a bright boy who one day would be a highly successful bank manager. His parents, good practising Catholics, insisted that he be reconsidered on the basis of his first-year performance there. Mick was duly transferred to the Grammar School, albeit now a year older than his classmates. His father had another row with the parish priest over this transition to an Anglican school, and reached an accommodation that meant Mick would be allowed to avoid Assemblies, where prayers largely featured, and Religious Instruction lessons. By some inscrutable process Mum, always on what she liked to call the 'qui vive', got me incorporated into this arrangement, a happy chance for us both, now partners in crime. Each Thursday evening after school, we would troop down the hill to St. Mary's church to receive our instruction. I came to look forward to this immensely. We were always greeted by the priest's housekeeper, initially with somewhat pursed lips, clearly of a mind to expect that two cherubic-looking young boys were likely to be up to no good if given the opportunity. But once our work with the priest was done, she would treat us to a quite magnificent tea of scones, sandwiches and cakes. This prospect was enough to keep us on time and up to the mark.

The priest was Father Lawrence Spiller, a Benedictine who had taught at Ampleforth before his move to the Knaresborough parish. He was a kindly, amiable man who carried his evident learning very lightly, and managed to turn the dry-as-dust teachings and rites of the Church into interesting questions for three intelligent people to discuss. He never patronised us, and never once questioned our involvement in a non-Catholic school. I began to perceive dimly (as I was doing with Molly Sawdon) how stimulating a good teacher could be; ironically, Molly was a committed humanist, quite at the other end of the philosophical spectrum. For me, just opening up to the world of ideas, all this was genuinely exciting, if also very confusing. Mick, a practising but irreverent altar boy, introduced his own types of confusion. Once, in our formal recitals of bits of the Latin mass, I heard him deliberately mutter Orate Fartres (instead of Fratres). We both instantly went bright red with barely suppressed laughter. Perhaps wisely, or perhaps a little deaf, the saintly Father Spiller seemed not to notice.

# Chapter Nine
# The Good of the Village

*The English temper refuses to give up its rural nostalgia*
A. H. Halsey

Meanwhile we had all settled into our new Roecliffe village world, one which to me grew ever more exciting as I progressed through my teenage years. I began to feel that I was inhabiting two worlds: the rural agricultural world of the village and its nearby small town of Boroughbridge: and the rather more sophisticated society I was beginning to experience through the grammar school and its solidly middle class, more unfamiliar environment. Roecliffe was a pretty place, with houses set round a large village green, the parish church slightly set back, perhaps deliberately to avoid noticing the clearly godless village pub, The Crown Inn. At the far end of the green lay a small row of council houses, largely inhabited by workers at the brickworks just down the road towards Boroughbridge. Two or three farmhouses were also ensconced around the green, their respective acres constituting a green hinterland, on one side running down to the River Ure, a bit higher upstream from the stretch I had explored at Ellenthorpe. There was only one grand Georgian house, home to a well-connected outsider who was, however, a local magistrate. The farms were mostly tenanted for the Lawson Tancreds, local and long-established gentry who lived in Aldborough (the old Roman camp and Brigantes settlement) some miles away. This would be my local, family world for six years or so, until I would move away, first into National Service, then to Cambridge, finally to London, all constituting very different worlds and cultures. The village world is the one I remember with most affection; but I also recognise that as I grew older, more observant, perhaps more sensitive to the increasingly complicated social undergrowth that hemmed in my winding path to the future, I could see more clearly the hard and bitter nature of the conditions in which my parents were caught. While I was happy at this time, and in this part of my rural life, I was increasingly resolved to escape from it, immensely determined to avoid the poverty trap that had so constrained my parents. This trajectory would be underpinned in no small part by my mother's persistent and driving encouragement, buttressed by my father's stoic resolve and support.

But there was much to enjoy too. Though relatively poor again after our heady interlude at Allerton, we lived in a rather large farmhouse with four bedrooms and three rooms downstairs: cold and draughty, rather run down, but spacious. And now, at last, in 1952, electricity, running water, and a proper bathroom seemed here to stay. Life centred on a roomy kitchen with the usual coal-fired range for cooking and baking: this is where we ate and spent most of our evenings. The scullery off it, opening out on the milk shed and farmyard is still memorable to me as the setting for my very first world-changing shave, or so I felt it to be. There was a sitting room which one day would contain our first rented television, Mum's eclectic and often surprising collection of books, and where we would have occasional 'blow out' teas, usually when we had family visitors: the proper Northern kind with tinned salmon sandwiches, home-baked jam tarts, jellied trifle, tins of cling peaches, malt loaf, and Battenberg cake: it is still to us children an inexplicable miracle that my mother managed to produce these admittedly occasional feasts on such skimpy wages (Hoggart, in *The Uses of Literacy,* gives considerable attention to the eating habits of working class families in 1930s-1950 Hunslet in Leeds, and the items favoured in my mother's teas feature strongly in Hoggart's list). The room in between kitchen and sitting room served no clear purpose, but I would in summer do my homework in there; in winter I would sit isolated in the kitchen, trying to draw warmth from the kitchen range. Upstairs, I had my own bedroom, with its own grate and chimney. On one never forgotten occasion as I woke drowsily, snug beneath my blankets, I sensed a movement inside my pyjama top. Finding a small warm body sitting on my chest, I drew it out and inspected it: a terrified harvest mouse. I was fairly terrified myself for a bit: even more so, when I would listen in dread to the sounds of farm rats gnawing inside the walls: the famous Room 101 scene in Orwell's *1984* rang utterly true to me when I came across it.

Roecliffe village and the surrounding farms formed a genuine village community that in the latter decades of the twentieth century has been steadily eroded, in common with rural communities across the country. Primary school (doubling as a community centre), traditional pub, church, Womens' Institute; all were focal points for village activities which brought people together and let them engage with each other in ways much diminished since by a combination of middle class gentrification, and the deadly night-time grip of television. Back in the 1950s the generations would often meet together to dance, to participate in whist drives, to have a good time in The Crown, to commune more solemnly together in the parish church. Most people in the village joined in all this: I can only think of two or three families who regarded themselves as too grand to do so. For a while, given the impossibility of taking holidays, the highlight of the year was the Annual Mystery Trip, organised by Gladys Crozier, Secretary of the WI. My sisters and I were tremendously excited at the prospect, as were Mum and Dad. We piled into the coach at 5:30 pm with a significant proportion of the population of the village on board. After an hour's bumpy ride, we arrived at our destination: Stokesley, a small market town on the way to Middlesbrough. It turned out that Gladys Crozier's sister lived here, and Gladys disappeared to see her, with a stern remonstrance to us all to be back on the coach by 9:00 pm. Stokesley is pretty enough, but then was something of a one-horse town: by the time we arrived most of the shops had closed. Many fathers went missing, presumably in the local pubs. Women and children wandered around in little groups, the chief excitement being when we kept bumping into each other. We all ended up in the same fish and chip shop, still suitably mystified. The following year we did the Annual Mystery Trip again, under Gladys Crozier's careful prompting, and there was much speculation about where we would end up this time. To general disbelief, we once more found ourselves in Stokesley. I expect Gladys's sister was pleased.

Dad had now settled into his new job. His boss was Jim Driffield, an untypical farmer who had been a tank commander during the war, and still suffered from back injuries sustained then. He had red hair and a fiery temperament. He also had a much younger wife called Stella. At this time, we acquired an 18 year old lodger called Sidney Scholey, the son of a Bradford mill worker, wanting to escape a grim urban environment. The handsome Sidney was a real urban smartie in our unsophisticated rural setting, and he soon had the local girls' heads spinning. There was some evidence that he had set the attractive young Mrs Driffield's head spinning too, but at the age of 15 this was still somewhat above my innocent gaze: even when I once saw them talking together in a secretive manner behind the barn, I was quite unable to put two and two together and make it add up to something. I knew that it was making Mum very cross, but then she got cross with me if I so much as looked at a girl, so I didn't think that amounted to anything. Complications set in when Stella Driffield's younger sister made visits, and soon I glimpsed Sidney communing with her behind the barn too. Even now, older and more worldly, I cannot reliably report any real wrongdoing, and certainly the two young Driffield daughters both had their father's fiery red hair, though they were always affectionate with Sidney. Affection is something I felt for Sidney too, for it was like having an older brother, and he was full of fun. He always managed to charm Mum, whatever his indiscretions (a degree of leeway not allowed to me). He got a Charles Atlas Book of Body-Building, and we would spend hours heaving bits of old iron and measuring our arm muscles. Dad, the only one with any real muscle, would chaff "Now, you lads, y'ave muscles like spider's kneecaps". We practised standing on each other's shoulders, invariably collapsing in a heap of blankets and giggles.

Then in early 1953, the village was galvanised by Queen Elizabeth 11's Coronation. Mum and Dad, as openly anti-royalist as any in the country, threw themselves into the celebratory fray. The Fancy Dress competition was regarded by Mum as a challenge to her creativity. She decided all our roles and organised all the costumes. Maureen, pretty as a picture, with black wavy hair and lovely blue eyes, was installed as Queen of the May; six years old Sally was decked out as a Coronation Mug, trapped in a sort of cage made of chicken wire, glue and paper: a more grumpy, uncooperative chicken it would have been difficult to imagine. Sidney and I were allocated the roles of Ancient Britons, Neanderthal men (pretty much Mum's view of the essential character of all men), dressed in skimpy rabbit furs over our underpants; from the town butcher she had procured two large cow bones, which we brandished fiercely. Unhappily it was a very wet morning as the Yorkshire weather did its best to rain on this essentially Southern parade. We all shivered as the Chairman of the Parish Council and his Good Lady Wife interminably inspected a bedraggled row of sopping kids in various states of disarray: it would have been none too easy to determine, by this stage, what many of the entries represented, as costumes and spirits drooped in the persistent drizzle. To no one's surprise Mum's creations won two of the first three prizes.

The final event and highlight of the day's proceedings was the Race Round the Village Green, involving all male members of the village between 12 and 50. A clever system of handicapping was deployed. Sidney and I attracted penalties for the sheer fact that we wore shorts and gym shoes: I was known to have won real races at school. We were placed together at the very back line, along with Johnny Crozier, also known as a likely local athletic lad from

Boroughbridge Modern School. The older men were given quite substantial starts. Naturally, no one knew of Dad's youthful prowess at running: indeed, I didn't know this myself until I read his diaries after his death. Still, he was now 43 and dressed in his best trousers, shirt and shoes. He couldn't possibly win... could he? We lads at the back surged forward, confident that we would soon overtake all these useless kids and old fogies. We steadily reeled them in, but Dad was flying out at the front, cheered lustily by everyone except Mum, who always wanted me to win any race I was in, including the race of life. Sidney was fading behind me; "Bloody hell, Martin" he gasped "you can't let your Dad win". And I couldn't, though I now wish very much that I had. I caught him, a few yards from the finishing line, his shirt tails streaming out behind him, one of his shoelaces undone and threatening to trip him up. Johnny Crozier was third. "I kept wondering when you'd turn up" Dad remarked, as he wandered off to join the single wicket bowling competition.

Roecliffe had never shown much interest in village cricket until Dad arrived. He found a willing accomplice in his boss, Jim Driffield, who had apparently been a fine fast bowler before his back injury. We put our heads together, me acting as Hon. Secretary. I wrote begging letters to anyone who might give some money to us: magistrates, tradesmen, the vicar, farmers, the retired military (we had both a Colonel and a Major in the village, the former running a grumpy village shop: small boys and vagrants would have been shot at dawn could he have had his way). A special letter was concocted for the local squire, (he of the Lawson Tancred family) who owned most of the farms, inviting him to be President. The response was heart-warming: envelopes poured in containing cash and cheques. The grumpy Colonel offered a free score-book from his rather ancient stock of stationery. The Squire graciously consented to lend his name. There was enough to buy a bag of kit: bats, balls, pads and gloves, wickets. Roecliffe Cricket Club was born, a latecomer in a long Yorkshire tradition.

Our first match was memorable. A newly mown cornfield outside the village was inspected and approved as our pitch. A heavy old steam roller was trotted out by a local farmer and this puffed up and down until a 22-yard strip of stubble-strewn earth could be regarded as somewhere near flattened. Our first match was against an XI drawn mainly from Minskip, a neighbouring village with a proper cricket team for whom I had already played in the Harrogate League. They batted first, sledged constantly not only by our own players but by a motley assembly of villagers who came from the Crown carrying crates of beer, and thought the whole thing a fine entertainment. When we were fielding they even tried to kick the ball back into the field of play before it crossed the straggly white washed boundary line. They failed to prevent a rather large score by the opposition against our somewhat unpractised bowling. Jim Driffield charged in aggressively and had several testy altercations with the opposition umpires (another venerable strand in the weave of the Yorkshire village cricket tradition was that umpires were often unoccupied members or supporters of the competing teams). Our own secret weapon here was Old Frank Winn, actually not much older than 50, a farmer who had the odd habit of repeating everything he said: "Good mornin', Ah say, good morning", "Nice day, Ah say, nice day". Our village postman, Jack Harland, delivered his overs rather more quickly than he normally delivered his letters and parcels: at least these arrived, but his very slow spinners were carted into the next field. After the agreed 20 overs, we were left to get the unlikely total of 144, a very high score by Yorkshire village cricket standards, where people were not supposed to hit boundaries until at least ten overs had been played, and remarkable in the light of the utterly unpredictable nature of the wicket.

I knew Minskip to have a wild young fast bowler called Les, and privately thought someone's life and limb would be severely threatened as I went out to bat with Jim Driffield. Les's first ball not only soared over my head but the wicket-keeper's too, without even bouncing on the way. His second scuttled along the floor and cracked into the base of my stumps. I retired red-faced, my reputation in tatters. The Major now entered, wearing a very natty cummerbund in his old school colours. He looked as apprehensive as he might have been in the trenches, and probably wished there was one to hand. Happily, Les sent his remaining four balls either side of a despairing wicket-keeper. At the end of the first over we had scored 20 byes for one wicket. There were one or two collector's items: the Major was hit hard in his private parts and given out lbw by the Minskip umpire, who was roundly jeered by the increasingly well lubricated spectators. Our own reply to all this was Old Frank Winn, who leaned on his stick and scornfully dismissed every appeal. This bought us significant time and though a win was out of the question, we would get a draw if we could see out the 20 overs. An unexpected cameo was provided by Sidney, who hailed from the cricketing part of Bradford known as Pudsey, home to the famous Len Hutton: in a completely un-Huttonesque style, he flogged the ball to all parts until unceremoniously stumped trying to smash a six. Enter Dad, the last man, only one good hand but a heart of oak. For the three remaining overs he set out to demonstrate the meaning of 'they shall not pass', interposing every part of his body between ball and wicket. He must have been black and blue but never flinched. Every appeal was met by a stern "Not Out! Ah say, Not Out!" from Old Frank Winn. Dad met the last fierce effort from Les with (unusually) the middle of the bat and we had won a famous draw. Dad was a most unlikely hero, given his modest batting record. We held a beery celebration in the pub car park: Old Frank Winn didn't drink alcohol but stumped about on his stick grinning broadly and declaring at intervals "Not Out! Ah say Not Out!"

Dad would shortly wrong-foot us all again, for he had an even more modest record in practical household matters, to my mother's frequently expressed irritation. Dad never in his life, to the best of my recollection, mended an electric fuse, plug, or appliance. Most of his domestic life had been lived without the benefit of electricity, and his Irish father proclaimed it an invention of the devil, nightly, in his old age, pulling out every plug he could find before retiring to bed. Dad inherited this distrust and didn't intend to find out how it all worked. Matters electrical were, as much else in the house, left to Mum, but she wasn't much better informed than Dad. Once I came home to find her standing on a wobbly chair in our sitting room, grappling with a recalcitrant ceiling light. The light simply would not work, though she had put in a new bulb. Tight-lipped, she jumped from the chair, marched out, returned with a pair of garden shears, and with an expression of no little ferocity snipped the light cord clean off. She clearly felt, as I have always done, that *things* have a distinct personality, usually hostile. Things can be for you or against you, they must not be so much managed and repaired, as fought against and subdued. This posture was to some degree self-contrived, and had its benefits. I have avoided all manner of unexciting and awkward tasks just because no-one in their right mind would have dreamed of entrusting them to me. Dad was much the same, simply preferring to avoid the aggravation that comes from trying to mend things broken by other people (my bike, Mum's mangle), but not because he couldn't do these things: he was, after all, a highly skilled craftsman on the farm.

The truth of this was borne in upon me, and, possibly to her chagrin, Mum, shortly after I had been expelled from my woodwork class on the grounds that the school couldn't afford to waste so much wood. I was immensely destructive with a chisel and tenon-saw in my hands, and brought my woodwork teacher, Mr Metcalfe, to the brink of hysteria. He told the headmaster that if I didn't go, he would. I went, to the art class, where the amiable and gentle soul Jenks (we met him earlier) had long gone past the stage of being fazed by anything a child might do; anyway, paper was cheaper than wood. Mum wasn't pleased with this development, though, and somehow her tirade about my fecklessness broadened out to include Dad. He too, she implied, would have been thrown out of any self-respecting woodwork class, why, he couldn't even mend a snipped-off light flex, ordinary everyday things like that. Dad would normally display the proverbial duck's back to such floods of wrath from my mother, which were by no means uncommon, but for some reason this particular charge got through the thick skin he had developed. "I could do it if I wanted to," he asserted stubbornly "I used to be good at woodwork". Disbelief was general. Dad didn't say any more, but the next Monday evening he took himself off to the local Modern School, and this became a regular Monday evening fixture. Curious, we pressed him for information. "You'll see, soon enough," he would mutter darkly. After six such Mondays, as Mum and I sat warming our legs in front of the blazing hearth, there was a loud knock on the front door. It opened to reveal Dad, grinning with pride and self-satisfaction as he wheeled in the most perfect, highly polished, sweetly rolling tea trolley you could ever hope to see. "Y'see", he kept saying to no-one in particular, "Y'see". And indeed, we did see, but we still couldn't believe it. Mum had gone very quiet: a polished wooden tea trolley was one of her dearest dreams, one she never thought to have realised. Dad looked at her uneasily, shifting from one foot to the other and back again. "I thought, like, you'd be pleased with a tea trolley. Y'know..." Mum rapidly left the room: she hated to cry in front of the children. Dad never again, to my knowledge, made or mended anything domestic; but Mum never again mentioned this deficiency. The tea trolley made up for a great deal of frustration. Moreover, Dad had demonstrated that he could do practical household tasks if he wanted to: he just didn't want to.

Around this time, politics reared its head again. Since the glory days of 1945, Dad had kept his counsel, happy enough with the post-war settlement and the creation of a welfare state that promised to bring greater social justice and security for working class people, freedom from worry about health, better educational opportunities for ordinary families. At the same time, a Britain bankrupted by war and ill-equipped to manage the economic aftermath, became increasingly impatient for an end to gloom, continued rationing, and scarcity. Memories were all too short, and soon people were thinking that the grass might be greener on the other side of the political fence. Labour had just scraped home in the 1950 election but were unable to prevent a Conservative victory in 1951, despite our sitting up all night listening to the results on the radio, and keeping count of gains and losses with red dots and blue dots in the list of parliamentary constituencies. This time Labour won many of the battles but lost the war, the Conservatives obtaining a relatively narrow majority of parliamentary seats, despite Labour getting a majority of the popular vote. Mum and Dad were less than pleased to find themselves once again under the premiership of Winston Churchill, the old class enemy. Things went from bad to worse in the 1955 election. The results when they came were a huge disappointment for my Labour family, and for me, though I then thought of it a bit like a football match, our team against their team, red goals against blue goals. The Tory team had increased their majority to 54, bringing to Downing Street Anthony Eden, who would soon mastermind the fiasco of the Anglo-French Suez invasion in late 1956, then be compelled by American and international opinion into an ignominious and rapid withdrawal from a campaign that left behind a significant number of Egyptian dead and wounded, and a thousand dead civilians. He would be succeeded by Harold Macmillan, for whom one day I would help to write a televised speech. This all lay in a future I could scarcely imagine.

Frustrated by these political defeats at the national level, Dad decided to pull out all the stops at the local level, and stand for the Roecliffe Parish Council, mounting a political campaign in this most unpolitical but conservative (with a small 'c') village. He liked nothing better than to try to search out the often hidden sources of revolt, usually among downtrodden farm labourers, but Roecliffe had something passably akin to a factory in the form of the Brickworks, which produced distinctive russet handmade bricks for houses for many miles around: the workers there got little more money than farm workers, while working in a dusty, hot environment. Dad felt sure he could swing a few votes, and that the spirit of '45 might prevail again. His first step was to produce a large red poster: 'Vote Labour!' hardly an original message but one hitherto unknown to Roecliffe. He pinned the poster up on the oak tree at the side of the village green, facing the school, which traditionally made do as the village noticeboard. The next day the poster had disappeared, torn down in the night. Dad put up another one. The same result. That evening we had a visitor: Henry Cambage, Chairman of the Roecliffe Parish Council, another local farmer. Henry liked and respected Dad, a courtesy which was returned, but felt (it seemed) that he must do what a Chairman of the Parish Council must do. "Now, Martin," began Henry, jovial in the certainty that he knew how to handle The Men. "Now, Henry," said Dad. "Had a good day?" enquired Henry. "Had a good day", rejoined Dad, as if democracy required an equality of words between opponents. "Well, Martin", said Henry, "I think folks are a bit worried about this political goin' on, posters an' all. It isn't for the Good of the Village to have folks fallin' out. Look at Yon Place (a reference to a nearby village), Yon Place is always full o' bickerin' and gripin' and upsets. When you think of it in that light, the Good of the Village, I think you'll see what should be done." "Oh yes?" said Dad, in tones laden with obstinacy. Henry went a bit pink. "What I mean is, the Village isn't used to elections being *political.* We just get on with things like. Major agrees with me." This was a tactical mistake, but anyway in the context of a strategy that was disastrous. "Oh yes?" Dad's voice was rising, his gaze at Henry unwavering. Henry wriggled uneasily. "Will you perhaps stop puttin' up any more of them political posters on t' tree: after all, it is the parish council noticeboard." Dad rose to his feet: "I will not, not for you, and certainly not for that Major. What do you fellers know about the Good of the Village? When, in the last 20 years, did you lot do anything for the good of anyone except yourselves, Tories pretending to be Independents? Well, those days have gone. We workers had to fight to get the vote, and it's high time this village decided to use those votes, and decide for itself what its own good is. And I'll tell you somethin' else" he offered, though Henry clearly had already heard enough, "this will be no parish pump election, this election will be fought on a National Platform." Henry stared at Dad's feet, perhaps expecting the National Platform to materialise beneath them.

Dad's next step was to enlist the aid of Wilf Choppin, a tiny bandy-legged silver-haired old chap who worked with Dad. He was married to Annie, a story in itself. For twelve years Wilf had courted Betty, a farm worker's daughter and elder sister to Annie. Since twelve years seemed a reasonable period of notice, Wilf took his courage and his cap in both hands and asked the Old Lady for permission to marry Betty. The Old Lady was uncompromising; "Nay, tha' cannot, Betty's stayin' wi' me: but tha' can ha'e Annie". So Annie it was. Wilf and Annie now lived in a house overlooking the green, and those bright blue, slightly malicious eyes missed very little. It just so happened that, surveying the village world at midnight before turning in, he had seen a figure steal up to the Village Tree and pull down Dad's National Platform. Dad wondered aloud who it might be. "Ah'm sayin' nowt," said Wilf, eyes sparkling with mischief "but you'd better consult wi' yon Major's wife."

It so happened that Dad in his spare time did a bit of gardening for the Major's wife, a pleasant and unworldly woman who had very little understanding of her husband's politics, and probably only the haziest recollection of how she had come to be married to him. But not for nothing was she a Colonel's daughter, and knew when to obey orders. All went as smooth as a military operation, and she had crept back through the rhododendrons clutching Dad's poster. But the Major's wife, poor soul, was in no way prepared for Dad's frontal assault: never once had she known Dad to be other than quiet and courteous. Now here he was wagging an admonitory finger under her nose. "I've been puttin' notices up on the Village Tree, and someone has been takin' 'em down. I know who that someone is, and if it happens again, I shall withdraw my labour from your garden". This was a real body blow, not to mention the first time industrial action had ever been declared in Roecliffe. Both the major and his wife were wedded to their garden, and their prowess was yearly accoladed at the local show. Fundamentally they were urban outsiders: their garden was their passport to rural and communal acceptance. A truce was declared, and Dad's posters now went unmolested.

And so came Election Day. Our house was gay with red ribbons: the only one in the village. Polling day turned out bitterly cold and wet. The polling station was the school, and it opened at 7:30 am. After feeding a gaggle of pigs and hens, all of whom would have voted for him without a qualm, Dad went to the school to vote. There he got a surprise, for the opposition, running scared, were keeping a check on the voting, through the person of Horace Daniel. Horace lived next door to us and exchanged gardening hints and potted plants with Mum and Dad. A burly bespectacled man, he had some of that Yorkshireman's stubborn streak that afflicted Dad from time to time. Horace was seated next to the school's roaring stove, chatting with the polling booth officer. Dad didn't immediately say anything but collected his voting slip, completed it, and posted it in the little brown box: he did all this slowly, almost reverently, for he had a very rare sense of what the seemingly insignificant ritual stood for, of the blood and tears out of which the right to enter into it had been created: after all, he could remember the first ever election by universal suffrage in 1929, which had returned the first Labour government with a majority of seats, though not an overall majority in Parliament. Then he turned to the polling station clerk, forefinger stabbing the air in front of that startled official's face. "That man," he said, without once looking at Horace, "has no right to be in here. It's against the electoral law. I'm off home now to fodder t' calves, then I'm comin' back, and when I do, I don't want to see that man in here or I shall ask for all the votes here to be declared invalid." Dad being Dad, he knew the rules precisely, and was determined that this bit of the election should be done by the rulebook. When he duly returned, it was to find the unfortunate Horace shivering on the school doorstep. But Horace, if out, was not yet down: when he saw Dad he produced a pencil and the 'reading list' of names of those eligible to vote. "Now then," he declared purposefully, confronting Dad, "can I have your name please?" "Never you mind what my name is," said Dad. "Nay, Martin," began Horace, but Dad broke in "Oh, you seem to know my name after all?" "Well dammit," snorted Horace "I know your name as well as you know mine. Don't be so bloody daft!" Dad was unmoved, even in the face of such an untypical outburst from Horace. "I'll tell you somethin'," he said, determined to sustain his non-recognition policy, "I don't know *you*, not officially, and I'll not tell you who I'm votin' for, because this is a secret ballot, and if you think that people in this village will tell you who they are really votin' for you don't know them any better than you know me." Horace gave up, shaking his head.

We all gathered in the school at the end of the day to hear the results. Dad's judgement had proved right: many of the farm labourers and brickyard workers who would never have dreamed of declaring any political affiliations in public, nor probably had any enthusiasm for the Labour Party, had voted for Dad, one of Us, and a poke in the eye for Them. From now on, Henry Cambage and his fellow Independents (truly very thinly disguised Conservatives) would need to take care with Dad's beady eye on them. I can't say that a radical revolution broke out in the handling of our small rural concerns, but certainly democracy had broken out, to general satisfaction.

# Chapter Ten

## Growing Pains and Pleasures

*If thou of fortune be bereft*
*And of the earthly share have left*
*Two loaves, sell one, and with the dole*
*Buy hyacinths, to feed the soul*
Childhood rhyme, quoted by Sir Alec Clegg, Chief Education Officer, West Riding Education Authority, 1945-74

As I approached the iconic age of 16, I was on the cusp of two possible futures, though at the time any possible future seemed clouded and obscure. As I have tried to show, I was enthralled by the imaginative vistas opened to me by my various studies and enjoyed the recognition that seemed to flow: in those days you were not tested to destruction as would be the case now, but work was consistently marked and the scores added up in such a manner that you were placed in a pecking order in every subject, and I flourished under the joint influences of a dreamy involvement in learning, and an inner, quite tough competitiveness, both characteristics inherited from my mother, and a resoluteness of spirit drawn from my father. Apart from Art (24th out of 24) I managed a sufficient number of 1sts and 2nds to satisfy even Mum. I was constantly doing battle with a clever and lively girl called Catherine Gandy, another Catholic. As we approached the formal School Certificate examinations, we were also being asked to decide whether we would stay on into the Sixth Form, which would open up paths either to University or (more usually then) Teacher Training College. My parents were made aware of this looming choice. Most unusually, they summoned me into the 'best' room for a quite formal discussion. They wanted to know what I wanted to do; but they also wanted me to know what a difficult prospect this would be for them personally, for with three children and a farm worker's wage, things would be very tight. Mum said that they had decided that she would have to get a job, not so straightforward with seven years old sister Sally to be looked

*Josie, sous chef at the Crown Hotel, Boroughbridge.*

after. They would expect me to help Dad with his overtime stints, and help Maureen with housework when Mum couldn't be there. None of this had really occurred to me in my utter self-absorption but I knew, and made clear, how very badly I wanted to stay on at school. Dad quite gravely and formally said how very proud my academic progress had made them, and they had only wanted to be sure that I was serious about my commitment. I discovered later that Molly Sawdon had already spoken not only to my parents about all this, but also to the head of my local Education Authority, Alec Clegg, who would become famous for his efforts to encourage schools to single out children from underprivileged backgrounds who might be candidates for university. A few years later he would meet my parents personally at a School Speech Day, and the epigraph for this chapter sums up his approach to education.

But I look back now and remember what this meant for them - and me - in all its hard reality. By day, Mum would go off early to the Crown Hotel in Boroughbridge, where she had a position as what is known as a commis chef: her speciality was teas and cakes, but she could turn her hand to any kind of cooking. This new dispensation was a bit miserable, for it too often meant that she was not waiting to greet us when we came back from school, quite a change for us. Dad again took on extra overtime harvesting cabbages and root crops, paid as usual by acreage. I joined him on frosty weekend mornings, and a very painful learning process it was, for your hands would soon be numb with cold, and slashing the tops off swedes with a sharp sickle-like blade quite a risky process. Another task was to help out by feeding the farm stock at weekends: hens, calves, pigs, cows all watched with interest as I made a botched job of delivering their provender. The newly born but fast-growing calves were the worst, quite capable of wresting from my feeble grasp and spilling over the floor the buckets of milk I offered. I lived in mortal fear of the enormous sow I had to feed in the fold-yard, for she was known to be aggressive when feeding her brood, and quite capable of lumbering towards me with what always seemed like menacing intent. Milking the cows was more straightforward. Dad had taught me at the age of 12 how to do this by hand, but by this time we had electric milking machines, so you only had to get the milking machines fixed to their teats, but you always had to look out for the inevitable one that would try to aim a crafty kick at your head while you were stooped alongside her. I had to grit my teeth more than once, but I much preferred any of this to the business of washing eggs. This was Mum's task, assisted by all three children (we all dreaded it), and paid by the number washed in any given week. Huge buckets of dirty eggs were washed in cold water, in a bitterly cold outhouse, and placed in paper trays for despatch to the Egg Marketing Board. Worse was the clinging, unpleasant egg smell which was exacerbated by the inevitable breakages. The stench would cloy for hours. I didn't touch an egg for a long time, but years later would find myself deeply moved by a poem my sister Sally wrote, called simply 'Washing Eggs', with a clear trace of Seamus Heaney in it. All this hard work affected Mum's health quite badly, and only a year later she would have an operation (a hysterectomy), after which she spent six weeks in a convalescence home. Maureen, only 13, struggled resolutely and bravely to keep the house going but complained on a visit to my mother that when she baked jam tarts, Dad and I would keep eating them. But we were all at sixes and sevens until Mum was happily restored to her rightful place.

I have kept for the end of the list of tasks I had to endure during my school years the most memorable, because I have never forgotten the nightmarish quality of it. One night, my father asked me to join in a rat hunt. This involved attracting rats from the corn stacks they inhabited, in order to kill them. Nothing could have prepared me for how this experience would play out. Men and boys stood at intervals along the side of the stack, me included. We were all given a torch, and a hefty stick. We then shouted loudly, while beating the sides of the stack, and directing the torch beams upwards. Soon hordes of rats were scrabbling and leaping down into the bright beams, and the forest of sticks, and they seemed to me to be jumping straight down onto my head. I thrashed them in a frenzy of fear and horror, hitting the bodies in mid-air, while the ones any of us missed were pursued by snarling farm dogs. To me this was a vision of hell, and has stayed with me as one of the most traumatic of my experiences at any stage of my life.

A rather different narrative took shape through football. Having been unable to play games until the age of 10 I had, thereafter, made up for lost time. I became the youngest ever player to play for the Grammar School 1$^{st}$

*The stackyard at Roecliffe, by day, minus the rats.*

XI at the tender age of 13, accompanied by my pal Mick Harper aged 14. By the age of 15, I had been drawn into the Boroughbridge Town football team, a leading light in the local Harrogate League. Amazingly, I would turn out for my school team on Saturday mornings, then rush back in time to play for the town team in the afternoon. This was challenging physically, not least because I was playing with and against some tough adult men and it could get rough. I can remember our centre half, Alf Stokes, a long distance lorry driver, once picking up the opposition centre forward by the throat with one hand and threatening to rearrange his features with the other; his opponent seemed to lose heart after that. In another match my opposing full back, who wore a mane of black hair in a hairnet and was known as 'Mad Dog' (though never to his face), instantly kicked me into next week whenever, and often before, I got the ball. At half time I took my boots off and my feet swelled up so much that I couldn't get them back on again. Six weeks later, Mad Dog was banned for life: he had kicked a man on the floor in the face and broken his jaw. A rather mixed blessing in all this was that Mum and Dad wanted to come and watch me play, at least at home matches. At one level, of course, I was pleased to win their approval, but my mother could be quite embarrassing, stalking the touch line and freely offering advice to me, my opponents and the referee. Once when I was getting 'the treatment' from another mean-eyed full back, and left in a heap on the floor, Mum ran on waving her umbrella, shouting "Leave him alone, you big bully, he's only a schoolboy". I was mortified, and hissed at her to keep quiet. Dad led her away, remonstrating mildly: "Nay, Josie". I might add that in these mid-fifties days, when very few people yet had television, we played in front of substantial crowds, and local loyalties were strong. The Boroughbridge crowd were so notoriously loyal that they had once chased a referee they took exception to down the lane, threatening to throw him into the nearby River Ure. He retired the following week. I

*Boroughbridge AFC, me far right of back row.*

soon learned that the best way to avoid injury from hulking defenders was to run away from them very fast, preferably with the ball. I would then look up and cross the ball on to the unerring forehead of Big Harold Sadler, our tall and muscular centre forward ('striker' now). In my first full season this combination helped Harold to 72 goals, I think possibly a League record that has never been broken.

I also was selected for the Harrogate and Craven District Schools team to play in the England Schools Trophy, scoring four goals in my first game, then playing and beating Sunderland Schools at Roker Park. All this got me noticed by a local ex-miner who scouted for Wolverhampton Wanderers, then the Manchester United of the day and top of the First Division (now the Premier League). I was asked to play in trials, then for an 'A' team against Wolves Reserves. Out of the blue came a letter from Stan Cullis, the famous Wolves manager, offering me a schoolboy contract, the stuff of schoolboy dreams nurtured by Baldy Hogan. I was wild with excitement. Moreover, I was asked to play the following weekend for a Wolves X1 against a Newcastle United X1. The match would be played at Wallsend, on the very ground behind Granny Simpson's Hopper Street house where, as a young lad, I had crept across the roof to watch the matches. Mum instantly wrote to our Tyneside family so that they could watch me play.

Then the dream castle came tumbling down. When I told my sports teacher that I would not be able to play for the school team that Saturday, he immediately took me to the Headmaster. Douglas Stevens was an immensely

*A cartoon from the local paper.*

tall man, who had come to King James's Grammar School from a public school post. He held strong views about instilling a public school ethos into the Grammar School, and told me in no uncertain terms that my loyalties must be to the school, where I had just started my Sixth Form work. To be fair, too, he made clear to me that in the opinion of my teachers I could look forward to a good University career and all that went with it (remember that at this time only some four percent of the nation's young went to University). He advised me to consider this carefully with my parents, and think about the unpredictable nature of professional football. Then the iron fist in the velvet glove: if I went ahead and played for Wolves that weekend, I would never again be allowed to play for the school. This would also mean that I would be withdrawn from the Harrogate Schools representative team, shortly due to meet Sheffield Schools in the Yorkshire Schools Final (which was also to be regarded as the next round in the England Schools competition).

I went home tearfully to my parents. Mum was angry with the Headmaster and couldn't stop thinking of the uncles, aunts and cousins who might be waiting to see me in Wallsend. Dad was cannier: "When we talked about goin' into t'sixth form, you said, like, that you really wanted to go to University one day". But they would support me whatever decision I made, and I must be the one to make it. I doubt if I slept that night. Surprisingly, I realised that what was weighing with me most was not the rather distant prospect of the University, but the immediate probability of my grammar school world, in which I thrived, turning to dust and ashes. With a heavy heart I told Mum and Dad, then Mr Stevens, that I would be playing for the school that weekend. My Geordie relatives would look for me in vain at the Wallsend ground. My Headmaster was right, of course. Even had I succeeded at the Wolves, professional footballers in the 1950s were wage slaves, earning not much more than double the wages of the average working man, and with the expectation of a quite short, injury-strewn professional life. My prospects as a University graduate would be considerably better, and I would not be liable to be bought and sold. But I have always felt some regret, nonetheless, that I never got to emulate the stirring deeds of Baldy Hogan. To rub salt in the wounds, our Harrogate Schools side was defeated 5-0 in the Yorkshire Schools / England Schools fixture, all five goals headed in by a lofty bean-pole who towered head and shoulders above our hapless goalkeeper.

I now settled down to life in the Sixth Form, and the task of moving in a serious sort of way to Advanced Level and Scholarship papers: the Scholarship paper was regarded as a higher level, and could be used as additional evidence of superior ability in the university entrance stakes. My strong subjects were English Literature and History, the former presided over by Molly Sawdon, and the latter by a new History master, Bill Murphy (naturally soon known as Spud, with the complete absence of originality only schoolboys can produce). Molly, as I have tried to make clear, was simply inspirational; but I was equally fortunate to find in Bill Murphy someone with a genuine enthusiasm for his subject, and a determination to prove himself through his charges. He had a wonderfully critical eye, and taught me above all to temper my flashy judgements with a due regard for argument based in evidence and respected texts. His preferred periods were the Tudors and Stuarts, this driven to some degree by his own strong interest in religious history, being himself a practising Roman Catholic: you see how impossible it was for me to escape this religious stuff. My third subject was French: I was excellent on the literature (the set texts being Racine and Moliere) but trundled along at a much lower level when it came to the rather crucial language bit. Not least of the problems here was that the very kindly Miss Dixon taught the whole subject pretty much in English: no language labs in those days. Though she was supported by a French *assistante*, the pretty and manifestly foreign Nicole Vallier was more of a distraction than a help, at least to the male half of the study set, already struggling with the onset of raging hormones.

Perhaps one of the most liberating and genuinely educational features of our grammar school was that it provided opportunities outside the formal curriculum, particularly in drama and music. I had not been on a public stage since my lamentable five-year-old war time stage fright, but this was about to change. Molly Sawdon and Paddy Wansbrough were the leading lights and organisers of a newly established school Drama Society, and they produced a play for public performance each year. Molly directed and rehearsed, while Paddy did everything else from painting sets to providing tea and buns. Our first effort was *His Excellency* by Patrick Hamilton. I recall this play mostly because as ADC to a colonial governor, I was obliged at one point to kiss the governor's daughter. Neither I nor the girl in question much wished to rehearse this, not being all that keen on each other. By dress rehearsal, we still had not managed a solitary peck, but time was now up. We both stared soulfully into each other's eyes for what seemed like a very long time. From Molly's directorial chair came an irritated shout: "Oh for heaven's sake! Get on with it!" We did, and then couldn't seem to stop, finally parted only by ironic applause and laughter from the rest of the cast. It was all right on the night, and we had all now been bitten by the theatrical bug. The following year Molly chose, adventurously, Christopher Fry's 1930s free verse play, *The Lady's Not for Burning,* with a sixteenth century setting of conflict between new libertarian ideas, and old witch-burning practices. I had a wonderful time with the part of the pompous Mr Justice Tappercoom, and his wordily dismissive 'stultiloquential fiddle-faddle!' I had mixed feelings about my first ever theatrical review, which declared: 'the prelatish waggery of Tappercoom (Martin Minogue) was good, if it sometimes had the inevitability of a music hall gag'. Our next play was remarkable for its revelation of a true acting talent, Desmond Gill. Des was a year younger than me, in the lower sixth, but I knew him well as the son of a Boroughbridge farmer. I knew from my mother that the Gills were an unhappy family, the father very often drunk. Des always took our bus, as it passed the end of his farm track. Often we would see him sprinting down the track, and we would crowd to the windows on that side, making bets with each other on his chances of making it to the end of the lane before the bus swept past. I think he had almost as many late attendances as I did.

Des surprised everyone, including Molly, by his sensational and naturalistic first ever public performance as a carousing Samuel Pepys. He transformed a very ordinary play into something hugely funny and riotous, in such a way that an audience beside itself with laughter were in on the act. I think he probably surprised himself, and knew that he had discovered the only thing he thereafter wanted to do. A year later I would return, now having left school, to watch him play what remains in my memory an unforgettable and dramatic Hamlet, a triumph for Molly's direction and the brooding intensity of Desmond's acting. It was no surprise to anyone that he now won a place at the prestigious RADA, one of the first of a highly talented group of young working-class actors who would soon enough make their mark, including Tom Courtenay and Albert Finney.

A word here about music. I came from a family with strong musical traditions. Each Christmas, my grandfather had sung to his gathered children songs of loss and mourning for the Irish countryside; my own Dad continued this tradition at the drop of a hat, any high day or holiday would do, never mind Christmas. But he preferred the humorous songs like 'Phil the Fluter's Ball' and had off every one of the tongue-twisting roll call of Irish participants. My mother's Tyneside family inherited both the Celtic dances and songs associated with Catholic communities, and the working-class ballads and protest songs rooted in the mining and shipbuilding communities. After my sister Maureen's wedding in 1963, we had the most hilarious evening where each side of the family tried to out-sing and out-dance the other, my Uncle Jimmy triumphing over all with a stentorian version of 'The Blaydon Races', while Mum executed a perfect and agile Ceilidh dance to the astonishment of her children. But these traditions did not embrace classical music, so it was a revelation to me when Molly and Paddy, as background to our theatrical rehearsals, played Beethoven's Pastoral Symphony as soothing mood music. Later they introduced the Fifth Symphony, doubtless anticipating our triumphant finales. At around the same time the school choir drew me in for performances of Coleridge-Taylor's 'Hiawatha's Wedding Feast', and C.V. Stanford's 'The Revenge'. I had a decent voice but couldn't read music, so had to mouth the words until I learned the music by heart. Again, participating in public performances of these pieces was a delightful experience. I was hooked, and began painstakingly to collect records out of my own part time earnings. Before long I was having to choose between Mozart and The Beatles.

My life in the sixth form was marvellously full and enjoyable, a heady mix of sport, drama, music, and a growing interest in the world around me. There were girls to learn about too, a learning process quite heavily policed by my ever-watchful Mum, prone to give out stern but essentially vague and inexplicit warnings about the disasters that could flow from too close an acquaintance with the opposite sex. Any such remonstrances were a sign for Dad to disappear from view: I could expect no help there. My pal Mick was eager to offer evidence in the form of stories, but these appeared to be second-hand and neither of us could be sure of their reliability: we decided to concentrate on our football, a considerable advantage being that we would be in no danger of an embarrassing confessional with Father Spiller. Maureen good naturedly allowed me to take up with one of her friends who had just been crowned Miss Knaresborough. I was putty in her hands for a while. Smelling danger, Mum introduced draconian restrictions on my movements, which meant that on no account could I be home later than 10:00 pm, 11:00pm at weekends. When I responded with a sort of dumb resistance, arriving home late, she locked the doors. I was dumbfounded and had to bed down in the adjacent barn. After a row or two (and Mum could make a row last for days, often involving a stubborn refusal to speak to me at all) Dad intervened: "Nay Josie", and a resolution was arrived at whereby if I was late she would lock the door, but Dad was allowed to leave a downstairs window open for me to scramble through. Honour was satisfied all round and peace prevailed. I might add in my own defence that living out in the sticks put severe pressure on my timekeeping, not least because I would now be out with schoolfriends in Knaresborough, some nine miles distant by road from my home in Roecliffe. If I missed the bus (a fairly constant feature of my youthful life) I could not avoid being late. If I missed the last bus and had to hitch-hike, I could be *very* late. My sister Maureen had the good sense to attract young men with cars, who soon learned that if they incurred Mum's wrath by bringing Maureen back late, they were unlikely ever to be allowed to see Maureen again. In those unenlightened days, girls didn't have cars, so were no help to me as a taxi service.

I was soon to hear gossipy rumours about Molly and Paddy, with hints of some sort of sexual relationship, fired in part by the undoubted fact that they had written a banned novel together, *Sons of Normandy*: why, it wasn't even set in England! Again, I was more than mystified: I had scarcely worked out what boys and girls did together, and was utterly disbelieving about the possibility of girls doing something (always unspecified) with each other. I stoutly disregarded the smutty innuendoes beloved of the other boys. I probably came across as a bit of a prig. I disliked the demeaning ways in which these were directed at girls: and a bit later became aware of an unpleasant streak of homophobia, not an uncommon aspect of a determinedly masculine Yorkshire culture, whether in boys or adults. We all knew in our village about Colin, a twenty-year-old who was obviously gay (though this term was not then in use, 'queer' being the preferred disdainful designation, though local lads used the even more scornful term 'shirt-lifters'.). Colin always went off to the shadier parts of the bright lights of Harrogate to pursue his inclinations, and was never, to my knowledge, treated as other than normal in our village setting, despite homosexual activity being at this time strictly illegal, as I knew from the lurid headlines in the appalling News of the World. But I was aware that this was an area that smacked of social danger: for example, when I was about 14, Mum had a decidedly sideways sort of conversation with me about the need to 'keep away' from a Boroughbridge parish vicar, for reasons she declined to elucidate further. Her warnings were confirmed in my own imagination when, one Saturday evening, as I took a bus to some schools event in Harrogate, the said vicar boarded wearing a colourful tie and smart suit instead of his usual black robes and dog collar. Clearly, I thought, Mum was right, he must be up to no good. Such was the nature of our confused and confusing social prejudices. It was about this very time that the Wolfenden Committee was in the throes of a public investigation which would recommend the decriminalisation of adult male sexual relationships, but it would be another decade or more before more enlightened attitudes prevailed, and the Sexual Offences Act 1967 would mean that Colin and the Vicar could then at least be sure that they would no longer risk being sent to prison.

Another manifest social prejudice in our part of Yorkshire was anti-Semitism. The nearest large city of Leeds had a sizeable Jewish population, owed largely to late nineteenth century migration from central Europe, and added to by the Nazi-driven migrations of the 1930s. Even at this tender age, I was well aware of the terrible treatment and mass killings of Jews during the war. So it made me uncomfortable, if somewhat uncomprehending, to hear casual anti-Jewish remarks from the other boys, the sneering description of one or two local citizens as 'Jewboys'. Doubtless this reflected a parental prejudice, common enough in the local society of small businessmen and shopkeepers, but it was shocking to me to hear this sort of thing being parroted by children who were supposed to be the best and brightest in our small community. On the other hand, I can recollect no other manifestation of racism or bigotry: my mother had talked in a general way about the hostility suffered sometimes by Irish Catholics, though she could summon up a fair amount of anti-Irish hostility herself if Dad got on the wrong side of her. Later in my life, I would discover unsuspected and strongly expressed racism in my beloved Auntie Sadie; given that she was a woman of great kindness and generosity, and came from a part of the country where people of any colour other than white were at that time seldom to be seen, this remains somewhat baffling, but a reminder that racist prejudice was alive and well in some sections of the working class, no less than in the middle and upper classes.

At a point where I was undergoing a great deal of what might be called social learning and adjustment, not least to attitudes and behaviour with which I was unfamiliar, I drew confidence from two sources: my parents and some of my teachers. I see now, as I could not have formulated it then, that I was fortunate to have parents who possessed and lived by extremely solid values: tolerance, humanitarian sympathy, generosity, a sense of social community, an even stronger and politically rooted sense of social justice and fairness. These attitudes had come to me and my sisters through their example and their conversation, their lived life, and were deeply embedded in us in consequence. Yet at school, essentially a middle class setting which felt like a foreign country, I often felt shy, unconfident, uncertain as to how I should behave and desperate to fit in. Ironically, this brought some sense of dislocation from my parents, as I became aware of the social and economic distance between them and the parents of the great majority of the boys and girls I now mixed with. This was brought home to me memorably by my father's employer, Jim Driffield. While working alongside me sorting potatoes on a machine which graded the crop into different sizes and qualities, he suggested that it was a mistake for me to try to go to university: people who progressed in this way always and inevitably rejected their parents once they had made their way in the world. Was this what I really wanted? How would that make my mother and father feel? These were already real anxieties with which I was privately struggling, but I had no wish to debate these, and was well aware of a real malice behind his goading of me. I am fairly certain that he did not like the idea of his farm hands getting above themselves socially, or their children doing rather better than his own were likely to do. I fear that my only response was a sort of mute, red-faced and humiliated silence.

In this situation, I needed guidance that my parents were unable to give me: indeed I could not have asked them for it, for I knew that for me to have expressed that distancing would have been too hurtful for them. Naturally, I felt a good deal of guilt, which made me moody and uncommunicative, though Mum and Dad probably just thought it went along with being a teenager. My saviours were Molly and Paddy, who seemed to divine my moral and mental struggles. Molly took it on herself to polish some of my rougher social edges, helping me to speak and conduct myself in ways which made me feel more self-confident; at the same time she also talked to me about my parents, telling me of her to her about my mother too often being bad-tempered with me, and insensitive to my own feelings. Molly told me in no uncertain terms that I was ungrateful, and didn't seem to understand how hard my mother had fought and worked to ensure the opportunities that I now had; I should stop feeling sorry for myself and repay her by working as hard as she and my father did. I had never seen Molly so angry, and to my consternation saw tears in her eyes as she turned away from me. Childless herself, she had a considerable emotional investment in her favourite charges, of whom I was one (along with Desmond Gill, and his best friend Rex Taylor, a clever latecomer from Orkney), and this was my first, unforgettable glimpse of an involvement with all of us from her and Paddy which would be immensely influential for a lifetime. In a way, I had two sets of parents, one in each sector of my divided life, each helping me to learn who I was, each contributing to who I would become.

*Molly and Paddy in retirement in their 90s, life-long friends.*

The next two years flashed by in a haze of activity at school and at home. I was kept busy in various ways, being Head Boy for two years, editing the school magazine, the Challenor (I wince now to read my callow sub-journalistic prose and clunking poems, though greatly amused to find in a back issue a 'Poem to a Parent', attributed to me and my sister Maureen, but with my mother's signature versifying all over it). I had to adjust to a new Headmaster, one Frank Brewin, who came to us, like his predecessor, from a senior public school house position. Why, I still wonder, did our Board of Governors think we should be turned into an anaemic and pretentious version of a public school? Mr Brewin, a stern and stubborn Scot, possibly of a Presbyterian persuasion, was not much liked or admired, but Molly as de facto Headmistress kept him in check and if many of the detailed changes were irksome, the essential character of this small, intellectually modest, but socially lively bit of rural Yorkshire's education system was not much damaged. During this time, my sister Maureen left school for a secretarial training and career. My younger sister Sally, arriving in the year after I left, would prove to be something of a prodigy, and would follow in my earlier footsteps, becoming Head Girl and Editor of The Challenor, then winning entry to St Hilda's, Oxford at the age of 16. The 1957 Challenor pays tribute to 'Mr and Mrs Minogue for generously offering to continue the Coronation Prize for the best [academic]... achievement ...for the next five years'. Only we children knew what an enormous gesture this was given their financial circumstances, a gesture moreover that was rarely replicated by the many well-heeled middle-class parents. The grammar school successes of their children were the only reward they desired, and they wanted to express their gratitude to a school which had so much helped us to progress. But before I could make any further steps forward, I would have to make a step backwards, as I served two years of military conscription, known to all as National Service.

# Chapter Eleven

# Making Men of Us

*It seemed as though I had been plunged into a Dantesque hell*
Keith Thomas

Conscription found me unprepared and unwary. I had been so busy just living my grammar school and Yorkshire village life that the outside world hardly seemed to signify, apart from occasional forays to Tyneside, which anyway to me always appeared somewhat disconnected from the rest of the country. Moreover, despite my childhood experiences of war, the military too seemed like a world apart. I should, I suppose, have had some inkling from Uncle Jimmy, Mum's brother, a soldier from tip to toe, who during the Second World War had not only risen from the ranks to an officer's commission, but was said to have served in the fabled 'commandos'. I knew that he was something of a rough diamond, who had led a tough life. Captured by the Japanese after the ignominious fall of Singapore, he survived three years in prison camps, including a long spell on the infamous Burma Railway, on which around 13,000 Allied personnel died, including 6,904 British prisoners of war. He had also been an Army boxing champion and once boxed an exhibition match with a former world champion, Gene Tunney (I have seen the gloves Tunney presented to Jimmy, now in the possession of my cousin Joe's son, Steve). There is a good family story that Uncle Jimmy decided after the war to teach my 16-year-old cousin Russell how to defend himself, and invited Russell to hit him. Russell did, quite hard, and Uncle Jimmy responded by knocking him out cold with a single punch. Russell's mother, Aunt Meg, didn't speak to her brother for weeks. Mum's other brother Tommy served in the RAF, but I gleaned from family conversations that he was vaguely disreputable, a heavy drinker, and often in (unspecified) trouble. On Dad's side, the picture was rather chequered. Dad himself avoided military service by being in a reserved occupation. His elder brother, John, who didn't fancy the drudgery of farm labour, had early on left home with a travelling circus and family anecdotes suggest that later he may have joined the British army, though I have not been able to find evidence of this, other than a photograph of him in a security guard's uniform, this being a common job for ex-servicemen. If so, it would have been to his Irish father's dismay, since this was an army notorious in Irish eyes for the many brutalities perpetrated during 'the troubles' in Ireland in the early part of the twentieth century, (though of course some 300,000 Irishmen served, very honourably, in the British army during the First World War). Meanwhile, during the Second World War, Dad's youngest brother Bernard was at Dunkirk, but somewhat ingloriously as a member of the Army Catering Corps. To complete an odd set of military connections, Dad's youngest sister Pat after the 1939-45 war married Kurt Brogatski, a German POW who didn't much feel like returning to an East German home now occupied by Russian troops. I recall him well as a warm and mild-mannered man, with a smile made more flashing by the presence of two gold teeth: he turned out to be an excellent father and husband, who helped Pat and her sister Agnes to look after Granny and Grandad in their final years.

So not exactly a family military tradition then, and what there was seemed far outside any possible world I might inhabit. It surprises me now, looking back, and considering my developing interest in national politics, that I appear to have given so little consideration to the implications of military service. Britain was still suffering from the delusion that it was a Great Power, and sought to keep a place at the so-called 'top table'. It was also in the process of trying desperately to hang on to a fractious and disintegrating Empire, so vividly illustrated by the Suez canal crisis, and Anthony Eden's disastrous invasion of Egypt, together with the French, in November 1956, after secret collusion with the Israelis over military action. Given the continuing antagonisms in Europe and the various colonial bush-fires to be dealt with, it was always quite likely that if you were conscripted you might end up putting yourself in harm's way, or even shooting somebody. None of these thoughts seems to have registered with me, despite my early political awakening during the Suez crisis (this was when I first cleaved to what was then the Manchester Guardian for its outspoken opposition to the British government's action). Doubts stirred briefly in conversations I had with my predecessor as Head Boy, John Rathmell, another Molly favourite who had won a scholarship to read English at Jesus College, Cambridge. He too would be obliged to take two years out, but in his case he had registered as a conscientious objector, and was able to prove to the satisfaction of a sceptical tribunal that he had held such views for some time: according to Vinen's definitive (2014) study of National Service, by the 1950s such tribunals were taking a much more relaxed attitude to those with pacifist views. In consequence John was allowed to spend two years working as an agricultural labourer, which included for some of the time working on his own parents' market garden. I must confess that the thought of two years of being an agricultural labourer seemed to me just as miserable a prospect as being in the armed forces, and you were quite as likely, I knew now from personal experience, to be shot at by our own ruling classes: better the devil I didn't know than the devil I did.

The steep learning curve began with an initial registration and medical examination in a gloomy subterranean part of Leeds Town Hall. Mum escorted me protectively, always deeply suspicious of bureaucratic authority, and ready to go to war herself if she thought my welfare might be threatened. But even she was helpless to influence matters once it was established that I had no reasonable grounds for rejection, such as flat feet or other physical disability, and I was not tested on my ability to mend an electric plug. I had a desultory discussion with a very bored official about which branch of the services I would prefer to be in. I had already decided that if pugilistic Uncle Jimmy was an example of what the army might have in store, I should best avoid it. As to the navy, all I knew here was based on horrific stories from Uncle Bob, married to Auntie Sadie, who (by Mum's account) during the war had twice been sunk by torpedoes while in the merchant navy; since I was quite unable to swim, I felt that this was a risk too far. By default, this left the Royal Air Force, still invested in my mind with some residual glamour from those Battle of Britain days, and characterised by that handsome French-Canadian boyfriend of cousin Molly. I had also recently read Paul Brickhill's *Reach for the Sky*, a stirring account of Douglas Bader, the famous WW2 pilot with two false legs, a book acquired by Mum through the Reader's Union Book Club, which provided cheap editions on an instalment payment basis. So the boys in blue it would be, their motto *per ardua ad astra,* an apt enough guide to my own long term ambitions.

The first step on the two year journey took me to RAF Cardington in Bedfordshire, a camp rather bizarrely but attractively festooned with large Second World War barrage balloons, which still look to me as though they had been designed by Salvador Dali. Cardington had originally been home to the famous R101 airship project, abandoned after the prototype crashed with considerable loss of life; Cardington is still active now in these matters, the largest airship ever built having made its maiden flight there. Here was where all new recruits to the service were kitted out. Essentially this was also the first move in the ambition of the senior military to turn a large number of assorted individuals with their own particular personalities into a uniform mass of zombie- like creatures who would do whatever they were told to do without hesitation or contradiction, whether that be to shoot the enemy on sight, or march over a cliff. To erase individual differences seemed to mean initially that everyone should look exactly alike. Hair was the first target, barbers without any apparent acquaintance with their supposed craft our first persecutors. Men came to them with a glorious variety of lengths and colours, most at this time favouring the so-called D.A., or Duck's Arse, where otherwise luxuriant growths were trimmed and shaped to a neat point well down the back of the neck. As the floor was covered in a mass of black, brown and blonde waves and curls, a tide of glum, shaven-headed robots shuffled out, regarded with dismay by those still waiting. Next up was the fitting of uniforms. The word 'fitting' is quite without meaning here. The corporal in charge would examine each arrival with an experienced eye and yell 'Long 40' or 'Middle 36'. I had never got beyond the well below average height of 5 feet 5 and a half inches. I owed this either to that premature birth, or to simple genetics: Dad was a reasonably standard (for those days) 5 feet 9, but Mum barely crept over a straight five feet. On the other hand, my sister Maureen was taller than I was, and I could be quite sensitive about the whole business, the received Hollywood norm being a tall handsome chap with a svelte and notably shorter girl on his arm. So I blushed furiously when a beady-eyed corporal took one look at me and yelled happily: 'short-arse 30'; a pretty accurate guess at my inside leg measurement. We each got a blue serge suit, shirts (at least you were allowed to indicate your own neck size), shoes and boots (ditto), abrasive underwear, black tie, a soft blue beret with a brass shield, and a rather natty hard-peaked cap a bit like those worn by Scottish policemen. We then had to change into all this stuff and give up the civilian clothes we had arrived in, which we then bundled into parcels, addressed to be posted back to our homes. Vinen tells a good story of how the aristocratic sons of the Duchess of Richmond gave their parcels to a corporal who cried: 'look here, these lads are sending their gear home to a pub'.

The final stage in this primary phase was a trip to a long low brick building which turned out to be a medical unit staffed exclusively by trainee sadomasochists. We were required to doff the shirts we had just put on, stand in a long alphabetical line, and receive injections against various possible contaminations. Looking back over the whole service experience, the most useful treatment would have been a vaccination against boredom, though one against so called 'bullshit' i.e. the constant pursuit of mindless and meaningless tasks, would have been first on most people's list. To my astonishment, a handful of the men could not cope with being vaccinated in what was admittedly a rough and ready manner, 'right arm out, lad', needle plunged unceremoniously in. A big strong looking chap just in front of me, before any plunging could be administered, sank to the floor in a dead faint: "It's no good lad," said the orderly to his prostrate form, "that won't get you out of your two years".

The whole notion of two years seemed like a never ending bad dream: how could we possibly take another 729 days of this sort of thing (many men faithfully recorded daily how many days were left before a merciful release)? The first night made it all seem worse. Herded in groups of some two dozen, again alphabetically, into Nissen huts which for a week or so would be our sleeping quarters, we had for the first time a chance to pause and take stock of what was happening to us, as well as to appraise each other. The forced de-individualisation that came with stripping us of our normal hair and clothes was certainly a shock to the system. Some met the changes with a show of bravado. As we lay awake in the dark, a butcher's boy from Hebden Bridge began a long account, replete with obscene detail, of how he had spent his last night with his girlfriend. Others joined in with their own favourite dirty jokes. While Hebden (as he was ever after known) had the saving grace of a dry humour and a rich Lancastrian accent, the rest were merely tedious. Many of us stayed silent, in my case suddenly overcome by strong feelings of loss, the loss of the familiar company of my parents and sisters, as the realisation dawned that for the first time in my life I was on my own, in most uncongenial circumstances. I could not weep in this surrounding, but my heart felt wounded. Hebden eventually quieted, various snorings and harrumphings broke out: I did not sleep for a long time. Keith Thomas, then a Welsh grammar school boy, now a most distinguished social and cultural historian, in a recent account of his National Service experiences refers to 'the horrors of the barrack room... surrounded by miners, steelworkers, and labourers... whose conversation was an unbroken stream of obscenity'. My own background had made me quite hardy in the face of such rough and not unfamiliar behaviour. In any case, I also divined in it a desperate attempt to avoid seeming too soft, or giving way to unmanly feelings. Later in life I would become friends with men who went through a similar uprooting as they entered their public schools at the age of seven. I still cannot imagine how they coped with this, and even less can comprehend how or why their parents should banish them from their homes so precipitately. When I had left home at the age of 19, my parents had faces of stone, my dear sisters looking grief-stricken, as if they thought never to see me again. I had then felt uncertain, embarrassed by their show of emotion, trying to keep a cheerful countenance. Now, in the dead of night, I felt utterly bereft and miserable, and so I believe did many of my seemingly tough-skinned companions.

Come the light of day there was nothing to be done but put the best face on things and survive whatever was in store. We already knew that for the next six weeks we would be doing what was known as 'square-bashing', since most of our waking hours would be spent marching up down and around a tarmac square as we learned how to put our best feet forward. We were all issued with a travel warrant indicating our destination: West Kirby, in the Wirral peninsula, just across the water from Liverpool. We were marched raggedly to the station, possessions in our kit-bags, mine now stamped with my identity, not a name, but a simple number: 5046489. It is said that, like those incarcerated in concentration camps, national servicemen throughout their lives, whatever else they forget, will never forget their official number. Before long I would be a pert little 489, but for now I had to use the full number when addressed by anyone in authority over me, which meant pretty much everyone, from Wing Commanders to Leading Cooks. Two trains came and went carrying their reluctant cargoes: then another train pulled in, labelled West Kirby. We were on our way to what Vinen terms 'the hellish chaos of basic training'.

The Wirral is a very beautiful part of the country, West Kirby a solidly respectable and attractive coastal resort. RAF West Kirby seemed quite out of place, an undistinguished pile of buildings and parade grounds a couple of miles out of town. Here we would spend the next six demanding, tedious, sweaty, weary weeks. We had to learn quickly what were the priorities if life was not to become completely unbearable. The first priority was to avoid anything whatever that might incur a punishment, thus adding to what was in any case an extended punishment regime; for any really serious offences, time spent in close detention would be added to your two years. Given our initial ignorance of the little ways of services life, it was all too easy to transgress, and those in authority over us were quick to take advantage, regarding such punishments as their principal reason for existence, their function to 'make soldiers of us' as soon as possible. One early minefield was the business of saluting, since we were not yet familiar with the rules, and the insignia of ranks. If you failed to recognise and salute an officer, you were liable to a humiliating dressing down (they well knew how to do humiliation).

On my second day, playing safe and ready to salute anything that moved and wore funny dress, I mistakenly saluted a warrant officer, sufficiently powerful people but not commissioned officers. I was asked to identify myself by number and training unit. I knew the first but had no idea that I was even in a training unit. I was told to report to Parade Ground number 3 in full kit at 5pm. There I was met not by the warrant officer, but by what appeared to be a schoolboy dressed as a flight lieutenant, accompanied by a scowling corporal. These turned out to be Flight Lieutenant Brown, and Corporal Mills, the officer and NCO in charge of my unit. They would make my life a misery in the weeks ahead, and wasted no time in getting started. Later, as I got to know the system and its workings a bit better, I realised that officers and NCOs in charge of one unit would delight in taunting their counterparts in other units by catching out the airmen for whom they had formal responsibility. This would produce an annoyed response that was visited upon the unfortunate offending airman. In this case it was me, and I was made to march up and down the long parade ground endlessly. At each turn I would be confronted by one or the other, and required to salute the officer and give my number and training unit, but to avoid saluting if confronted by the corporal. The worst aspect of all this was that they now, literally, had my number, and would mark me out for special attention. In the case of the corporal, this became a fairly standard litany of uncomplimentary remarks, jibes, and swearing, all at full throttle and often with a red face stuck an inch or two from yours. Eventually this abated, especially as he found other unfortunates even less adept than me in the matters of drill and dress. My friend Mick, who had gone off to the RAF (and Malaya) two years before me, told me that in his unit he was friendly with Francis, a very devout Catholic, and a gentle giant of a man, who had trained initially for the priesthood, but on deciding against this path had been called up. When his NCO swore at him on the parade ground, he immediately asked if the Corporal would please not talk to him like that, he didn't agree with swearing and saw no need for it. The furious NCO thrust his face forward and shouted: "I'll decide what's needed, you fucking shower of shit." With that, Francis knocked him to the ground, doubtless demonstrating his unsuitability for the religious life. My Uncle Jimmy would have been proud of him.

When it came to retributions, dress was another minefield. You had to be ready to be inspected at any time, and this meant that anything you possessed must be in perfect order, boots highly polished, webbing belts Blanco-ed an improbably pristine white, trousers sharply creased, rifles (when you got them) perfectly oiled. Any shortcomings were likely to land you with extra duties, or extra drills under the jaundiced eye of the congenitally bad-tempered Corporal Mills. Our unit was distributed in low wooden huts, a stove at one end, a rack in which our rifles were locked at the other. We were, I think, 20 beds in all. A junior NCO slept in a separate little office at the entrance and was nominally in charge of the hut, though he showed little interest except at formal kit inspections. These were made by Flight Lieutenant Brown and Corporal Mills twice a week, so we knew when to be ready for them. They included inspections of our beds, which had to be perfectly made, with any possessions not being worn laid out formally on top of the bed. This pattern persisted, though less frequently, throughout our service life. In the latter year of my service, by then feeling more than a little bored and rebellious ('bolshie' was the phrase my companions would have used) I laid out my books too, as required. As if to justify the epithet, on the left I placed an evidently thumbed copy of *The Communist Manifesto*; on the right, a copy of T.S.Eliot's *Selected Poems*: and suitably centre place, a recently acquired copy of Richard Hoggart's *The Uses of Literacy*. On that particular occasion, we were being inspected by the Acting CO of the station (RAF Lindholme), a red-faced Wing Commander. He paused by my bed, took in the book display, and went even redder: but he passed on, after bestowing a glacial stare, and a curt word to the accompanying Warrant Officer. As it happened, I worked under this NCO, and got on well with him. Later he told me I'd better keep my nose clean for a bit, as he'd been told to keep an eye on me.

Those in charge of us in the Wirral were considerably less friendly, and gave us all a hard time. An interesting group response emerged, as we realised we had to help each other, and especially one or two weaker brethren who seemed quite incapable of observing the simplest routines. Johnny, a rosy cheeked lad who still appeared to be emerging from the chrysalis of late onset teenage, could not get the hang of marching, quite unable to coordinate arm and leg movements. He proceeded with each arm stiff at his side, which induced a duck like meander. This put him entirely out of line with the rest of us, those immediately behind him likely to trip over his feet, and eventually a milling cohort would simply stop in the middle of the parade ground. This was liable to send the NCO into a hysterical rage, directed at Johnny (who once, appallingly, burst into tears) but with threats that the whole lot of us would be placed on potato-peeling duty, or 'spud-bashing'. This was very much a fate to be avoided, as you had to sit at the foot of a huge mound of potatoes, the peeling of which took a good three hours of the precious spare time you longed to spend merely lying on your bed to rest aching limbs. So we all rallied round the hapless Johnny and took turns to march him up and down, desperately trying to get him to swing his arms backwards and forwards alternately with each stride. Eventually he got it, and grinned with huge embarrassment when we all gave him a lusty cheer.

We learned to share our tasks by the rather efficient method of determining who was best at what, and allocating the tasks accordingly. Hebden was still with us (happily he had now exhausted his sexual reminiscences) and it turned out that he had started out his working life as an apprentice tailor, and was a dab hand with a flat iron. So before inspections, we'd all take off our trousers and dump them beside Hebden, and he would by the end of the evening return them to us, beautifully smoothed and with razor-sharp creases. In this fashion, four men polished all the boots, three Blanco-ed webbing, others made up our beds with hospital corners (which of course we didn't sleep in the night before inspection, staying wrapped in blankets on the floor to avoid disturbing the neatness), and so on. Jock, an experienced regular army soldier who was there because he had just been transferred from the army to the RAF, taught us all, after illegally liberating the rifles locked up at the centre of the hut, how to handle them. It was quickly established that I was quite useless at most practical tasks, and I was relegated to floor polishing, which largely meant, after a certain amount of elbow grease, skating vigorously about on footpads to buff up the wooden floor of the hut. We had quickly learned that the twenty of us had to survive as one unit the daily ordeal of being kicked about from pillar to post, constantly bawled out, and punished for the merest infraction (even a sardonic expression didn't go down too well with Flight Lieutenant Brown). Mostly, you had to keep your head down and avoid drawing attention to yourself. Some, like Johnny, seemed quite unable to manage this, and some NCOs were mean-spirited enough to make their lives an utter misery. I shall never forget the shock and disbelief I felt when someone in our wing reportedly jumped from the top of a water tower. Three weeks later another man ran away from the camp and threw himself under a train. This dreadful combination appeared to force the remoter parts of the command structure to take notice, and there was a distinct if reluctant muting of the day to day bullying.

By degrees, we were turned at least outwardly into obedient, disciplined troops who could march properly. We began to learn more demanding skills, like map reading for targets, and disassembling light machine guns (Bren guns), and reassembling the parts in the correct order: by no means easy, as you had to meet a strict time limit. Most bizarre, in some ways, was bayonet practice. Bayonet practice had not changed since the Great War and was based on the same assumption i.e. that warfare consisted mainly of running hell for leather across muddy terrain, a bayonet fixed to your extended rifle, while uttering unearthly screams, then trying to pin a vaguely defined opponent to the floor before he could do the same to you. In the training version, the enemy was a large stuffed sack suspended from a gantry. Even the least athletic of individuals would have found it difficult to miss the sack, which complaisantly failed to move or jab back. Several men, however, having slammed their bayonet into the sack with much ferocity, were then quite unable to extract it. The NCOs in charge of this exercise gleefully pronounced them as captured, having surrendered their weapon, and fit only for potato peeling duties, for which, no doubt, the bayonet might have come in handy. It's unlikely they could have served any useful operational purpose. The principal conflict then being waged was against Malayan insurgents who were often Chinese and regularly designated as 'wily' in the desultory briefings given to us. I could not imagine that they would be as cooperative as the stuffed sacks, nor that bayonets would have been their weapons of choice. Vinen found that bayonet practice was the most hated form of training, perhaps because the most psychologically daunting. He also records that 'in Glasgow during the early 1960s gangs fought with bayonets that had been liberated from Highland regiments by enterprising national servicemen'.

The actual shooting of rifles was quite exciting. We all had been issued with a Lee Enfield .303 No 4 rifle which was still then the services issue, having first been introduced in 1941 (though an earlier version went back to 1895). We were marched to the shooting range. The targets were smaller than the sacks, but just as immobile. However, we had been reliably assured that 'in the field' we might at any time find ourselves under attack (the wily opponent, of course, rarely gave convenient notice), so our rifles, and their attached bayonets, might one day save our lives. There was a more significant incentive: if you hit an appropriate number of 'bulls-eyes' and 'inners' you would qualify as a sharp shooter, and could wear a special marksman badge. I think it might even have produced a small bonus on your pay (itself as vanishingly small as the targets). We were all keen to win these marks of favour. Personally, despite my rural familiarity with shoots, I had never before handled anything bigger than an air pistol. Under a careful experienced eye, I loaded and aimed, then responded to 'Fire!'. We were to do this six times. I pressed the trigger, slowly, as instructed. The next thing was a tremendous blow to my right shoulder, such that I almost dropped the rifle. We had been warned about the degree of recoil, but nothing could prepare you for the reality. Second time round I was ready, and hugged the rifle-stock to me more tightly. Same result. My shoulder burned with pain, and my eyes began to water so that I could not clearly see the target for the last three shots. When my target was collected, my first three shots had hit two bulls and one inner; the last three shots had missed the target altogether. I would have felt downcast, but was too busy gritting my teeth against the pain in what proved to be a highly discoloured black and blue shoulder. I thought that if it came to a showdown with the wily opposition, I might be better served by the bayonet after all.

The weeks went by, and we would soon pass out at a special parade attended by proud families and friends; not mine, since none of us felt there was anything much to be proud of. Before that finale there were some remaining hurdles, called Reliability and Initiative Tests. We were divided into teams of eight, each with a designated Leader. Thanks to my possession of school A levels, this accolade was bestowed on me. The first test involved working out how to build a bridge from bits of wood and rope, then getting this bridge across a shallow ravine filled with mud and water: the Leader would then triumphantly march his men across to the other bank. First, the Leaders went to a central point where the building stuff was explained to them by some engineers. Then the Leaders, having memorised all this, would go back to their men and get them to put the bridge together and throw it across the ravine. This seemed to work out well enough, as we soon put together a convincing looking apparatus: happily, my men were unaware of my dubious background in woodwork or earlier failure to qualify for the Scouts. The next bit involved me picking on someone who had to wade waist high across the murky waters, catch the leading edges of the wood and rope structure manhandled across to him, and secure it to handy trees I had espied on the other side. Then I lined up my men, put myself at the front, and ordered them forwards: 'by the le-e-eft, qu-i-i-ck MARCH!' Mr Reliability himself, I led them boldly on to the bridge, which began to sway in an unreliable manner. Halfway across, I felt the rickety framework begin to give way under my feet. Turning instantly into Mr Initiative, I yelled the order 'Run!!' and made off. I got to the far bank, and turned just in time to see the remaining seven members of my little platoon, unaccountably slow off the mark, collapse helplessly into the unforgiving mud below, inextricably bound together with bits of rope and timber. Obscenity ruled for some time, not least when the team discovered that they would have to parade a few hours later in spotlessly clean kit.

This performance did little for the team's confidence in my leadership potential, and they were understandably edgy when we came to the second test, which covered skills in map-reading and traversing terrain. Again, we Leaders were summoned for a cursory briefing. Each one was given a different map reference, and instructed to lead our men to it, secure evidence of having been there, and return to the camp. We were to use our initiative in achieving this task as quickly as may be, and it was regarded as a competition between training units, with unspecified rewards for the first team back at camp. I quickly worked out that the reference point was actually the site of Chester cathedral, some 20 miles across the Cheshire plain. The group conferred. I had devised a plan: if we walked the shortish distance to West Kirby, we could surely find a bus service to Chester, locate the Cathedral, get our evidence of having been present and correct there, and return in the same stylish manner. Doubts were expressed: surely we were meant to march, and map read our way to our destination, rather than travel in style? And we had no money to pay the bus fares. I pointed out that there was a clear absence of rules about how we should proceed, only an assertion that we should use our initiative. That's what we were doing. As for the buses, leave that to me, I was confident I could talk our way onto them. There was a certain amount of restiveness among my charges, but an unthinking acceptance of authority, even so slenderly based as mine, was already well embedded after weeks of learning to do whatever the man placed above you in the scheme of things told you to do, even when it landed you in the drink. Undeniably, the prospect of an easy ride to our target, and no chance of getting hopelessly lost in unfamiliar country, played a part. We duly set off, marching smartly along the main road to West Kirby, in high spirits to be actually out of the dreary confines of the camp. We found the bus station, and we established that there was indeed a direct service to Chester and our target. The business of payment was remarkably straightforward. National Service affected all communities and classes, and national servicemen were treated with considerable sympathy. The friendly bus driver knew lads from his home district who were doing their bit, and once I had explained our purpose, saw no problem about giving us free transport. We bowled along merrily through the Cheshire countryside, on a lovely sunny day. I tucked the redundant map into my knapsack and relished the warm approval of my team. When we reached our destination, nothing could be easier than tracking to the Cathedral: when we alighted from the bus, we could see its spire lifting above the skyline of the town. We just walked straight to it. Happily, it was open to the public, and we got the young woman minding the office to sign and date a piece of official Cathedral notepaper with all of our names (and numbers) on it. We ate our rations in the precincts, basking in the sun. Easy-peasy, this reliability and initiative stuff.

We returned by the same bus routes, even had the same driver on the return to West Kirby. We marched smartly back to camp, and up to the orderly office. At first, we couldn't find anyone to report to, because they had not expected anyone to return yet: the exercise was expected to last all day, and we were the first back by some four hours. A clearly disgruntled officer dismissed the men but kept me back for a debriefing. When he heard of our manoeuvres, the complete absence of any travel across difficult terrain, the almost complete absence of any record of map-reading, he was visibly angry. Summoning an officer (a Squadron Leader) more senior than any I had so far been acquainted with, he made me repeat my account, which was received by the senior officer with disbelief. What kind of leader was I, if I failed to give my men practice in the reading of maps, and sharpening of their physical skills by traversing difficult ground in hot and demanding conditions? I protested that the only instruction I had been given was to ensure the use of initiative in undertaking our task, which was to reach a defined target and return to base in the shortest possible time. The Squadron Leader fixed me with the sort of blimpish glare he had presumably been taught at Officer Training School, though possibly it might have been copied from the numerous films going the rounds in those days set on the North-West Frontier in Victorian times. But he had a forcible point he wished to make: "The armed forces of this country do not go to war in *buses*," he said icily, "and you will not find a church spire to guide you in the Malayan jungle. Your team will be recorded as having failed in every aspect of the exercise". The team didn't care that much and felt that we had somehow pulled a fast one when we observed the moans and groans of those who had done some 40 miles of hard marching all day. My reputation might be in tatters with the command, but had triumphantly recovered with the lads.

We could not, though, avoid a much sterner physical test, our last hurrah before the end of square-bashing. This would take us for three days and nights into the Brecon Beacons, the wild hills in the middle of Wales. This time our map reading was a serious requirement, and often had to be done in the dark, and in pouring rain. At night, each individual had to sleep in a sorry-looking shelter constructed from sticks and a solitary canvas groundsheet. We were part of an official military exercise, and this time my little team, which rather surprisingly had not been removed from my questionable supervision, had to defend a wooded ridge. Other units, 'the enemy', would at some point in the days and nights ahead, attempt to infiltrate our ridge. At first, we were full of enthusiasm, keeping sentry duties like hawks and jumping to alertly at the slightest noises, usually caused by badgers or night birds. Happily, we had no ammunition for our guns, presumably in case we contrived to shoot each other (there had been some dreadful cases of deaths by 'friendly fire' in Malaya at this time). But by night two we were incredibly wet and cold, for it had rained without pause since our arrival. We had been quite unable to light fires or cook hot food. We were all thoroughly miserable and could scarcely see the point of being there, in this wet wilderness. Down in the valley, below the ridge, was a long, low-slung farmhouse which looked as though it might have stood defiantly there since the Middle Ages. The windows glowed brightly, holding a promise of warmth and hospitality. "Look, lads," I said, "why not go down and see if we could beg a hot drink, it would take an hour at most". We stumbled down to a surprised but tremendously friendly welcome from a ruddy faced hill farmer and his gently spoken wife. They had a son in the regular army ("He'll not be looking to follow me," said Mr Williams, somewhat sadly) and positively mothered us with hot cocoa, soup, and Welsh cakes smothered in farmhouse butter. We bade them goodbye and climbed cheerfully up the steep slope to our guard posts. Inevitably, the opposition had passed across the ridge at the very hour we were down in the valley. We pleaded that we hadn't seen a thing, and indeed we had not. Our warrant officer sighed heavily, but didn't appear to have considered fraternisation as a likely explanation.

# Chapter Twelve

# Marking Time

*Grammar school boys never fitted neatly into the armed forces.*
Richard Vinen

In the light of my demonstrated incapacity for leadership, it was no little surprise that I was called for an interview with the hated Fl. Lt Brown, who wanted to persuade me to apply for a three-year commission. The RAF at this time were giving very few commissions to national servicemen, but were keen to use short term commissions as a potential source of higher quality officer recruits over the long term. They were even prepared to add financial inducements to those who, like me, still had to go to University. This was Brown's own chosen path, Cambridge our shared destination. He used quite the wrong tactics with me, declaring that I'd be a much happier man in the officers' mess, detached from the low life and low intelligence of the average airman. I told him curtly that so far as I was concerned, I would be happier and better off where I was, and that two years of this stuff, let alone three, was already a complete waste of anyone's time. He flushed angrily at my evident scorn and suggested that it was people like me who contributed to low morale, unforgivable at a time when the country was at war, and needed firm and intelligent leadership. I expressed the hope that we might one day debate his assertions in a Cambridge pub, where he would not have the temporary advantages of rank he was so keen to deploy. He replied haughtily that it was most unlikely that we would be moving in the same circles. This must have been the case, for although I kept a keen look out when at Cambridge, I never saw him again. There were plenty more who exhibited his kind of social disdain: Vinen tells that the famous John Peel, a national service private, had a sister whose fiancé was an officer, and who made Peel address him as 'sir' at family gatherings.

Since I had declined the opportunity of a primrose path to officerly privilege, I was thrust back into the ranks, where we were able to express preferences as to our future service occupations. Most of us had no clue as to what was on offer. I nominated the Education section, the only choice with a conceivable link to my usual life. Second, I opted for Radar, as there were rumours that this held out possibilities of training to be a Flight Navigator in real aircraft. Both were regarded as a 'cushy' number. Least popular was the Catering Corps, which we had observed so far only as a form of punishment. There was no explanation of, nor any appeal against, the final allocations. A small group of five of us, all grammar school boys, were issued with orders and travel warrants. First, we would complete the official Passing Out parade. This was a jolly affair, our spirits raised not only by relief at the knowledge that this was the very last act in our initial round of punishment, but also by the public applause for our new smart skills as we marched crisply to the strains of our station brass band (even Johnny could now do this, thanks to his hut-mates). The next day, we five were to proceed to RAF Hereford, enlisted on a four-week training course as Equipment Accounting Clerks: no real aeroplanes for us.

Equipment Accounting is pretty much as boring as it sounds. It involved learning the various means by which the RAF kept track of its physical resources, from very large to very small. This produced the kind of joke beloved of we Equipment Accounts Clerks. One of the accounting processes we had to master was stock control, which meant in effect ensuring that the quantities of things you had down on paper tallied with the number of things you could physically identify on the ground (so to speak, as some at least of our stock was frequently to be found high in the air). The joke was that on paper, you could 'lose' a Hangar: Aircraft, by offsetting it against an extra Hanger: Coat. In theory, you could sell the now spare aircraft hangar without anyone being any the wiser. The joke seemed to depend on the presumed inability of those in charge to spell properly. I think it was probably a typical national serviceman and grammar school boy joke.

But it was probably a typical regular RAF staff joke to place we military innocents in the same camp as some tough RAF Regiment types who were more army than air force, and would be succeeded (in 1960) by the Hereford-based SAS. This was also a time when the IRA were actively planning operations on the English mainland, and to our dismay we were assembled one day to be told by a grave-faced officer that because of 'intelligence' about a potential IRA raid to steal weapons, the camp was now placed on a state of High Alert. We would all take our share of regular security patrols at night round the camp perimeter. I thought it best to keep quiet about my Irish connections. Lists were posted and I was down to patrol with a cheeky chappie cockney called Dave. He was no bigger than me, and the state of our nerves was not improved when, on reporting for our Saturday night patrol, we were issued with wooden staves. This was not much better than being issued with coat hangers. It seems all too comic now, but at the time we were thoroughly scared, and jumped out of our skins at the slightest sound: I perceived the wisdom of not issuing nervous troops with real guns, but withholding this defence against presumed real terrorists seemed unfair. Of course, no IRA attack ever ensued. Indeed, I can reliably report that we were far more at risk of bodily harm from the local Hereford lads than from the IRA. Fights in town were regular events, and we national service lads, blushing violets all, kept well away. However, I did get quite knocked about playing football for the station team in the local league, which was not all that far removed from the open warfare in the fractious colonies we were then trying to suppress.

Football, though, would do me a huge favour. As the end of the training course approached, we waited with bated breath for news of our subsequent posting. Naturally, no one wanted to be sent to real war theatres, of which the most serious at that time was Malaya. Any day in that final week you could see a small line outside the orderly office, all set to plead recently dead grandmothers or other sudden family emergency. On the final day of the course, a senior officer came in and portentously pinned up a notice of posting, but could not conceal a huge grin, knowing how the news would be received, as it was, by a chorus of groans of dismay. The whole group had been posted to Singapore, then onward to the Malayan mainland. But wait a minute: at the end of the list, under a separating black line, was my name: posted to RAF Hereford. I wasn't going anywhere. The reason was that the RAF Hereford football team had reached a Command cup-final and I had been kept back to play in it. As it turned out, I suffered more physical harm as a result than most of my erstwhile colleagues. During the match, I leaped to head what would be a glorious winner, and headed the wooden goalpost instead, at full speed. I was led off concussed, my nose cracked and bleeding. But I would now be safe at home, where that wily enemy couldn't reach me.

I was badly homesick by now, and discovered that there was a system of voluntary exchanges which allowed you to swap jobs of equal rank and description. I found in the listings system someone in the West Midlands who wanted to be in his home town of Hereford. Once my football skills were no longer required there, I was free to go. But this was something of a frying pan into the fire move. I found myself at RAF Cosford, in the Midlands. Though undoubtedly nearer to Yorkshire, it was then the base for the training of Boy Entrants, who signed up at the age of 16. They came more or less with their own set of training staff: officers, NCOs and military police. It soon became clear why the latter were needed. These young recruits were a pretty hard lot drawn generally from the big city slums. The forces represented a means of escape from intolerable, poverty-stricken and broken backgrounds. Many had used entry as a sort of plea bargain against sentences in young offenders' institutions, so were in spirit if not quite in practice what were in those days known as Borstal Boys. During their training they were confined to camp, so this was the only place they could let their hair down. Weekends were sheer mayhem, as they took their boredom out on each other. They had their own 'Boy' NCOs who were much disliked. On one occasion, some of the boy trainees locked their boy corporal into a small wardrobe, then flung it from a second-floor balcony, breaking both his legs. The worst event was when some of them set fire to their living quarters, and several local brigades had to assist the overrun station fire crew in extinguishing the blaze.

For putting up with this unlovely lot we were paid the grand sum of 19 shillings a week and scarcely dared to go out after dark. There was one moment of light relief when the station received an inspection from an Air Vice Marshal: really high up the food chain. It was decreed that a Guard of Honour should welcome him, formed from the camp personnel, since the Boy Entrants would be having their own separate ceremonies. I was amazed to be nominated as one of the hapless dozen, since Guard of Honour types are usually chosen from the tallest men available, but the truth was that there were few regular staff to choose from. We had to practise incessantly, though we were already well versed in sloping and presenting arms and so on. But we were an odd bunch, with a line straggling from lofty six footers at each end down to me in the middle. Since all our rifles, when presented, had to be on the same level, I had to tuck in my elbows and push my wrists up unnaturally high. On the day, we also had to fix bayonets, rendering the mute rifle a potential hazard. The bigwig walked down the line to inspect us, twice lingering, rather as royalty does, to conduct meaningless small talk. By the time he reached me my arms were aching intensely, and I could feel them, and the bayonet, wavering. I thought that if I had to talk too I might well collapse into him bayonet first. Mercifully he sized me up with an expert eye, smiled sympathetically, and passed on.

I badly wanted to get away from this dreary and rather menacing camp (now the site of an RAF Museum). The exchange lists brought me relief in the shape of another equipment clerk who wanted to be in the Midlands. I gave a studiedly neutral description of Cosford: it was, I thought, every man for himself. And so, in December 1957, I fetched up at RAF Lindholme, a dozen miles south of Doncaster, and not far from my dear old Great North Road. I would be able to hitch-hike the 50 miles home and back on my free weekends. RAF Lindholme is now a state prison, and served a not dissimilar function as far as we national service inhabitants were concerned. It was then part of Bomber Command, which still enjoyed no little prestige because of its wartime exploits, tarnished though this brutally earned reputation has subsequently become. The nearest camp, a few miles away, was RAF Finningley, a main base for the nuclear armed Vulcan bombers. These extraordinary flying triangles were on 24-hour patrol. They flew over us each night and were deafeningly noisy. For my first week in Lindholme I simply couldn't sleep, but after a while this noise faded into a familiar environment and ceased to disturb me. Just as well, for this is where I would spend the remaining 18 months of my service.

RAF Lindholme's function was much less grand but quite significant, for it was here that new pilots received their first flying lessons, starting off on the comfortingly familiar and famous old Lancaster bombers. This could produce some nerve-racking moments. The landing strips were in a vast open space separated by service roads, and bounded on one side by a hedge alongside a public road which ran from Bawtry on the A1 to Goole on the east coast. The planes had to come in and land over hedge and road, and not infrequently would fall short, taking the hedge with them. The public road was wisely closed to traffic when landings were in prospect. But inside the airfield, we servicemen had our football pitches alongside the runways, and there were frequent inter-section competitions. We all knew that from time to time the trainee pilots would miss the tarmac altogether. Often we would simply freeze as we watched a big Lancaster coming in, swaying about drunkenly as some hapless trainee sought to keep it straight, often enough pointing it straight at us. Normally the experienced trainer would take over at the last to avert disaster, but we were quite unable to trust to this, and many a time we would be found literally taking our eye off the ball, a particularly trying affliction for the goal-keepers.

I now began some serious clerical work, simple routines which rapidly became tedious. I was both fortunate and unfortunate as to those in authority over me. The unfortunate bit was the officer in charge of my section, a regular Flying Officer who had been to an undistinguished minor public school in the Home Counties. He couldn't seem to come to terms with my Cambridge destination, and would often have me into his office ostensibly on office business, but then ask questions about my grammar school, my family background, how I would cope with university, all with an apparently amiable manner, but one which concealed attempts to goad me with supercilious remarks. I fumed inwardly, but already knew better than to give people like this any opportunity to punish me. I was much more fortunate in my immediate boss. He had seen active service overseas in the RAF Regiment, with the significant rank of Flight Sergeant. Though he never ever spoke about this, someone told me that it was rumoured that he had been badly wounded on secret operations in the desert, and had been unavoidably returned to a desk job. Flight Sergeant Morris was, on first acquaintance, extremely formidable, a large bull of a man with heavy blue jowls and dark brown eyes which gave him a slightly menacing expression. He had a certain stillness, a way of considering you quietly, which lent him a natural authority. I think that initially we regarded each other a little suspiciously, unsure of what would develop. I quite soon began to realise that we were going to get on fine. He wore his rank very lightly if you gave him no nonsense, and also left me to get on with my job without any interference. It was in all conscience a very straightforward set of tasks: exchanging old kit and equipment for new, making sure the sums added up, and selling off the used products to external contractors. Nothing interesting ever happened apart from the rather prickly sessions with Flying Officer Trent. Football saved me from this boredom to some degree, as I was again selected for the station football team, and the quite fanatical officer in charge, Squadron Leader Dawson, negotiated large chunks of time out of our jobs for training. We had rather a good team, in which I was the only amateur: all the other players had professional contracts like the one I had been obliged to forgo with Wolves, though generally in the lower leagues of Third Division North and South. Our fixtures meant that we travelled widely to play other RAF teams, the highlight being a match against RAF Cranwell, the officer training station (where one of my youthful heroes, Lawrence of Arabia, served for a time in anonymity as an ordinary aircraftman: I had read *The Seven Pillars of Wisdom* at school, and had been astonished to discover that after losing the whole draft on Reading railway station he had written it all again from memory). Several of the mostly industrial working-class lads in our team gleefully took this opportunity to put the boot into the nascent officer class.

To do them credit, the young officers gave as good as they got physically, but we outclassed them in the end. We then progressed to the final of the Bomber Command Cup, against RAF Waddington in Lincolnshire. Squadron Leader Dawson contrived to get all of us released from working duties for the three weeks before the final, so it was a bit like being on holiday. Sadly, our opponents, another team full of contracted professionals, inflicted on us our first defeat in a year.

Life at Lindholme, for most national servicemen, as in so many other RAF stations, was a mix of undemanding and boring work, occasional rehearsals of our basic drills, some repetitive guard duties, and spells of time off. Since most of us had very little money, we were in the evenings more or less confined to the NAAFI bar. Servicemen tended to form small groups based on the billets they shared, and in our case, this meant an all national service group. We were usually a quiet and law-abiding lot. The liveliest was Gus, a small Scot with curly blond hair and a cherubic pink face. His constant companion was another Scot, always Mac to us, a physical giant of a man who was by temperament an absolute kitten, usually gentle and courteous. One Saturday night trouble sparked, with a lot of drink having been taken. Gus, always inclined to a cheeky sarcasm, said something taken exception to by a group of regular servicemen, who didn't much care for the conscripted cuckoos in their midst. Remarks were made casting certain inferences as to Gus's sexual preferences, and fighting broke out. Mac was transformed into a raging bull as he sought to defend his pal Gus. Maddened, he picked up a chair and almost brained two people at once with it. We realised that we had to stop him before he seriously injured someone, and four of us tried to hold him back. I recall holding on fast with both arms to the right arm with which Mac was intent on wielding the remains of the chair. He simply lifted me off the ground, but at least our combined efforts made him miss his target. The military police arrived to prevent any further mayhem and I hid in a dignified fashion under a table to avoid further attention. In the result, Mac was sentenced to two months in detention for causing actual bodily harm, which meant he would now serve two years and two months: he was mortified.

To avoid the wrong impression, I have to say that this was the only violence I ever saw during the whole of my national service, apart from the horrendous incidents at the Boy Entrants camp. And indeed, there were other ways to spend your leisure. I was drawn into an amateur dramatics group run by two of the officers, Phil Bennett and Jim Shield, the latter on a short-term commission. They were friendly enough to the 'other ranks' involved in the plays, but I reflect now that they never ever invited us to their homes, and were in effect unable to invite us into the officers mess. Phil always took the juiciest parts, and Jim acted as director. Gus did all the lighting and practical stage management. I did minor roles. The highlight was a performance of *The Duke in Darkness* by Patrick Hamilton, set in a mediaeval castle keep, surrounded by a moat. At one point I had to help to throw through a window high up in the keep the dead body of the Duke's jailer. A mattress had been placed behind the stage to catch the 'body'. Gus, doing sound effects, would then after some seconds produce the sound of a loud splash. Our adrenalin levels high, we swung with abandon, the body disappeared and missed the mattress, so there was a loud bang followed by a groan, immediately followed by a splash. At the tensest moment of this melodrama, the audience bellowed with laughter.

We celebrated the end of the theatrical season with a very alcohol-laden party. The next morning I felt quite ill, and threw up twice: but we had to turn out in full kit for a visiting inspection by an Air Commodore. It was a wet, sultry day and he was late landing. We were kept standing at the ready inside an aircraft hangar. I felt unwell. The next thing I knew was coming round in a dentist's chair, getting an injection. I promptly passed out again. Apparently, I had keeled over and fallen flat on my face on the concrete hangar floor, breaking off a tooth. Flight Sergeant Morris had picked me up, unconscious and bleeding, and carried me in his arms to the medical centre. Once the dentist (another short-term officer) had extracted the broken tooth and patched up my bleeding mouth, he wanted to put me on a charge, because he smelt the alcohol still on my breath. Flight Sergeant Morris told him quietly but firmly that I was his responsibility and he would handle it. He helped me out, and all he said to me was "Go to bed and don't come back to work until you feel normal again, or what passes for normal with you, you daft bugger." There was considerable kindness behind that fierce exterior.

The main reason for transferring to Lindholme in the first place had been to get nearer home, and this worked out well. I could join my constant life companion, the Great North Road, at Bawtry, then hitch-hike directly to Boroughbridge. In those days hitch-hiking national servicemen were a common sight, and many drivers sympathetic. I rarely had to stand for too long. The people who gave me lifts covered a whole social spectrum, from an upper-class brigadier going on leave himself, to long distance lorry drivers with quite incomprehensible Glaswegian accents. One of these picked me up more than once as he did a regular night-time North-South run. On the first occasion, he told me he didn't want me to make any conversation, which seemed odd, but I wasn't about to quibble. When he stopped at a lorry-drivers cafe for a break he left me and made off to sit with the other drivers. But to my pleased surprise, a waitress came over with a mug of hot tea which my silent travelling companion had sent over for me. Another regular saviour was a commercial traveller who warned me on my first lift that he would drive extremely fast, and advised me on how to adopt the crash position if the situation might require it. I need to explain that at this time, most of the A1 was a single-track road with very heavy traffic, which this impatient traveller was intent on overtaking, given the smallest window. I closed my eyes more than once, but Mum's favourite guardian angel was watching over me. Again, friendliness intervened: once, needing a break, he stopped at a smart wayside hotel, took me in with him, and treated me to a slap-up afternoon tea. My humble position seemed to attract acts of kindness.

The best example of this was the Ice Cream Man. He had been a regular visitor to Roecliffe and surrounding villages for a long time. Mum discovered one day that, astonishingly, he was based in Doncaster. A tall, thin, lugubrious man, he would be happy to give me free passage to Doncaster on Sundays when I was at home for the weekend. He was as good as his word, and I could spend a good long Sunday without worrying about the long hitch-hike back south. However, this turned out to be a bit of an ordeal. The only place for me was in the back with the ice-cream, and there was no proper seating. Worse, there was some sort of freezing system which kept the whole back of the van and its contents icy cold: this included me, and when we reached Doncaster I would stumble out onto the street walking like a zombie, and frozen to the core. My travelling companion soon realised that Doncaster still left me a dozen miles adrift, late at night, so he took to calling in at a transport cafe he frequented, and arranging my next lift down the A1 to Bawtry. He was an uncommunicative man and we scarcely ever exchanged a word other than greetings and goodbyes, but here is another example of good fellowship from ordinary people so typical of my time in the services. I'll always remember the Ice Cream Man, and for years afterwards Mum repaid him regularly with a warming mug of tea before he departed in his frozen vehicle.

The months crawled by at the slowest pace, though at least I finally got my teeth into more interesting work, since I was given responsibility for the direct negotiation of contracts with external businesses who took used equipment off our hands. I heard many stories of airmen making a lot of money on the side through such contracts, but I can honestly say that I was never ever offered a single bribe or inducement; my reward was elevation to the giddy heights of Corporal, two stripes on the arm and a few shillings extra in the pocket. My last hurrah in this capacity was to represent the station in an inter-command athletics meeting being hosted at RAF Lindholme. Since I had been a useful cross country runner at school, I volunteered for the 5000 metres steeplechase, an event I had never before experienced. It involves running round and round a track leaping over hurdles and water jumps. I spent as much time in the water as I did on the track, and once slipped underneath a barrier and had to go back and jump over it again, to sarcastic but warm cheers from my many spectating mates. Sheer cussedness kept me going and I came home third, approximately half a mile behind the first two runners. The tannoy announced 'and third, Corporal Minogog'. After nearly two years they still couldn't get my name right. Fred Inglis, an old friend of many years' standing, still jovially addresses me as 'Corporal Minogog' whenever we meet; it is, perhaps, a suitable epitaph, military service as a joke.

*Corporal 'Minogog' not looking happy after two years of military service.*

On a warm late summer's day in 1959, I passed through the camp gates for the last time, taking with me a kit bag full of uniform and the like, since in theory number 5046489 might be summoned again at any time during a three year period 'on reserve'. But it was already clear that this would not happen: National Service itself was on the way out, and the last conscript (what an unlucky fate) entered in 1960. Had I been allowed in 1957 to defer for three years and take up my University place instead, I would have avoided it altogether. I devoutly wish still that this had happened.

You often hear the argument that National Service took in immature and often badly-behaved youths and 'made men of them', somehow performing a service to society. But Vinen's masterly and detailed study concludes that National Service principally taught a whole generation how to avoid work and responsibility, as well as how to subvert authority and demonstrate disrespect in a thousand ways. This exactly sums up my own experience, and I still regard it as a complete waste of two years of my time which, so far as I can judge, contributed nothing tangible to the national good. For those young men who jumped from water towers or under trains, or died in action, National Service destroyed them, and the happiness of innumerable families, principally to ensure that an ageing and discredited imperial system could prosecute colonial wars and kill many other people in far flung places like Cyprus, Malaya, and Egypt. I deeply regret having had any part in this, however small.

I also acquired another type of experience of the pervasive British class system, which in the armed forces takes a very open and heavily institutionalised form. Granted, it promotes a certain degree of social mobility, not least because there is some acceptance, since the disastrous leadership of the Great War, that the upper classes are wont to be 'donkeys leading lions', and cannot be wholly trusted for effective leadership in real war situations. However, the literature on national service demonstrates how the upper echelons of the armed services were in the late 1950s still dominated by people with a public school background, and in the case of the more prestigious regiments in the Army, by specific prestigious public schools; Vinen quotes figures for the Rifle Brigade where 49 of the 50 officers selected went to Eton, with only one being non-public school. He also demonstrates that such bias was the norm in officer selection processes. It is clear that the RAF was the least class-bound service, and several officers came from the ranks of grammar school boys. Speaking personally, the rigid divisions made between officers and other ranks, and the clear expectation that there could be no fraternisation between the two, rankled. I had no wish to join the officer class, but was irritated by the assumption that everyone else was by definition inferior and should be treated as such. It will not, I thought confidently, be like this at Cambridge. I had a shock coming.

# Chapter Thirteen
# Life at Cambridge

*We grammar schoolboys were the interlopers.*
Alan Bennett

It was Molly Sawdon who first suggested to me that I should be put in for the entrance examinations to Cambridge University. King James's Grammar School had rarely put people in for Oxbridge, one a year at best: very few of the teachers had an Oxbridge background, or were interested or knowledgeable enough to push forward bright pupils. Since Molly set the bar very high in this respect, her nominations were usually successful, but tended to be infrequent, and confined to the humanities. Two years before me, John Rathmell had been awarded a scholarship to Jesus College, Cambridge to read English, and would eventually be elected to a Fellowship at Christ's College. The most successful old pupil before him, some ten years previously, had been Professor Kathleen Gough: the daughter of an agricultural machinery contractor in a local village, she had become one of the world's leading anthropologists, and would be a distinguished campaigner against America's war in Vietnam. People rarely seemed to go to Oxford.

Cambridge seemed to me to be in a different universe than the one I inhabited, and I was both excited and apprehensive when such an opportunity was placed before me. My biggest decision was what subject I should pursue. For five years I had blossomed under Molly's guidance and inspiration in English Literature: but I was finding myself increasingly drawn to the study of history, and even to archaeology, fascinated by the many examples close to home of the Roman occupation, and also of pre-Roman artefacts, such as the megaliths standing in the farm fields my father worked. Folklore had it that the devil had fired them at Aldborough but missed, and hit Boroughbridge, hence their local designation as The Devil's Arrows. Another story suggested that they had been erected by the Romans as markers for chariot races. It was my mother who first told me of their more probable history as Celtic monuments of some kind, probably with a ritual significance similar to that of Stonehenge, something now confirmed by contemporary scholarship. They were thought to have been brought there by being floated downriver from the nearest source of millstone grit, then erected in an alignment relative to the rising and setting sun. Dad once, when reaping corn in the field that contained two of these standing stones, explained all this to an attentive Wilf Choppin. Wilf took off his cap and scratched his silver head: "Now, I can see 'ow they might 'ave brought 'em down t'river like, but 'ow the 'ell did they get 'em ower yon railway line?". It was indeed a puzzle, to which I sought answers in many happy hours of reading in the York Archaeological Museum. My new history teacher, Bill Murphy, encouraged and fed my interest. I decided that my Cambridge application would be for history, much to Molly's disappointment. I also had to choose a college for this purpose. I settled on Christ's College, for no other reason than that my new Headmaster, Frank Brewin, had been there and knew the Senior Tutor, a Dr Pratt, who had taught him Mathematics. I only discovered later that this might not have been much of a helpful connection as Mr Brewin had scored an extremely modest class of degree.

One cold, crisp December afternoon in 1956, I took the train to Cambridge, books and notes stuffed with my clothes in a bright, new, cheap suitcase. There I would spend some days being interviewed, and taking written entry examinations in history, and Latin. This last had occasioned no little panic. My scratchy 'O' level Latin was long behind me and happily, but unfortunately now, forgotten. The Latin master, a quiet, self-contained man called Frank Jowsey, had made his best efforts to get me up to scratch, but I had not been a receptive pupil. I arrived in a fairly anxious state, not helped by the clear self-confidence of the boys around me in the train, most of them seemingly from public schools. But I was bowled over by the unexpected and unknown physical beauty of the Cambridge colleges, and the wonderful Backs along the Cam. Christ's itself, an ancient foundation, took my breath away. I knew instantly that I badly wanted to get myself there. The night before the first history paper, I sat up until three in the morning, compulsively combing through my notes and the special essays I had written for Bill Murphy. Slightly dazed, I emerged from the history papers feeling that I had not let myself down. But Latin set me a different set of questions which I struggled to answer. The final stage consisted of two interviews. The first was with a noted historian, J. H. (Jack) Plumb: it was in itself extraordinary to me to find myself face to face with someone already known on the written page. He started out in a gentle way, asking me about my school. He then asked me when Knaresborough had last sent a Member to Parliament. This almost did for me straight away. Had he asked me which Roman cohorts were stationed at Eboracum, and how their skirmishes with the local Brigantes had played out, or which mediaeval king had been pinned down in the now ruined Knaresborough Castle by rebellious northern barons, I would have been in no difficulty (it was Edward 11, and the castle had been 'slighted' in 1646 by Thomas Fairfax, of my old Appleton stamping ground). However, not one of my history teachers had ever thought to follow the nineteenth century electoral history of our home town. My mind raced through the relevant Reform Acts (1832, 1867, 1884-5), trying to recall not just what had happened to the franchises, but which Ministries had preceded them. I made a quick stab: "I believe that would be 1865, with Knaresborough, in effect a 'rotten borough', being disfranchised by Disraeli's 1867 Reform Act." Dr Plumb smiled kindly, doubtless able to trace from my horror-struck expression that I was flying by the seat of my pants, and didn't press me any further on this. Checking later, I discovered that I had been half right and half wrong. Knaresborough had indeed been a classic 'rotten borough', with only 284 voters, and one of the smallest in the country to send two members to Parliament, the same number as nearby industrial urban Leeds with an electorate of 9,000. Knaresborough had survived the limited 1832 reforms. The 1967 Reform Act took away one of the two members, so Knaresborough continued to participate in parliamentary elections, largely in the Whig/Liberal interest, until eliminated in the 1884-5 reform legislation. In a debate on the 1832 Reform Bill Henry Brougham, a Whig grandee who had been nominated by the Duke of Devonshire as a Member for Knaresborough, said wryly "you may be returned for this place but it is at your peril that you show yourself among the inhabitants".

Despite this unnerving start, the rest of the interview was relaxed and interesting, and I felt quite upbeat as I passed on to Dr Pratt, the Senior Tutor. I did not know at the time, but learned much later, that Dr Pratt had ruled the Admissions roost at Christ's College for some considerable time, and had a reputation for using this power to build obsessively the best possible sports teams there. Reputedly, according to a Cambridge sporting friend of mine, when one of the outstanding rugby stars of his time entered the Senior Tutor's room at Christ's for his admissions interview, Dr Pratt instantly hurled a rugby ball at him, he caught it, and was in: according to this, possibly apocryphal account, the said rugby star entered Cambridge without A levels, and left it without a degree. On the soccer side, Pratt would attend English Schools Trials and encourage likely lads to enter themselves for Christ's, pretty well without much reference to their academic expectations. In theory, this should have helped my case, given my national service successes. Evidently this was not a sufficiently high standard. In a perfunctory interview, and with little discussion about my background and academic record, his chief question was: what did I consider my greatest weakness as a footballer? Disconcerted by the unexpected focus of the interview, I joked that I was one-footed, and only used my left leg to stand on. I was rather curtly dismissed.

Two weeks later the school had a letter turning down my application. I had been awarded an Exhibition Scholarship level mark for History, but my Latin paper was regarded as too weak, many other more deserving candidates etc., etc. Bill Murphy was furious. After discussion with Molly, he wrote immediate letters to four other Cambridge colleges, pointing to my excellent history performance (and my 'unusually humble background': I can still hear Mum snorting at this description, nothing humble about her). We quickly received three offers of interviews, from Gonville and Caius, Trinity, and Magdalene Colleges. Back I went on the train. The first interviews were to be at Caius, initially with Philip Grierson, the college's Director of Studies in History. I would come to know Philip well, a soft-spoken Irishman with a stunning command of European languages, many of them self-taught as an aid to his principal research interest in ancient coinages. Having established that I had a strong interest in the mediaeval period and English monastic history, he launched into a disquisition on the Cistercians in Yorkshire, with such a wealth of detail and assured grasp that I sat riveted. After 40 minutes in which I scarcely got a word in (though I did rather wrong foot him by telling that the history book that I was currently reading was H. G. Wells' *Outline of History*) he more or less patted me on the arm and sent me off to the Caius Senior Tutor, Dr Ian McFarlane. Where Pratt of Christ's led with football, McFarlane of Caius led with cricket. He had a theory that England might do much better at Test level if they were to think outside the box, and open the bowling with slow spinners instead of predictable fast bowlers: what did I think? What I thought was that Cambridge Admissions Tutors were a very odd lot, seemingly preoccupied with sport: but I thought it politic to show some enthusiasm for his ideas. Much later, I would learn that Dr McFarlane rather fancied himself as a slow left arm bowler, and all was clear. It quickly became evident that he and Philip had already decided to offer me a place on the strength of my Christ's papers, and a supportive reference from the generous Jack Plumb. The only condition was that I would take up the place on offer in 1959, after completing my two years of National Service. He was, I think, pleased by my instant decision to accept, without seriously exploring any further the possibilities at Trinity and Magdalene. I hugged myself in wordless delight all the way home. Mum and Dad hugged me in wordless delight too: it was due reward for all their selfless efforts, all those hours labouring in lonely fields and hot, exhausting kitchens. I never forget any of that selfless labour and love. I also owed much to Bill Murphy, who looked seriously embarrassed when I thanked with him a present of a cheap, and probably tasteless, painted pottery ashtray. Not long afterwards, Molly and Paddy invited me to a tennis party at their attractive house alongside the River Nidd. Molly was delighted to see another of her favourites make it to Cambridge, but told me firmly that I had better not turn up there in the dirty tennis shoes that I was wearing that afternoon. "Right ho, Miss," I responded cheerily. "And you had best not use expressions like 'right ho' to your tutors", she added severely, at pains as always to soften any rougher edges she detected, and determined that I should not be allowed to get above myself.

I still had to learn a lot about good taste and accepted norms of social behaviour, but two years in the armed forces had not offered much help in this respect, so that I arrived in Cambridge for the Michaelmas Term of 1959 all too uncertain about how I would fit in to my new and, for a rural Yorkshire boy, wonderfully grand surroundings. Gonville and Caius was one of the oldest and most centrally placed colleges, alongside the Senate House, next to King's College Chapel. I had the luxury of rooms to myself (sitting room, bedroom and small kitchen) on the second floor in the newer St Michael's Court, across Trinity Street; baths and toilets of a spartan kind reminiscent of my national service days involved a trek down to the basement. My 'staircase' was cleaned, dusted and polished by Mrs Flood, known in the Cambridge argot as our 'bedder'. Ma Flood, as she became to us, though only out of her hearing, was very small and almost comically spherical, her height and width being about the same dimensions. Of indeterminate age, probably in her mid-fifties, somewhat gruff, and sporting a wispy moustache, she brooked no nonsense, having sorted out several cohorts of 'my young gen'lmen' over the years.

The young gentlemen who would share my college life for the next three years were a mixed lot. Caius enjoyed a broader intake than some other

*Gonville and Caius College, Cambridge, probably in the 1950s.*

colleges, and I would find a fair smattering of grammar school boys (no girls entered the college until the 1980s). But the majority were undoubtedly from public school backgrounds, with a sprinkling from the upper crust, hailing from large family estates of the kind my family had worked on as labourers and servants. I knew no one initially who was, like me, from a working-class background. I found myself inordinately anxious about this, worried about how to fit in, and immediately conscious that I stood out because of my clear Yorkshire accent. The first week involved a grand dinner in college at which we would be expected to wear formal dinner dress, something I had only once done before. Hiring the right clothes, putting them on correctly, were small nightmares. Somehow Mum and Dad had never got around to teaching me how to tie a black tie. At least Mum saved me some potential embarrassment, having taught me all the right place settings and uses of cutlery and glassware, based on her experience of setting upper class dining tables, so that at least I knew how to cope with the complex array of knives, forks, spoons and glasses that confronted me. I still looked covertly around me, carefully watching what my peers were up to before making a move myself. My overriding impression was how utterly self-confident and socially at ease were these new companions. Early exchanges in conversation were usually about which schools people had come from. A man opposite was from Harrow, a second from Winchester. My own contribution, Knaresborough Grammar School, elicited faintly surprised looks, and a tactful change of conversation. Occasional references to 'my people' passed over my head; it took a little while to realise that they were talking about their families. I had a whole new language to decipher. I went back to my rooms a little tipsy, but was unable to sleep since on the floor directly beneath me a very loud party was going on, with much laughter and some shouting. Next day I was up early and found that the staircase and landing were carpeted in champagne corks. This was a scenario I had half expected, upper class yahoos who would look down on me and waste their time having drunken parties, to which I would not be invited. I made careful note of the name on the door: H. S. Johnson. To cut a long story short, Hugh Johnson would become a life-long friend, and I would one day be best man at his fashionable Versailles wedding; but right there and then, I deeply resented all the privilege he and his companions stood for in my mind.

As I got to know a bit more about my new fellow students, I came to realise that a surprising number of the public school cohort had very modest 'A' levels, often inferior to those of some of my erstwhile Sixth Form companions in Yorkshire such as Catherine Gandy, who had never been remotely considered as suitable for Oxbridge entry (at least she made it to Durham, along with Bristol and St Andrews one of the few universities regarded as appropriate by upper class people not quite bright enough for Oxbridge). The bias often seemed to be towards those of modest academic records, but possessing sporting talent. Another surprise was the evident strength of an Anglican Christian culture, also reflecting the prevailing public school culture, each college with its Chapel and Chaplain. I soon realised how strong a grip Christianity had in the University at this time, and how actively evangelistic many of its proponents were. Somehow the Catholic Society discovered me, but I found the welcome party I went to stuffed full of demonstrably well-bred types. The smooth presiding priest, Monsignor Gilbey, seemed to lose interest once he knew of my origins in a grammar school that was not even Catholic, but I had lost interest in him and his Society too (I was not one bit surprised to discover recently that when Monsignor Gilbey retired, he took up residence in London in the exclusive Travellers Club in Pall Mall).

It was clear to me that class discrimination of the most obvious kind was alive and kicking so far as Cambridge college admissions were concerned. Even the best students from respectable grammar schools struggled to win admission to Oxbridge, as I had done. While public schools in the 1950s and 1960s accounted for between 5% and 7% of the schools population, they invariably commanded more than 50% of Oxbridge places. This meant, of course, that a substantial number of applicants who were not from public schools got places; however, in the early 1960s the representation of manual working class students was a fraction of one per cent, while the representation of the children of farm workers was too tiny to be recorded. I suppose I should have counted myself fortunate, and indeed I did, but felt angered then, and still do now, by the inequalities of opportunity and reward that remain deeply entrenched in our class dominated system of education.

My anger was mixed with anxiety. I was prepared to dislike at first sight anyone who seemed cockily self-confident and brash (and there were plenty such) or who were openly condescending and snobbish. The latter usually came from the ranks of the upper class, with impeccable social pedigrees. Conscious of their elevated status in Cambridge and in the College, they treated those they deemed to be socially inferior with a sort of frostily polite disdain. There were several self-defining groups in the College: one was this tight knit social set who mixed only with each other, and tended to pursue the pastimes of their rurally based estates, such as hunting, shooting and beagling. For many of them Cambridge was an expected rite of passage before they (or their families) awarded each other lucrative jobs in the City or politics, or went on to inherit and manage their country estates. Their past, present and future were seamlessly laid out, in part at least from no more than the accident of birth. While I had to admit to myself that many of these chaps were damned clever, it was difficult for the offspring of a father and grandfather who had worked their whole lives for such people for pittances, to contemplate these gilded youths with equanimity.

A more congenial grouping might be called the intellectuals, centred on my set of history students. I saw little of Philip Grierson at this stage, as the first-year students fell to the charge of Neil McKendrick. One day, Neil would become a highly effective Master, but in 1959 he was only recently appointed as a College Fellow. I was astonished to learn many years later that at this point he was, at 24, only a couple of years older than me: astonished because he seemed even then to carry himself with a sort of middle aged gravitas which stood him in good stead in his eventual Mastership. He was a tall, slim fair-haired man, who Ma Flood referred to as 'that long yellow man'. His interests centred on industrial history, and he was always about to write a book on Josiah Wedgwood, though he never did. While he never became in any sense a notable historian, at least he had a clear desire to create and attach himself to a strong college tradition of excellence in history, attracting a string of superior candidates. In the 1950s and early 1960s, Cambridge did not always pay much attention to teaching, or worry so much as they would later about the relative standings of examination performance across the college system. Teaching methods were still somewhat old fashioned. You went to lectures each morning, and had a face to face tutorial with a college fellow once a week, based on an essay that you had written and would read out. In Caius, we did this in pairs. My 'pair' was Colin Jones, a very quiet and self-contained Welshman with whom I had no other interaction whatever. In this first year I didn't get much interaction from Neil either, since he offered little comment beyond an unrevealing 'Yes, not bad' or 'you seem to have covered most of the ground'. He would give us a title and recommended reading for the next week's effort, and that was it. Even here the references were scanty, as you were pretty much expected to read around the subject on your own initiative. But having to write a substantial essay every week was a strong discipline which required and shaped good habits, which, fortunately for me, had already been instilled by Molly Sawdon and Bill Murphy.

There was a Caius History Society where the history students across the whole three years congregated. In this way I got to know my peers. At first, I was a little overwhelmed by their manifest talent, cleverness and articulateness. I hovered silently on the edges of this group, too shy to intervene, and more than a little dazzled. I gravitated (as did many) to the rooms of Quentin Skinner. I knew from mysterious college grapevines that Quentin already came with a reputation for brilliance. As with so many other of my new acquaintances, my initial reaction was a curmudgeonly one, ready to think him yet another child of privilege to whom success had come too easily, and who would (I expected) look down on me and my Yorkshire accent. For me it was at first a sort of love-hate relationship (he would never ever have guessed this) since fundamentally Quentin was who I wanted to be: clever, witty, self-confident, and academically brilliant. Just recently, nearly sixty years on, an internationally well-known academic I met at Quentin's house, when he heard that we had been in the same college as undergraduates, asked with a mischievous smile: "Now tell me, what was Quentin really like in those days?" I didn't then know how well this man knew Quentin. Turning away, I said "Why, he was intolerable, utterly intolerable". This was meant to stonewall, to prevent any revelations that might somehow embarrass Quentin. Afterwards I felt tremendously angry with this clumsy response, for how must it have sounded to my friend, standing within earshot? Yet I had unconsciously reverted to the ungenerous feelings that I had on first meeting, all those years before, generated by my own deeply felt insecurities.

But to my good fortune I was drawn inexorably into Quentin's orbit, and through him into the orbit of John Barnes, a more senior college member who was a prominent student Conservative (later an LSE academic and author of a well-received biography of Stanley Baldwin). Through them, and their connections, all kinds of Cambridge luminaries would be seen and heard. I first met there, if somewhat tangentially, since I was too shy to say boo to a goose, let alone a luminary, men who would take the top posts in the Cambridge Union (a sort of upmarket debating society), go on to long political careers, and serve in senior ministerial office in a series of Conservative administrations that were simultaneously increasingly right wing and increasingly mediocre. The most appallingly self-satisfied of these future Tory grandees (we thought even then) was John Selwyn Gummer, now most memorable for having, as Minister of Agriculture during the 'mad cow disease' food crisis, insisted on his young daughter publicly eating a beef burger that for all anyone knew may have carried the fatal infection; and later, in the parliamentary expenses scandal, for having claimed £36,000 for garden maintenance. Politically he was something of a Vicar of Bray, changing his political position to suit whichever leader might reward him: Heath, then Thatcher, Major, and finally David Cameron. An admired intellectual, briefly glimpsed, was the eventually ill-fated Leon Brittan, who enjoyed a meteoric political rise to be the youngest Cabinet minister in Mrs Thatcher's second administration, and later presided over the brutal and secretly-organised policing of striking Yorkshire miners in 1984 (ironically he represented a Yorkshire constituency). An obituary in 2015 judged that he was too often 'seen as trying to do and say what the Prime Minister would prefer': much good it did him, for in a later policy disaster in 1986 he was sacrificed to save Mrs Thatcher's Prime Ministerial face, though later rewarded with a peerage by John Major. Ken Clarke, a law student at Caius, then a rather run of the mill student politician, was another who flourished variously as Education Secretary under Thatcher, as Chancellor of the Exchequer under John Major, and even in his seventies in Cameron and Clegg's coalition government as Justice Secretary. For a man both then and now characterised as a moderate Tory (a label derived largely from his pro-European stance) he managed to espouse and carry out some deeply damaging right wing policies, and as a former lawyer seemed intent, in his Justice administration, on wreaking some sort of revenge on the law profession. He was also actively involved in British American Tobacco, essentially securing considerable financial rewards from products that killed very large numbers of people; this company has also recently been identified in a UN report as exploiting child labour in Africa.

I don't recall meeting any serious Labour Party students at this time, and I was altogether too anxious about the demands of study to entertain any idea of spending time on political activities: and heaven knows what my Dad would have made of my hobnobbing, even so mildly and at a distance, with the political opposition. But the irony of these Tories seeking to be in some sense part of the informal circle around John Barnes and Quentin Skinner is that Quentin himself was then, and has remained throughout his life, solidly Old Labour. This was one of the things which soon made me begin to see him through eyes unobstructed by the sizeable chip on my shoulder. I came to know Quentin at all because of our common membership of the Caius first year history set. I could not have known at the time what an exceptional group of people this would turn out to be. Quentin Skinner, after getting a starred First and an instant appointment as Fellow of Christ's College, would become Cambridge's Regius Professor of History (later turning down the offer of a knighthood in line with his political principles), and famed internationally as a leading historian of political ideas. Norman Stone, a gifted linguist who for most of the time affected a world-weary cynicism unbecoming in one so young, would one day become Professor of Modern History at Oxford, and a notoriously right wing commentator, acting as policy adviser and speech writer to Conservative Prime Minister Margaret Thatcher. John Sclater, a self-assured, snobbish, disdainful and coldly clever upper class man, loved to stride round the college in a resplendent beagling outfit; one day, he would end up at the highest levels of corporate finance, as President of the financial giant Equitable Life. At the time, all I could think was: my god, they really are ridiculously brilliant here at Cambridge, how on earth will I keep up? I resolved that I would spend as many hours as it took, like my dear old Dad among his turnips and my dear old Mum in her hot hotel kitchens. Frequently I burned the midnight oil, putting all I had into the weekly essay. Neil McKendrick's languid responses didn't tell me much, so I was never sure whether I really was keeping up.

I must not give the impression that history had become a chore for me: far from it. I loved all this side of my new life: cycling madly each morning to Mill Lane, where the history lectures were given, and enjoying with the mass of new history undergraduates the remarkable mix of people who lectured to us. We had economic history from a slightly unbelievable man called John Saltmarsh, who specialised in a sort of economic-historic anthropology, making much of the habits and behaviour of early communities such as the Windmill Hill people. Saltmarsh was quite theatrical and had an oddly high fluting voice: '... and so we leave Windmill Hill man on top of his hill, his sword in one hand, milking his kine with the other'. We trembled at the bizarre possibilities, mostly with laughter. Saltmarsh was always extremely unkempt, but a late-coming student once reported to us that he had seen Saltmarsh pause before the entrance to the Lecture Theatre, carefully disarrange his clothing, and scramble his hair. Saltmarsh was never seen without an old army knapsack, and often over our post-lecture coffees we speculated on what it might contain. The Cambridge police may know. One night, having forgotten the precise address of friends who had invited him to dinner, he was apparently apprehended after reports of a strange man peering into back windows. He drew himself up and said to the unfortunate constable sent to investigate. "My good man, do you know who I am? I am the Vice Provost of King's". "I don't care if you are Napoleon Bonaparte," came the reply "you are coming down to the station with me."

A quite different performance came from a distinguished specialist in religious history called Walter Ullmann. Ullmann was a central European by origin and knew everything there was to know about the mediaeval papacy. Mum was delighted to hear, in one of my weekly letters, that the Pope was still on the menu. Ullmann's lectures were fascinating and very closely argued. The problem here was that he would become increasingly excited by the ideas he was expounding to the point where his already thick accent degenerated into a clearly impassioned but virtually untranslatable torrent of words. We would retreat to our coffee and buns dazed and exhilarated, but not always much the wiser. Still in the Middle Ages, we thrilled to the bloodthirsty accounts of the Crusades, issued with evident relish by R C Smail. We laughed along in the funny, joking lectures given by a visiting American professor, Clinton Rossiter, though I cannot now remember what sort of history he was meant to be imparting.

So I got much enjoyment and satisfaction from all this, despite my high levels of social and intellectual insecurity. More pleasure still came from membership of another significant group in college and university life: the sporting fraternity. I was soon involved in the college football team, discovering that they were anything but thick hearties: Clive James, in his later amusing account of Cambridge life, *May Week Was In June*, gets this stereotype badly wrong. In my final year, when Captain of Football, I could boast an eleven with six players who had scored Firsts by that stage.

In the summer of that first year I naturally gravitated to the cricket field. Again, I played regularly for the College first eleven, though with rather modest results, despite being able to bat on wickets so hard and true they would have graced a Test Match. I have to say in my own defence that I also was obliged to bat against real Test match bowlers, as in the early season, friendly elevens like I Zingari or The Authentics would come down from London to get a little easy practice. These teams were a mixture of City toffs who had played for their public schools and Oxbridge colleges, and doughty professionals who presumably at least had all expenses paid, and very likely found their boots stuffed with cash in the changing rooms. To sum up the experience, I was dismissed in three successive matches by England Test match regulars. In the first I was caught at short leg from a fast, lifting ball from Barry Knight, then a current England opening bowler. In the next, I went in first wicket down to face the famous Frank Tyson, who had just recently put the Australians to the sword. I was so late on the first ball that I inadvertently late cut it for four, definitely an act of *lèse majesté*. Tyson scowled. I saw the next ball only as a red blur before it shattered my stumps. Next up was Jim Laker, renowned for having only three years earlier taken 19 wickets in one match against Australia at Old Trafford. His wicket keeper was Keith Andrew, one of the finest ever to play international cricket. Again the first ball: with most un-Yorkshirely elan, I advanced down the pitch and smote Laker for four through midwicket. The second ball looked exactly the same, but as I confidently advanced again, it drifted away from me down the leg-side and I was left stranded and looking rather foolish. So I had not exactly covered myself with glory, but how many cricketers can claim to have hit Frank Tyson to the boundary? While the sweetest memory of my cricketing life is the score book that reads: M. Minogue, stumped Andrew, bowled Laker: 4.

*Captain of Caius College AFC 1961-1962, centre front of picture.*

Sport at Cambridge brought, as ever, a degree of recognition and acceptance that I welcomed, and that gave me more self-confidence, and brought new friendships, some of which lasted well beyond university days. I played several games of football for the Falcons, the university second team, though never made it to the level of the first team and the much sought-after Blues, awarded for playing in the Oxford/ Cambridge matches. I even had a couple of games for the Crusaders, the university cricket second eleven. But I didn't really enjoy Cambridge cricket: it was still dominated by men from public schools, inclined to treat people like me with an air of ineffable superiority. They knew how to patronise, and did condescension particularly well, as did my own college captain. Oddly, the rugby fraternity seemed altogether more democratic in spirit, and a couple of my friends came from that group. The different sporting fraternities often cheered each other on in the hotly contested inter college competitions known as Cuppers. One of my abiding memories is of Fred Inglis, a rugger Blue, scarcely known then but later a very good friend and a distinguished intellectual and biographer, catching the ball in his own half then racing the whole length of the pitch to score a try, owed not so much to his blinding pace and strong build as to an expression of such ferocity that the defenders deemed it wiser not to interrupt his progress.

The final summer term of this first year was a heady mix of pain and pleasure. The pleasure came from all that Cambridge has to offer on hot summer afternoons and nights: the dreamy click of bat on ball, the hilarious first ventures on to the Cam on punts along the sensational Backs, drunken sorties to a succession of pubs in King Street, known as 'the King Street run'; daringly going out without gowns and risking the disciplinary attentions of the University Proctor and his 'bulldogs', who patrolled the night streets to keep the 'young gentlemen' from bringing too much scandal to the Town. The pain came from the looming first examinations. I spent most nights in the College Library, going through my lecture notes and essays. Here I forged a first real friendship with Quentin, also a regular worker in this vineyard. We exchanged notes and ideas, playing the game of trying to guess from previous papers what likely questions would be. I was particularly anxious, given the still woeful condition of my Latin, about the 'Gobbets' section of one of the papers: this involved being able to identify and comment on Latin extracts from original mediaeval sources. Quentin was tremendously generous in helping me to understand what kinds of commentary were required. He also taught me, through example, to learn by heart apt quotations to impress the examiners (in the real papers I triumphantly offered one in Latin: take that, Pratt!). After a few hours of this, on Saturday nights, we would get a little light relief by melting into the raucous but good humoured undergraduate street life around the colleges. The actual examinations remain a blur, the overriding sense one of profound relief when they were over, and I could return to the bosom of my family.

# Chapter Fourteen

## Working Life

*As soon as a man opens his mouth everyone can tell to which class he belongs*
Ferdinand Zweig *The British Worker 1952*

I used to return to Yorkshire with alacrity at the end of each term of eight weeks, tremendously pleased to see my parents and sisters again. Sally, now 13 years old, and at Knaresborough Grammar School, was still a bit of a family pet, though apt to dance unwelcome attendance on me when I tried to take some local lass to the cinema. Maureen was now a very pretty 19-year-old, and our warring days were well behind us. We loved to dance together in our middle room, and around this time bought our very own first gramophone records, an odd mixture. Maureen chose True Love, the theme song sung by Bing Crosby and Grace Kelly in the hit film of 1956, High Society, wonderfully enriched by an improbably gravelly voiced Louis Armstrong. My choice was Mozart's *Eine Kleine Nachtmusik,* my first classical record purchase. We settled together on the hit of the year, Bill Haley and the Comets, with their single that had taken the country's teenagers by storm, *Rock Around the Clock*. We'd jive wildly, to the bemusement of our very traditional parents: Maureen and I are still capable of a pretty nifty jive in our old age, though I no longer throw her over my hips or send her sliding between my legs. The dances in Roecliffe were held in the school, which hosted all village events. These covered a wide range of activities, from Women's Institute bring and buy sales, to beetle drives and whist drives, card games being very popular before the spreading tentacles of television took such universal root. In my early teens I had loved these evenings, where the whole village turned out and you really got to know your neighbours much better. There were prizes too. I once got the most points in the whist drive, and went triumphantly home to Mum with my prize of two dozen eggs. She turned pale, fresh as she was from two hours of egg washing.

Old Time dances were a particular pleasure. Mum had already taught us all the dance steps but it was exciting to practice them on a real dance floor: barn dances, military two steps, the valeta, polkas, even the more modern foxtrots and quick steps. Not that the old school wooden floor provided much of a surface, and in addition you had to circumvent, halfway round the floor, the substantial obstacle of the large roaring stove which soon had everyone sweating buckets as they whirled around. Some of the traditional dances were 'progressive' which meant that the men moved steadily to their left to take new partners as the women moved steadily the other way. I was clutched to many an ample farm wife's bosom and blushed my way round the room. Old Frank Winn, the neighbouring farmer (and one time umpire) whose rather unresponsive son John I had tried unsuccessfully to coach through the eleven plus, would give a word of encouragement from his unmoving position next to the tea urn: "Well stepped, young Martin, Ah say, well stepped". One hazard at these local dances was the music. In the mid to late fifties this was provided by Norman Leathley, a shy bespectacled man who had been a professional pianist, but suffered from nervous stress to such a degree that he gave up his middle class life to be a farm worker, altogether more therapeutic. He could turn his hand to any tune or dance rhythm, and this gave him a respected role in his new community. But on one unforgettable and distressing occasion, as we danced around the schoolroom, the piano suddenly speeded up and became discordant and ever wilder. Soon, Norman was playing impossibly faster and faster, and ended in a crashing of chords as he slumped forward in a dead faint. It was nightmarish, both for him and for us. Though he returned to his farm job after several weeks in hospital, and was received in a kind and neighbourly way, he never ever played for us again.

Dancing was a constant entertainment for working class people at this time. There was a regular Saturday night one at Aldborough. Music was provided by records played on an amplified gramophone, a mixture of foxtrots and quicksteps, or the 'modern' waltz. Most were popular melodies sung by crooners in the post Bing Crosby mode. A collection of girls in pretty frocks would gather along one side of the village hall, facing a gaggle of nervous young men on the other, a mixture of red faced farm lads and junior clerks. It was a nerve racking business, since the man was expected to walk deliberately across the floor to ask a prospective partner to dance, risking the ignominy of a refusal. The prettier and more popular the girl, the more likely was she to refuse anyone who did not appeal; though often enough the convention prevailed that polite requests should be politely accepted. The crucial point of the night was to get a girl to allow you to walk her home, and again the convention was that this girl would be the one who would accept to have the last dance with you. There would be an unseemly rush across the floor at this point, focussed on the prettiest (or perhaps the reputedly most complaisant). Many, of both sexes, would be left on the sidelines, unfortunate 'wallflowers'. What I remember mainly is that you tried to catch a partner who didn't live on some farm miles away from your own home destination, for that would mean a long walk and a late homecoming, and for me, another climb in through the window.

Mum and Dad much preferred traditional ballroom dancing, and we'd all go together (minus Sally of course) to the 'big' dances held at the Crown Hotel in Boroughbridge, the hotel where Mum worked. Mum and Dad would quickly take the floor, and I always felt proud of them as they glided gracefully around the Crown's large ballroom, beautifully precise and in perfect rhythm. The music here was usually provided by a trio including two brothers, Ray and Willie Horner, who played with me in the Town football team. Ray was an excellent saxophonist, Willie a passable crooner. He would belt out 'embrace me, you sweet embraceable you', and give me an enormous knowing wink as I danced past with his sister Shirley in my arms. My friendship with Shirley didn't survive my National Service and University absences, but we all remained good friends, and Willie and his wife Lilian would often invite me to their home, and walk back to Roecliffe with me for company. Willie worked for the Gas Board, and was a voluntary part time fireman: the way this worked was that if a fire had to be dealt with, the old wartime air raid sirens would sound, and Willie and his pals would dash up to the fire station on their bicycles. It's fair to say that most fires had done their worst by the time the Boroughbridge fire engine arrived. This was sometimes welcomed, as one or two local farmers (including a middle class gent who was a leading local Conservative) had discovered the Trinidadian strategy labelled in V. S. Naipaul's *The House of Mr Biswas* as 'insurandburn'.

I was now, in the year 1960, and at the age of 22, much in need of paid employment to make up for the inevitable hole in my college finances. I still did work alongside Dad occasionally, his new boss Ken Clayton being another fellow footballer. I was now allowed to drive a tractor on the roads, and was happy to get behind a wheel and imagine myself to be Stirling Moss. And I always enjoyed the harvesting season, with its air of communal camaraderie and satisfying sense of age-old purpose. But work on the farm was irregular, and poorly paid. I did rather better when postman Bob Harland arranged for me to cover for him for his two weeks of summer holiday at the Boroughbridge Post Office. The downside was that I had to rise at 4:30 am to cycle to Boroughbridge in time to sort out the mail, delivered from 5.30 am onwards. Summer sunrises gladdened my heart as I raced down the country lanes. My postal round was quite far flung, taking in farms often a mile off the beaten track, but at least it was centred on Roecliffe, so that I could nip in for the tea and toast that Mum would have ready for me. My round would be finished by noon, leaving me free until the afternoon delivery at 4pm. I soon learned the tricks of the trade, one being to ensure that there was no daily delivery to two particularly distant farms, by keeping back the post for them during the week, then delivering two large bundles on Saturday mornings. The farmers and their wives must have wondered why their letters only ever seemed to come at weekends.

One day, while I was sorting the mail in the Post Office, the rather lugubrious postmaster shouted 'Martin, telegram for you!' So at 5:15am on a sunny July morning, I disbelievingly read the message from my college tutor, Neil McKendrick: 'You have been awarded a well deserved First. Hearty congratulations. Neil'. I rode back home delirious with relief and excitement. By this stage of my life, though, Mum and Dad took my achievements in their stride, pretty much expecting no less. "Is that good then?" enquired Dad, "Does that mean we might see you in 10 Downing Street one of these days?" Their pleasure and satisfaction, though, were enormous, as it would be three years later when my sister Sally, at the tender age of 16, won a place to read English at St Hilda's College Oxford, having turned down another offer from Girton, Cambridge. Not bad for an ordinary farm worker and his former domestic servant wife, a son at Cambridge, a daughter destined for Oxford. Needless to say, they were just as proud of Maureen, less intellectually inclined, but now a responsible and efficient legal secretary in Harrogate, and so pretty and personable that local likely lads were falling over themselves to catch her eye. Mind you, they were then likely to catch Mum's eye, and quail before it. After some years of being a bit lofty about my younger sisters, and not taking too much notice of them, I was beginning to enjoy unfolding relationships with them, relationships different each from each, but which would flower ultimately into deep and loving friendships. This was a sad time otherwise, for our redoubtable Irish Grandad had died. Dad records that when Grandad got married he earned 16sh a week, or approximately £38 a year: he was still doing paid work as a gardener at the age of 83, since he found it unimaginable to sit around, and I suppose this fine upstanding man simply wore out (Granny Minogue would die four years later, in 1964: Dad's account records ' people like her got little praise from the outside world, but they should have been in the Honours List').

I returned to Cambridge in the autumn of 1960 in a more confident and relaxed frame of mind. The First brought with it an Exhibition scholarship, which meant that I would be allowed to keep my rooms in College, and would not, as did most of my peers, have to scramble around finding digs in town. It also brought some degree of recognition in the college, for academic success was properly celebrated and widely known. I felt at last less anxiety about whether I truly belonged to this elevated community, and better able to accept that I didn't need to hate *all* the posh men, only those I disliked for other reasons. This was a defining moment for me, for it made me able to see and value people for what they were, rather than judge them by their social background. Significantly, my fastest developing friendships were with two men who initially I had treated suspiciously. Quentin Skinner had scored a brilliant First, and had played no small part in inspiring me by example and precept. I discovered too that despite his public school education (Bedford School) his social and political values were every bit as egalitarian and principled as mine, and though he mixed easily with all political and social types, he was as stout a supporter of the Labour Party as I was. Not least, he was an exceptionally warm and witty man, and an excellent companion. Through him, I would also later become friends with one of his closest friends, Fred Inglis, and would one day help Fred to fight the good fight when he stood as a Labour candidate for South West Derbyshire in one of the 1974 elections; here was another public school boy (Oundle) who didn't behave as I expected, though I have a notion that he didn't always behave as the public school expected either.

The other man who became one of my very best friends was Hugh Johnson, he of the champagne corks, and Sherborne public school. He too was close to Quentin, and I think our mutual friendships gelled together. He was someone with a delightfully anarchic sense of humour, and another who was enormously good company. We discovered a common interest in golf, and later would come together in fiercely fought contests ultimately characterised more by hilarity than skill. Hugh, on his mother's side, came from a solidly grounded Northern Irish family and had a quiet, but firm and confident sense of himself that was appealing to me, still hesitant about my own identity. To some degree, like my Yorkshire friend Mick Harper, he stood for the brother I subconsciously lacked. Moreover, with Quentin and Hugh, I could be more open in expressing who I was, and was strengthened immeasurably by their evident liking for who I was. Our relationships matured during the next two years, not least when we stayed up for a vacation term prior to Finals examinations. Though by this stage I had travelled a long social distance, I still had a strong sense of having differing identities: I revealed very little of my real background to my Cambridge associates, even to my new good friends. Most, I think, assumed vaguely that I came from a farm-owning family, since my address was Vicarage Farm.

Meanwhile back in Yorkshire, mixing again with my old school and football pals, I would slip relatively easily into a familiar world of sport, pub crawling, heavy drinking, a little light dancing, and occasional rough scrapes. The transitions might best be summed up by reference to my speaking voice. I had grown up, naturally, using the strong flat vowels, dropped aitches and lost final 'g' of my part of Yorkshire, while free with received slang: 'Aye', 'by gum'; 'now then': 'eyup'; 'lakin'. Progression through the grammar school had brought a rather more extensive vocabulary, together with corrections of pronunciation and grammar from Molly Sawdon's sometimes sharp tongue. The RAF had merely added in a new set of slang words which in effect were beginning to be quite old fashioned. At Cambridge, though, I was assailed by a plethora of accents, from mannered public-school drawls (I can still not hear someone say 'orrff' for 'off ' without wincing) to received BBC pronunciation. I was extremely sensitive to my own Yorkshire accent, because it was all too often evident that it made some of these well-bred chaps wince too. Quite deliberately, I determined that I too could do BBC English if I wanted to; and to avoid continuing embarrassment, I did want to, because I wanted nothing so much as to fit in to this foreign, heady, exciting, worrying new world. Writing in 2019 this may seem a very outdated concern: regional accents are now embraced and encouraged by the BBC, and the stigma accorded to them in the middle of the twentieth century is much less marked in the twenty-first century (though a recent survey found that half of the respondents felt that they were disadvantaged at work by their local accents). Upper class, public school educated politicians like David Cameron and George Osborne deliberately cultivated a kind of 'estuary' English to make believe that they were tuned in to ordinary people. The thought of Harold Macmillan or Sir Alec Douglas Home (the first Prime Ministers I worked under in government) dumbing down like this is laughable: and even by the 1980s, Mrs Thatcher felt it incumbent to take elocution lessons to put behind her any trace of her own lower middle class origins. I needed no elocution lesson, for I was quick, as ever, to learn on my own account. I adapted at this stage to my two worlds, beginning to develop some sort of version of BBC English at Cambridge, while reverting to a more natural and colloquial brand back in Yorkshire. I believe that it was only after Cambridge, moving in a Foreign Office world of decidedly cut glass upper class accents that I found that my received pronunciation, so arduously acquired, had become a natural speaking voice, my Yorkshire accent finally left behind. If all this seems unduly defensive and snobbish, I can only say that in those days and those environments adjustment of my way of speaking felt like a necessary protective colouration. After a time I simply didn't notice it, and if my Yorkshire friends and my family did, they never ever commented on this transformation; though I am now told that I give myself away by still, like the poet Tony Harrison, pronouncing 'us' as 'uz'.

Relieved of some of my social anxiety I began to enjoy myself, both at work and play. At the end of the second year I again received a congratulatory telegram, another First, and elevation to Minor Scholar. I would now move on to Part 11 of the History Tripos, and would have to choose from a range of specialisms, with advice from Neil McKendrick. The group of Scholars (Exhibitioners, Minor Scholars, and Major Scholars) got special treatment, since Neil would use his range of academic contacts to arrange supervision by leading lights in whatever fields we had chosen. This turned out to be a mixed blessing. One of my chosen topics was Ancient History, in part because of those early school forays into Romano-British times and artefacts. I was allowed to attend an advanced seminar in ancient history led by Professor A. H. M. Jones, and also involving the well-known American classicist, Moses Finley. These were people internationally famous in their fields, and talked about by us in hushed and awed tones. I think I was so drunk on the excitement of just being at the same table, that I scarcely took in many of the doubtless brilliant insights being offered. Ancient history also brought supervision by Guy Griffith, a Fellow in our own college. Dr Griffith had been famous in his early years at Caius, when he was awarded a much needed research fellowship. He was, apparently, a great gambling man. He wagered his whole research grant on a racing certainty. Pursuing his classical interests on holiday in Rome, he obtained a newspaper that told him that his horse had come in second. Faced by penury, he wrote a best-selling *Guide to the Classics* (the racing kind) that recouped his losses and saved his research career. Guy was also celebrated for his annual sideshow when, in the company of an Oxford friend, he would drive a splendid Rolls Royce down Senate House Passage, the narrow lane dividing Caius from the Senate House, to tumultuous applause from serried ranks of undergraduates. So it was something of a disappointment to find him a dry-as-dust, often incomprehensible lecturer. Quentin and I cleaved loyally to the course, but other members began to drift away. One day we arrived to find an empty lecture theatre. Unable to bear the embarrassment of meeting him as the sole remnant of his lecture audience, we looked at each other and with common consent made off to the nearest coffee house. I still feel more than a little guilty, wondering what he felt: probably relief, as lecturing was clearly purgatory for him. I still met him for individual tutorials, in which I would read out to him whatever essay I had been set. He would sit there with a kindly but rather glazed expression, and I would wonder if he was actually listening. Dramatic proof that he was attentive came when once he interrupted me, leaping to his feet: "Yes, yes, I believe Livy says something like that". He then got a small library step, climbed up to extract a volume of Livy from a top shelf and leafed through it. "I thought so, here it is..." and read and translated for me what did indeed reflect an idea I had just myself expressed. I remain astonished by the depth of learning displayed here, to be able to hear a sentence from a gauche undergraduate, and instantly go to the very page and line of a famous Roman author of which it reminded him: this was yet another instance of what a wonderful seat of learning Cambridge was (and still is). I would often re-read that essay, saying proudly to myself: 'Livy said that'.

My remaining two special tutors were a disappointment but for different reasons. I had chosen a paper in American history, in part because I had read an inspiring book by Frank Thistlethwaite (later to become the first Vice Chancellor of the new University of East Anglia). Neil had tried to recruit him to the tutorial cause but in the event, I was handed on to his wife, herself American. She was brisk and efficient but not inspiring. The final experience was rather an odd one. Pursuing the subject of imperial history in Africa, I was allocated to Ronald Robinson at Trinity College. Dr Robinson was co-author of a brilliant revisionist study of Victorian imperialism in Africa, along with John Gallagher and Alice Demmy, some of which I had already dipped into. When I presented my first essay, Robinson, a lugubrious and saturnine figure, puffed on a pipe as he listened. He made a few perfunctory comments, and simply gave me a list of sources and a subject for our next meeting. Feeling that I had not made much of an impression,

I burnt a good deal of midnight oil, making sure to integrate all the stuff he had recommended. I knocked on his door, no reply; knocked again and tentatively peeped inside: no-one there. After waiting for about 20 minutes I assumed that he wasn't coming: maybe I had mistaken the time. Returning towards Caius, I decided to have a haircut. Entering the barber shop, I saw a man seated in the barber's chair, reading a newspaper. He raised his eyes, and met mine: Ronald Robinson. I knew at once from his dismayed expression that his failure to keep our appointment was deliberate. I turned and fled, face hot with embarrassment. Robinson never contacted me, and I didn't return. Somewhat later, I learned that it was widely assumed by those in the know that Gallagher, a brilliant historian who would one day get an Oxford chair, had written the more original parts of the book, and that some of the rest had been put together by an assistant, Alice Demmy, who had insisted on being given some authorial credit. None of this surprised me, given Robinson's lofty treatment of me.

Back home for the summer vacation, I acquired a bit more tuition in the world of work. My Cambridge bills now regularly exceeded my income, and the gap had somehow to be filled. This was hammered home by my otherwise very supportive bank manager, who took me for 18 holes at Ripon Golf Club and spent much of the round resisting my feeble attempts to base a loan on as yet wholly imaginary future expectations (those were the days; I wonder how many students now get to play golf with their bank manager?) Next day, he contacted me to say he had persuaded the manager of the local brickworks to take me on as a temporary worker, six weeks of which would put me back in the black. The Roecliffe brickyard was close to home. All I knew of it was that most of the houses in the nearby villages were constructed from its pleasingly mellow red bricks: so was my own home. But I had no idea of the Yorkshire version of Dante's inferno that awaited me. The brickworks consisted of a series of low, seemingly quite dilapidated brick buildings set alongside a quarry, which supplied the raw clay out of which the bricks were shaped and produced. I saw very little of these parts of the enterprise. My job was in principle straightforward, to barrow the wet, moulded bricks to the firing kilns. This was not in any way straightforward. The kilns were brick structures set well above ground level because of local flooding risk. The 'barrow' was an odd, deep, almost triangular shape, made of wood and propelled by a quite large iron wheel. This had to be pushed up a long single wooden plank, angled quite steeply up to the kiln-shed entrance. When the barrow was full of bricks, it was pretty heavy and you had to take a run at the plank to get the load up to the top. After I had practised with a half load, the workmen gathered to watch me make my first real run. Halfway up, going quite fast, I ran the rim of the wheel off the plank and the whole barrow and its bricks plunged to the ground. The men, laughing and teasing, helped me to fill the barrow again, and off I went. I reached the top, and a rousing cheer rang out.

But a trickier problem awaited me. Laying the wet moulded bricks in the kilns was relatively easy, but taking red hot fired bricks out again was a nightmare, for this was a job you did by hand, and using gloves slowed you down tremendously; since the men were paid on piece rates (i.e. pay determined by how many bricks they could fire in a day's work), I was under constant pressure to keep up with them. I might be the son of a horny handed son of the soil, but my hands were the soft vulnerable hands of a would-be man of letters. By the end of the first real day's work they were raw and blistered; by the end of the second day they were bleeding, and handling the hot bricks was agonising. My work mates were sympathetic, but also anxious, since I was likely to lose money for them. I knew that I could not really cope, and so did the foreman. At the end of the week, he told me that he had found another job for me, working for a local window cleaner who cleaned their office windows and needed an assistant. More kindness, from a working class so often disdained, even reviled, by their so-called 'betters'.

The window cleaner, George Wright, was well known locally as a lay preacher and activist for the Jehovah's Witnesses. A small, wiry man with bright eyes and a brisk, no-nonsense manner, George was a strict but fair employer, who made sure windows were properly cleaned, but to a set time already calculated according to the size of the house and its number of windows. His watchword was 'time's money', and neither should be misspent. So far as I was concerned, washing windows was a doddle compared with the brickworks, and I was not about to complain. George came to trust me, and even taught me to drive in his large Ford van, in bulk not unlike the Fordson Major tractors I was already accustomed to driving, unlicensed, on public roads. George advised me to take the driving test in Northallerton, where the landscape was so flat that the examiners didn't bother with the tricky hill start. I was nervous taking the test, but when a car shot out in front of me and my quick reactions avoided what had looked likely to be a head on collision, the examiner was so relieved that he gave me a pass immediately, even illustrating for me in a pencil drawing the answer to a question on the Highway Code I was unable to get right. So I owed George, but had not counted on his evangelising zeal when yoked to a captive audience. From the top of his ladder, each day, he would drown me in Biblical quotations, determined to override my feebly proffered and rationally-based convictions about the origins and age of the universe. George had the true passion of one who knows himself to be one of the Elect, destined for future salvation, certain that the End Times would soon come, and sweep away his lowly window cleaning status. After a while I ceased to resist, preferring to lose the argument than my job. Once or twice I went back to his house for tea: his wife and son seemed as passive and beaten down as I had become.

George didn't hold with book learning, and waxed vigorously about the superiority of the University of Life. My Yorkshire setting was certainly a world apart from my University, and I was familiar enough with the relative poverty and meanness of many working class lives, but both on the farms and in the brickyard I came to know these workers as individuals, sometimes kindly, sometimes not, but always labouring hard to keep their heads honestly above water and their children in decent shoes. Oddly enough, I learned a darker side of local culture through my old grammar school drinking companions, mingled with footballing friends from Knaresborough Modern School. This usually turned on heavy drinking habits, and forays to town dances in Harrogate. I would invariably be drawn to the dance floor, hoping to captivate some blushing Yorkshire rose. But most of my male friends would remain at the bar until midnight brought the dancing to an end. On some occasions, the heavy drinking and local rivalries (Harrogate versus Knaresborough, town versus country) would end in fights outside. Amazingly, these were often punctiliously fist fights, no boots involved, and also from time to time the groups would be represented by specific 'champions', the result being respected by all present, as they enclosed the protagonists in a noisy human ring. Needless to say, if my Knaresborough group was involved in such a stand-off, my friend Mick Harper would step forward, and he rarely had to hit his opponent more than once: most unbefitting a respectable bank clerk, but he had been hardened in those vicious scraps with the Aussies in Malaya. Normally I would keep clear of all this macho action, hating such violence; but once I almost got myself into a fight outside the Crown Hotel in Boroughbridge. A large red-faced farmer's lad stalked the ring that had formed for an anticipated fight, asking aggressively if anyone wanted 'to hold my coat'. Naive, and eager to help, I said I would, not realising that thereby I was accepting an invitation to do battle. My friends pulled me away quickly, explaining to the rather nonplussed farm lad that I was a student and wet behind the ears, so saving me from a real beating.

On another occasion, six of us decided after an evening's drinking to invade the Young Conservative Association's Ball, held in the former stately home of Rudding Park (where in the 1930s my Irish grandad's brother Patrick had been a gardener). We had no tickets, and no intention of paying. Mick parked our taxi, his Dad's little green Ford van, alongside the park wall, and we infiltrated through the trees, across a cricket ground, and into the large marquee. Installing ourselves at the bar, we were soon spotted by virtue of the simple fact that we were the only men in the place not in dinner jacket and black tie. For some reason long forgotten, I decided to distract the hostile crowd by climbing up the central marquee pole and guide rope, right to the top, to cheers from my pals below. As I slid back triumphantly towards the ground, Mick was busy telling the Young Tory gentlemen that they should treat me with caution, as I was a Boxing Blue at Cambridge. This gave them due pause, and we all agreed to leave without causing any further trouble. Crossing the cricket ground again, we took possession of a large wheelbarrow, and took this trophy home with us, leaving it in the garden of Vic Boyce, another son of respectable Catholic parents. When we met again the next day to celebrate all this in the Mother Shipton pub, Vic was almost sick with anxiety, expecting imminent arrest, or even worse the full force of his father's anger. That night we smuggled the barrow out of Mr Boyce's garden shed and back across the Rudding Park wall; honour was satisfied, though perhaps not the brand of honour symbolised by the Gate of Honour at Caius College, through which Caius men traditionally trooped to be awarded their degrees.

That time was almost on us, just as I had finally discovered that there were more pleasures to be had than unremitting work. This included meeting a pretty, dark eyed, spirited German girl, Marlis Behr, taking a course at Bell's Language School, and I now spent with her much of the time I would have formerly spent closeted in either the College or University Libraries. The final year hurtled towards the dreaded Finals, and included a visit by my parents. My pal Mick generously drove them down from Yorkshire for a long weekend and I found lodgings for them all. I was playing cricket for the college that weekend, and of course they came along. To my consternation, in the field, I realised that they had got together with the Surrey stockbroker parents of one of my fellow players. I still cannot imagine the conversations that might have ensued: I thought it quite likely that Dad might harangue his opposite number on the iniquities of the income tax system, and what Labour would do 'to your lot' when they finally got in again (this was 1962, and during the thirteen years of Tory rule). When I sat down with them later in the afternoon, Mum was holding court about the virtues of the Women's Institute (of which she was now a local Secretary) and seemed to be getting on well with the Surrey wife. But still at the mercy of my inner demons, I was acutely conscious of her Geordie accent, and my Dad's dropped aitches. Mercifully on our own again, we had a thoroughly enjoyable time. Naturally I punted them up to Grantchester, my mother happy to find that there was honey still for tea. Dad, who hated water after a near drowning incident on the river Nidd at Knaresborough in their courting days, resolutely refused to get into the punt, and insisted on walking all the way to Grantchester and back. Mick characteristically found a pub that sold his favourite beer, and we dined there: he cast one or two scornful looks at the gilded youths around us, but thankfully wasn't in the mood to pick any fights. On yet another occasion my sister Maureen came for a weekend. She was an instant hit with my friends.

Another episode in my 'working life' experiences took place when I stayed in Cambridge for the final year Easter vacation to keep in touch with Marlis, who had now decamped to London. I got a job reading gas meters for the local Gas Board. This was in itself easy work, though considerably speeded up by the regular gas company workers. We had a block of streets to cover each day and would be free as soon as this set of meters was read (no clocking on and off). We practically sprinted from house to house. Naturally I was much less adept than my fellow workers. Reading a meter might seem easy enough but location and position made for delays. Outside meters were simple, but indoor ones might have all kinds of problems: a householder unable to find the keys to a locked cupboard, or you might have to move a selection of old boxes and bicycles before you could get to the meter at all. The worst problem for me was a type of meter so badly positioned that it could only be read by using a mirror and torch, i.e. reading the numbers in reverse. It took me some time to get the hang of this, and it is quite likely that some very unexpected bills were received during my brief involvement. But as ever my fellow workers were cheerfully uncritical, and after I had emerged rather dazed from the murky depths of some broom cupboard, it would be to find that one of them had meanwhile read the rest of the street's meters for me, another instance of the friendly solidarity I so often found in my work experiences.

During another vacation, I managed to get a job in central London, while arranging to lodge out near Crouch End with my cousin Peter Minogue, son of Uncle John ( once, in my teenage days in Yorkshire I had stayed with them and had refused all offers to take me 'hawking', anxious about coping with fierce birds: in effect, they were conducting 'rag and bone' ventures.) The London job was to be a temporary clerk at a credit agency in Bishopsgate, on a sleazy bit of the Thames. This was a truly Dickensian experience, lived out in what certainly must have been a working office in Victorian times. There were six clerks, including myself, and an office manager. We clerks sat at long tall wooden desks, the only light to work by coming from flat windows set high in the ceiling. Our task was to record painstakingly, in large ledgers (in pen and ink), the names and details of people convicted of debt and fraud offences. These details came mainly from County Court records from around the country. Some individuals would have several entries to their name. The office manager, who always came back drunk from an extended lunch, would receive credit queries in writing or by phone, (no computers then) and farm them out to us as we laboured to catch up on recording the voluminous county court judgements. The whole atmosphere was of fustian gloom and deep depression. Two of the clerks were elderly and infirm Hungarian emigres. One of them, Ferenc I think, already suffered from failing eyesight but dared not let on to the office manager for fear of losing his job. As the sun moved above us, the illumination he needed would move away from him, and from time to time we would carefully lift him and his chair to another sunlit patch. Here was yet another lesson for me in how the world of work could grip people in a vicious, unrewarding circle of low pay, abject conditions, and low expectations. Such experiences always made me conscious of the humanity of which people were capable even in such unpromising

*Three Cambridge friends celebrate their graduation: from left, Quentin, me and Hugh.*

circumstances, but reinforced my determination to escape the limitations and low hopes associated with such worlds. Now, with my privileged sojourn at Cambridge coming to a close, I would have to decide where my own particular escape route should lead.

# Chapter Fifteen

# Life in the Whitehall Village

*They always ended up by choosing Oxbridge men: you see, they speak the same language* Member of Civil Service Selection Board

Sadly for me, the academic outcome of my final year was a disappointment, producing an Upper Second Class degree rather than the hoped-for First. No telegram this time, though I did get a generous and consolatory letter from Neil McKendrick. I was not entirely surprised: I had finally learned to get the most out of my University life and had established friendships that would endure for a lifetime. Work, for once, had rather taken a back seat, not least to affairs of the heart, and inevitably I paid a price. But too much else was now going on for me to be too downhearted. In this final year we all had to turn our minds to an acceptance that life at Cambridge would come to a close, and we must gird ourselves to meet the outside world again, not least because grants (or in many cases deep parental pockets) would come to an end, and we would have to earn a living. What kind of living? When I was ten, I had wanted to be a train driver; at seventeen I thought I might like to be a Manchester Guardian journalist (and sometimes regret that I did not pursue this possibility); now, after two years of National Service and three years of Cambridge University, I realised that I still had absolutely no idea what I really wanted to do with the rest of my life. Neil had me along one day to raise the possibility of becoming a history teacher, since he knew I had no strong leaning towards a research career. It seemed he had a job virtually in his gift, through his connections with (I think) Repton, which needed a young history man with an interest in football. I had not really considered school teaching before this point, and realised what a good prospect was being held out to me. But I had a well-entrenched dislike of the public school system, both emblem and embodiment of the class differences and privilege which had painfully constricted my parents' lives, and still so dominated and soured the English social system. I believed that private schools should be abolished and much regretted the 1945-51 Labour government's reluctance to take on these deeply embedded discriminatory institutions. Already somewhat influenced by Cambridge style, I was too good mannered to embarrass my tutor by acquainting him with these thoughts, but I politely declined his offer.

What this encounter made me reflect on, though, was that I owed something to the Labour-created welfare state that had given me such far-reaching opportunities, and that a very honourable course would be to involve myself in public service, perhaps teaching in state schools, or some other possibility. A trip to the University's Careers office was less than illuminating, but a languid pipe-smoking chap gave me various bits of paper, one being an application for entry to the Administrative Class of the Home Civil Service, which was combined with competition for entry to the Diplomatic Service; those succeeding would be designated as 'high flyers', earmarked as likely material for the country's future Ambassadors and Permanent Secretaries. A handful of highly prized places would be fought over initially by some 3000 hopefuls, a good many of them successful Oxbridge graduates. I had little idea of what to expect, but might have been more optimistic had I known that in the previous year's competition, all but one of the successful candidates were from Oxbridge: and that at that time not a single Permanent Secretary was from a redbrick university. The 1962 process started rather unpromisingly (in yet another section of that gloomy Leeds Town Hall through which I had first stepped reluctantly into National Service) with a written essay examination, intended as a regional weeding out of the Northern candidates. I chose to discuss General de Gaulle's vision of European integration as a *'Europe des Patries'*. I'm fairly sure I scribbled some hopelessly woolly and ill-informed ideas about all that and was pleasantly surprised when I was invited to go forward to the Civil Service Selection Board. This was a two day procedure at the Civil Service Commission in Savile Row, with a further Final Selection Board where a very short list of hopefuls would be interviewed by a committee of distinguished people.

The two days consisted of a variety of role playing games and individual interviews. We all lunched together. The atmosphere was highly competitive, softened somewhat by the inimitable Oxbridge style of well-mannered bonhomie. My considerable experience by now in sitting back and being quietly observant, before deciding how to fit myself into whatever landscape I was in, stood me in very good stead. I think I was excellent at role playing, because I had been doing it most of my rather brief adult life, used to thinking myself into the shoes of the people I was dealing with. Our principal test was to act as a member of a committee tasked with making a difficult policy choice, based on extensive background papers we had been given a relatively short time to go through. Some people made the obvious mistake of trying to seem strong and decisive, rushing to take control, which seduced them into mistakes of detail which were quietly picked off by the many keen minds round the table. The wiser tactic, pursued by the better type of candidate, was to be collaborative and inclusive, ready to support or defer to rational arguments. A further related test was to act as the chair of a (different) group. I was fortunate to have seen the chair of my own discussion group do rather an elegant job of this, directing the debate firmly while ensuring that everyone had an opportunity to speak, at the same time decisive in formulating a conclusion that most people could accept. I simply chaired my group in exactly the same way, and brought the group home on the stroke of the time allowed. We were observed and marked for all these activities. Later, we were asked to judge our competitors, rating three people we thought were the most likely to make a mark in the top echelons of government, and the three we would most like to go on holiday with. Mischievously, I included the most attractive of the very few women candidates in the latter category.

We also had one-to-one interviews, ranging over our experiences, our policy interests, our academic specialisms. I recall best the required interview with the CSSB's chief psychologist. I had worried a little about this, thinking he might easily see through the carefully protective mental shield I had constructed to get me through my conflicted social world. I was surprised to find that the interrogation was of the gentlest kind, and the questions sometimes seemed rather risible, as in 'do you love your mother', though in fact this may have been closer to the heart of some of my social unease and private anxieties than I was then willing to admit. Turning to my sporting proclivities, the psychologist asked if I thought the style in which cricketers performed revealed their true character: 'does what is bred in the bone come out in the batting?' I replied that I hoped not, since on the cricket field I was a bit of a risk-taker and often got myself dismissed by trying to hit the ball out of the ground. Only afterwards did I reflect that I had probably, in evading the question, showed a degree of secretiveness. Later I heard from my final year Senior Tutor, Dr Macpherson, that the psychologist was an old college friend and had told him that I had an exceptionally stable personality: so I must have hidden my real insecurities rather well.

I had done rather well altogether, for I was on the short list that went through to the Final Selection Board. This consisted of a cross section of the Good and the Great, a favourite Whitehall description of people who had enjoyed successful careers in various categories of public service, and were now available to chair commissions, and committees of inquiry, and to choose their likely future replacements. They sat behind a table, in a slightly raised position, so that the aspiring candidates were compelled to look up to them. I felt nervous, but heartened by having got this far. The Chairman peered at me over his spectacles, and proffered a few easy questions about Cambridge, and my reasons for seeking a career in government. Then a man who turned out to be a current Ambassador referred to my working-class background, and asked quite directly whether I thought I might find it difficult to fit in with the advanced social circles I would encounter in the Foreign Service. I responded straightforwardly: I had very little experience of formal social occasions at such a high level, but would watch very carefully how my colleagues behaved, and take my cue from them. Since he nodded with evident approval, I seemed to have given an acceptable answer. If the asking of such questions may seem now rather ludicrous, and irrelevant to the issue of whether you might make an efficient and capable official, it may be noted that until only a couple of years or so before my interview, the form of testing was through a country house weekend, where your skills with cutlery and the passing of port were under close scrutiny. The Chairman then turned to the next inquisitor, a middle-aged lady so enthralled by my performance that she had fallen asleep. He hastily wound up the proceedings, and the ordeal was over.

Looking back, I now believe that this was pretty much a rubber stamping exercise for many of the candidates, already ranked in order of merit on the basis of the tests and interviews. In the final List (published in The Times, and, to my parents' delight, in the local Knaresborough Post) I was placed 6th of the 20 successful candidates. In due course, after a further examination in French, where the examiner and I were incommunicado for long periods, I failed to get into the Foreign Office section of the List, but was posted to the nearest thing, the Commonwealth Relations Office (ironically, within a year or so these two Offices would be merged into one Diplomatic Service and I would become a Third Secretary in the Foreign and Commonwealth Office, or FCO). On a fine autumn morning in early September 1962, I walked into Downing Street, and into the CRO, happily placed directly opposite the Prime Minister's Office, and on the other side of the quadrangle from the Foreign Office. I thought of my father, who at my birth had joked that one day I might become Prime Minister: well, at least I was in the right street. He and Mum could scarcely have dreamed that one day their son would travel from a poor farm cottage in Yorkshire to the very steps of Number 10. What a long and improbable journey that had been.

Part of the adventure was the opportunity to live in and discover London, an exciting and vibrant place to be as the Sixties decade advanced, though now regarded as more than a little decadent so far as public life was concerned. To my delight, Hugh Johnson and a close university and family friend of his, James Hetherington, had asked me to share a flat with them a mere ten minutes bus ride from Whitehall. The flat was small and congested, in what was then a somewhat down at heel working class district in Pimlico, just behind Victoria. None of us had much money at this stage. Hugh was to serve an apprenticeship as a trainee solicitor at a small but highly respected city law firm, Biddle and Co. James was training to be a water engineer at Binnie and Partners, a leading water engineering company based in Westminster. I was on what seemed to me an enormous salary of some £800 per year. We soon found numerous ways to spend what we had, very often in Gordon's Bar next to Embankment tube station, and a favourite watering hole for many years afterwards. The world - and London appeared to be pretty much the world - was our oyster.

I walked into Downing Street on my first day at work with my head in the clouds. Reality soon brought me down to earth. I found myself in a vaguely defined General Department housed in the bowels of the building, which looked splendid architecturally from Whitehall and Downing Street, but was something of an office slum internally. This being late autumn, heating was by coal fires; and, being the most recent junior staff member, I was deputed to light the fires each morning. Was it for this, I would reflect on bended knees, that I had laboured to get to Cambridge and into government: when would I Make Policy? At least my rural background was finally paying off: I was almost certainly better equipped for setting fires than any other member of the staff. One of my seniors was O. G. Browne (obscurely known as Phiz), an amiable upper crust-ish chap who always wore a fresh rose in his lapel, turned up at least an hour late every day after commuting from Cirencester, summarily distributed amongst us any work that happened to cross his desk, then spent the rest of the morning on the phone to his stockbroker. The man who bore the brunt of the daily load of responsibility was a lovely middle-aged Welshman called Pryce-Jones; though I got to know him quite well, I never did find out his first name. My roaring fires created a warm soupy fug in the office. One early afternoon I heard a soft thud from behind me and turned round to see Pryce-Jones slumped head first on his desk. Alarmed, I rose to help him, but was shushed by a young clerk, who told me that this happened regularly after lunch: Pryce-Jones' fatigued head would hit the desk, and after ten minutes or so he would come to with a start, look around furtively at our carefully averted gazes, and resume work.

Everyone simply took all this stuff as normal. No one in the Office seemed remotely interested in the latest group of highly qualified, expensively educated graduate entrants. At least this gave us time to get to know each other, and we took to walking over to the south side of Westminster Bridge to have long gossipy lunches in a greasy spoon cafe near the Middlesex Hospital. Friendships were forged that would last a whole career. I got on very easily with Michael James, a fine cricketer already famous for having taken a century before lunch off the touring Australians at Fenners (in 1956 while still only twenty-ish). After Cambridge he had taught at Harrow for a couple of years, and was a likeable, gently humorous, and self-deprecating person. I soon met his wife Sally, a lively and attractive would-be actress (who had trained initially with the young Judi Dench) and their two small sons, Tim and Andrew. They made me extremely welcome at their home in Guildford and I was considerably saddened when their ambition to go overseas as soon as possible was rewarded with a posting to Wellington, New Zealand, one of the first of several postings, including Sri Lanka, Guyana, and Barbados, where Michael's cricketing prowess and contacts came in useful. Friends of his from earlier days included Robin Butler, a Treasury man regarded as destined for great things. Another suave Oxbridge chap joined us in our outings but one day he simply disappeared. Michael knew only that he had been detached to the Intelligence service and apparently rarely saw him again. We also got to know the younger Admin Class entry from previous years: Robin Gorham, always ready to give sound advice about office politics; Richard Thomas, ever ready to poke fun at all that; Bryan Austin, with whom I would share a Whitehall flat for a period; and the man tipped to fly higher than most, Brian Gilmore, who was Private Secretary to the Commonwealth Secretary, and married to Rosalind Gilmore, Private Secretary to a Treasury Minister. They seemed heady company, already launched on promising careers (both Gilmores went on to stellar Whitehall positions, and Rosalind to very senior financial sector appointments).

But I was about to make my own step upwards and onwards. After what seemed like an interminable diet of fire lighting, long lazy lunches and desultory consultation of files one was not yet allowed to make any comment on, I was summoned by the Personnel Director to be told that they wanted me to occupy the position of Resident Clerk, an odd sounding title for what was in effect an out of hours Duty Officer (I had already helped out with this a couple of times). Since much of the work would involve highly secret communications, I would be subjected to Positive Vetting. This system, meant to establish whether officials were trustworthy, had been introduced in the wake of the Great Spy Scandal of the late 1950s: the defections of Guy Burgess, Donald Maclean, and ultimately (in 1963) Kim Philby to the Soviet Union, and revelations of their treasonous betrayals of intelligence. Most extraordinary was the realisation that these men were typical high level Foreign Office officials, upper class, public school and Oxbridge educated, right at the heart of the system, and privy to its secrets. Rumours were rife of other suspects, centred on a Cambridge group that included no less than the Queen's Collector of Pictures, Sir Anthony Blunt. Further flames were added to the fire in 1963 when John Profumo, a Defence Minister, was obliged to resign over a heady mix of activities involving scandalous country house parties, fast young women, and a Russian defence attaché.

Positive Vetting, smacking somewhat of locking the stable door after the horses had bolted, was intended to root out any such proclivities at source. I must say that I found it a rather laughable set of procedures. First, I was invited to sign a document declaring that I was neither a Communist nor a Fascist, and had no prior connections or sympathies of this kind, though it seemed clear that no would-be spy possessing such connections or sympathies would ever have declared them. I also was required to name two people who had known me for at least ten years, and who would vouch for my good character and absence of any suspect connections, or other alarming tendencies. I nominated my old school headmistress Molly Sawdon, and my friend Mick Harper's father, a reputable local builder in Knaresborough. Both subsequently gave me amusing accounts of the interviews by what Molly described scornfully as "a nondescript little man in a grey raincoat", presumably a parody of a disguise, designed to lure unsuspecting referees into unwitting revelations. Both of my referees confounded this attempt by speaking not so much about me as about my family, about how widely respected and trusted they were, and how their children had absorbed from them the best of values. In Mr Harper's case he went further back, to my Irish grandparents, and how they too had long been regarded as pillars of respectability in their local community. It seems that the nondescript little man coyly referred to the anxieties felt in high places about unseemly sexual orientation (as well they might after the Burgess scenario and other scandals linked to homosexuality, which despite the Wolfenden Committee's 1957 reforming recommendations, was still illegal). Mr Harper roared with laughter, and assured him that any such anxieties were as nothing compared to the anxieties of the parents of local girls when his son Mick and I were out on the town. The intelligence authorities were still not fully reassured. They called me in to interrogate me (and that's what it felt like) about my links with my German friend Marlis. I had declared this foreign connection as required to do, and they seemed quite disconcerted by the fact that she was now at university in Berlin, where the infamous Berlin Wall divided the city. I was able to tell them that she came from an impeccably correct, and politically conservative, middle class German family. Moreover, her father, Herr Doktor Behr, because he was part Jewish, had been obliged to continue his business under the close supervision of Nazi officials, and could in no sense be described as having a suspect political past or present. What I did not tell them, was that Marlis was involved in some sort of student activist group that helped East Germans to follow a secret 'freedom route' through the Berlin Wall into West Berlin. Since I never heard any more about it, I assume that they didn't find this out. In any event, I was informed that I had passed the Positive Vetting process and could embark on my initial 'bedding in' process as Resident Clerk.

While the duties of Resident Clerk meant that alongside the normal office day job you worked for several nights and every other weekend, the compensations were considerable. The Resident Clerk's flat was a tremendous perk: large and spacious, and part of the Foreign Office building, it had one of the best views in London, looking out over St James's Park and down to the rather staid grandeur of Buckingham Palace. At the side, a deep window opened out on to a semi-circular terrace overlooking Horse Guards Parade: on the Queen's birthday, you had a front row seat for the official Trooping the Colour (always an excuse for a party). The floor below contained the original India Office, at that time become the India Office Library, with an extraordinary and sprawling collection of documents and artefacts from the days of the East India Company and the British Raj. It was a historian's treasure trove (later to be sadly broken up and scattered) and I spent many happy hours looking through old colonial reports, diaries, and collections of drawings and paintings, mostly by former colonial officials and military staff. It was all a reminder of days of former glory, appropriately set in the aspic of the museum. Meanwhile, in our flat above, correspondence from real, live overseas posts came in continuously from all corners of the globe, or at least from those bits of the globe that were still, or had recently been, constituent parts of the British imperial system. The primary communications took the form of telegrams, received in a telegraphic section housed in the bowels of the CRO building, and printed out on differently coloured paper (pink, white, blue etc.) according to their degree of importance and levels of security: Urgent, Immediate, Confidential, Secret, occasionally a worrying Top Secret. They were despatched to the Resident Clerk's flat by a Heath Robinson arrangement of tubes and pipes, a noisy thud announcing their arrival.

I would soon find that Britain's imperial past had a way of administering a shock or two to those who might think it now had little effect on the present, and that very quickly included me. The drill was that if any crisis broke out after office hours the Resident Clerk was the first to hear of it in the form of emergency telegrams. You were expected to use your judgement on such occasions: could whatever it was wait until the next morning to be dealt with, or should someone more senior take that decision? You might find yourself talking to a very senior, Under Secretary level official who would take responsibility for any further action. But on occasion the Secretary of State for Commonwealth Relations himself might be involved; at my level and experience, this was a bit like talking to God. It so happened that I had a veritable baptism of fire, not one but two major crises in the international arena occurring simultaneously. The first of these happened on my watch (I was at this point preparing to share duties with Bryan Austin, the man I would replace as Resident Clerk once I had learned the ropes). I tumbled out of bed at the crack of dawn on 20th October 1962, summoned to examine an urgent telegram from our High Commissioner in New Delhi: China had just invaded India, and was now occupying long-disputed bits of Indian territory in the North East Frontier Area, and close to even more controversial bits of Tibet. The invasion of Delhi loomed as a possibility and Prime Minister Nehru was hysterically demanding urgent military assistance from Britain. He was holding a meeting in three hours with John Kenneth Galbraith, the distinguished economist and American envoy in India, with a similar request to the Americans. The High Commissioner wished us kindly to advise him as to the British position (even in an emergency the languid manner was sought after). The relevant Under Secretary was Cyril Pickard, a South Asian specialist who I would come to know as a level headed and unflappable man who reacted without fuss but decisively. Now, he took it on himself to wake the notoriously tetchy Commonwealth Secretary, Duncan Sandys, while I was instructed to get my opposite number in the Foreign Office, Kenneth Scott, to raise and brief Prime Minister Harold Macmillan's senior Private Secretary, Philip de Zulueta. So rarefied was the atmosphere I felt as though I needed oxygen; after all, I had only been in the Office for some six weeks. Happily (and wisely) the whole thing was taken out of my hands, though I was well informed about what was going on as streams of telegrams went back and forth between London and Delhi, with four days of fighting between Indian and Chinese troops spawning a great deal of intense diplomatic activity. This was an instant crash course in how the Office conducted itself in a policy crisis. Eventually the so called Sino-Indian war petered out (in late November) when the Chinese, having made effective cross-border interventions, and doubtless the point that they could have occupied Delhi if they had chosen to, withdrew and negotiated a ceasefire.

One of the reasons that neither the Americans nor the British were anxious to get too involved in this dispute, was that they were already deeply immersed in the Cuban missile crisis, which had flared just under a week earlier on 14th October 1962. The story is too well known now to rehearse here in detail. My friend Michael James (also with a whole six weeks' experience) was actually on temporary replacement duty when the crisis broke, but again I had a ringside seat as urgent messages and instructions flowed around the British foreign policy system. Essentially the whole crisis was played out between the Russians and the Americans, who demanded the removal of nuclear missiles and missile sites discovered in Cuba, while Russian leader Kruschev defiantly sailed Soviet ships towards an American blockade (carefully termed a 'quarantine' as a blockade was regarded in international law as an act of war). The most dangerous part of the stand-off between these two nuclear superpowers rolled out over the few days from Monday 22nd October, when Kennedy made a televised speech to the American nation setting out the stark possibilities, and indicating that he had ordered the Soviets to remove the missiles from Cuba or face an implied threat of an American invasion to do this themselves: his rhetoric included warnings of the possibility of direct nuclear conflict. Kennedy telephoned the British Prime Minister that evening to ensure the British were kept informed and on-side; the transcript of this conversation seems to indicate that Macmillan was treated virtually as a bystander, an accurate enough reflection of our post-Suez standing with the Americans. On 24$^{th}$ October,

Krushchev halted the Soviet ships in mid Atlantic, but was still refusing to remove the missiles. On Friday 26th October this crisis was still unresolved: since neither Russian nor American intentions were easy to second guess, and belligerent attitudes continued to be struck, nuclear war still seemed a real possibility. At 8pm that evening I came off duty and returned to Pimlico where my flatmates Hugh and James were hosting a party, and I still recall the hollow, sick feelings I had, trying to make small talk in a bright but brittle atmosphere, knowing that in the worst-case scenario we might not see the dawn of another day. As we now know, over that weekend Krushchev agreed to remove the missiles, a deal was negotiated, and the crisis was effectively over: nuclear war had been narrowly averted, even if Kennedy's famous success would later be put down to 'plain dumb luck' by one of his most senior advisers. By this time, I felt exhausted, having had to cope with the fall-out from the Sino-Indian crisis on the very day that ended with Kennedy's defiant speech to the American nation on Cuba, not to mention a party hangover. I was still only a couple of months into my new job and had jumped from lighting the office fire to being in a small way a part of two major international conflagrations. I was exhilarated to be so much at the centre of things already: I began to understand what being classed as a 'high flyer' meant, and how exciting foreign policy could be.

Early in 1963, I was confirmed as full time Resident Clerk, and exchanged my dowdy Pimlico flat for the splendours of Horse Guards Parade. The day job took me to a department headed by an extremely affable man, Kenneth East, my principal task to coordinate CRO relations and policy views with the Central African Office, (responsible for the affairs of the Central African Federation, a body bringing together the British colonial territories of Northern and Southern Rhodesia, and Nyasaland, later Malawi). The CAO was then headed ministerially by First Secretary of State Rab Butler, so I was now working in effect for the man whose 1944 Education Act had helped to project me into this position. This was not an entirely happy experience, for I was green behind the ears when it came to bureaucratic politics, and found that the Chair of the CAO policy group of which I was a member, Godfrey Bass, a slightly irascible Assistant Secretary, was disinclined to take any nonsense from such a newly arrived junior member, and would cut short or effectively ignore what were admittedly feeble interventions on my part. This all meant that Commonwealth Office perspectives were side-lined, and somewhat mortified I explained to Kenneth East what was happening. He pursed his lips: "Godfrey should know better," he said, "remember that it doesn't matter how junior you are if you have a representing brief, you are entitled to defend our corner. I'll talk to Godfrey if he doesn't play ball." Next meeting, I took a deep breath and girded my loins: "The CRO has a particular interest in this policy that the committee has so far not taken into account..." I sounded a lot more confident than I felt but Godfrey, after a slightly startled, appraising glance, thereafter treated me as an equal. This was another valuable lesson in the bureaucratic world of policymaking: it's not your rank that counts, but who or what you represent. Kenneth East's ultimate reward, if that's the right word, was to become Ambassador to Iceland.

I was enjoying my other life as Resident Clerk, though the working hours restricted my social life somewhat. The way to combat this was to host dinners, or parties, at one of the most impressive addresses in London. A particularly good party just before Christmas saw an excellent mix of my old friends and new working colleagues. Hugh and James came, Quentin too, even my old tutor Neil McKendrick. We (my co-host was the alternative duty officer, Bill Humphrey) had the good sense to invite Derek King, the big wheel on personnel and postings, a good man to know, but our evening was tarnished somewhat when he and I got stuck in the very old-fashioned lift, and spent longer at sweaty close quarters than perhaps either of us cared for. Just as well we had invited him, though, for he had to field the complaints

*Group wedding photograph, from left: Doug Oldfield, Stuart Herrington, Ann Davies, Me, Thomas Stanford Senior, Mum, Tom and Maureen, Dad, Rona Stanford, Sally, Vic Boyce, Joyce Grierson, Mick Harper.*

*Best man at Maureen and Tom's wedding in 1963.*

later as various bits of party debris turned up in unexpected parts of the Foreign Office. Another bit of *lese-majeste* took place when Michael James came up to have lunch with his friend Robin Butler of the Treasury, and we played a game of cricket in the long FO corridor outside the flat. Michael, probably one of the best batsmen in the country just then, smote to all parts the occasional leg-breaks of the man who would one day become Secretary to Margaret Thatcher's Cabinet, and Head of the Civil Service. In a foreword to a book by Michael's wife Sally about the trials and tribulations of a diplomat's wife (*Diplomatic Moves: Life in the Foreign Service* 1995), Sir Robin (now Lord Butler) records with some nostalgia that early cricket match in the corridors of power; on my thesis about the significance of cricket in the highest levels of establishment life, I rest my case. I'm reminded, too, that the Prime Minister I would soon work under, Sir Alec Douglas-Home, once commented: "I can never walk down a church nave without wondering if it would take spin."

Cricket intervened in a more personal way now, for my sister Maureen married Tom Stanford, not only a fellow Knaresborough cricketer, but a maths teacher at the Grammar School, thereby earning approval both from Dad and Mum. I shot back to Yorkshire briefly, glad finally to be able to see my father give Maureen away, relieving me of the need to sell her. We all enjoyed the happiest of family weddings.

Over the next year, I was lucky to find in both my fellow Resident Clerks, Bill Humphrey and Christian Adams, equable and friendly companionship, essential for life lived at such close quarters and often under considerable pressure. Bill was a brilliant economist and son of the headmaster of the well-known Leys School at Cambridge: a more upright member of the community would have been difficult to imagine. Nonetheless, he had resorted to a subterfuge during National Service intended to ensure that he would not be regarded as officer material suitable to lead men in any kind of military action, a thought that filled him with dismay. His outstanding academic record at Cambridge (a double First in economics) had seen him assigned to officer training and assessment in the Army's artillery arm. The first part consisted of simple maths tests for which Bill deliberately provided the wrong answers. The second part took him to Salisbury plain to direct his artillery section in the business of blowing up cardboard tanks. The standard procedure was straightforward: the officer calculated the range, then adjusted firing instructions according to whether actual shots went long or fell short. After a few such efforts, in those days of less advanced technology usually a half dozen or so, the target would finally be hit. That very day had been chosen by the General in command of the whole shooting match to inspect the officer assessments. Bill stepped up to the plate, looked at the distant cardboard tank, pretended to scribble a calculation, and then gave a completely random set of coordinates to his unit. They fired, and the tank exploded: a first time hit, almost unimaginable: "Good God!" cried the General, "Send that man to Malaya at once." They did, not only to Bill's consternation, but to that of his fellow officers there when they realised that he really didn't have a clue about military stuff, and was more likely to be a danger to his own men than to the enemy. They posted him to an accounting section where he happily did proper sums well away from the danger areas. Bill didn't take much to the Foreign Office either, and would soon find a niche for his real talents at the top levels of the International Monetary Fund in Washington.

Bill was succeeded by Christian Adams, tremendously lanky and likeable. He and his girlfriend became good friends to me, and I went to their somewhat high society wedding. Here I met a rather fetching woman who agreed to meet me for dinner the following week. I then discovered that she had been a debutante in the days when I had been serving the Queen in a rather less exalted capacity, and came from what you might call a very good family. Our brief relationship was severely compromised when I took her back home on the tube: she told me that she had never travelled in this way before and looked around her at the democratic masses with an appalled fascination. I think that it was clear to both of us that I was not suitable material for the debutante classes. I had a more chastening experience with another young woman met in the course of my duties, who worked as a Private Secretary to the Lord Great Chamberlain in the House of Lords. We discovered a common interest in the theatre, and began regular excursions. Mary, another Cambridge graduate, was pretty, intelligent, and had a quiet serenity that appealed to me. She said little about her own background, and I was disinclined in those days to say much about mine. She soon invited me to a party at her flat in Belgravia. A mutual friend who travelled there with me and who knew of my interest in her, told me that Mary was the daughter of the upper class family that owned Skipton Castle, not many miles from my Yorkshire home. Somewhat slyly, he made it clear that she had a boyfriend to whom she was quite attached. His name was Ian Milroy. I was dumbfounded. Could this be the same Ian Milroy who was the son of Lord Mowbray's unloved Agent, and had long ago usurped my batting position in the Hopperton village cricket team? By the time I stumbled into the party I was anxious and confused. My humble origins, carefully guarded in such company as this, would be revealed, doubtless to Mary's dismay and my own humiliation. Once inside, I simply froze, keeping to myself at the margins of the crowd. I easily recognised Ian and his sister, but wild horses would not have dragged me over to them. At one point Mary, clearly nonplussed, came over and gently asked if I was feeling alright, but I more or less waved her away. Soon after I walked out of the room without a word to anyone. I made no attempt to contact Mary again, nor she me. The two worlds I lived in were, to my mind, still incompatible, and they had come scarily close to interacting at a time in my life when I was not ready to cope with that.

It was not easy for me to adjust to the glittering social world in which I now found myself. Despite a career marked by constant success, and a clear demonstration that I was at home at the highest levels of public policy and action, my social self-confidence was still fragile. Where I met acceptance and friendship, as was often the case, all was well. If I met any sign of hostility or condescension, I would withdraw defensively into myself. This syndrome is well illustrated by my relation with the Foreign Office Resident Clerk, Kenneth Scott (who after a distinguished career involving 'cold war' ambassadorial posts in Germany and Yugoslavia, would be knighted and put out to grass as the Deputy Private Secretary to the Queen). Ken, ever friendly and hospitable, on our long weekend shifts would invite me regularly for a drink and a chat. He was an inveterate gossip and had some wonderful stories to tell about the various cock-ups perpetrated by the good and the great. During the summer of 1963 my mother, now a leading light in the Women's Institute in her part of Yorkshire, came to London for the annual WI Conference. I was delighted to be able to show her my fine office and flat, and she must have felt that all that grinding work to support my early progress had been rewarded. Ken Scott rang to invite me for a drink and he insisted on inviting her round too. I felt disconcerted and anxious: how would Mum cope with this minor grandee? How would I cope if she didn't? I need not have worried. Ken treated her as courteously as one day, no doubt, he would treat the Queen, and showed Mum round Foreign Secretary Rab Butler's inner sanctum (a bit of glamour for her next WI report). Moreover, Mum rose to the occasion like a trouper, displaying her always intelligent wit and no little poise. When Ken told an anecdote about the erstwhile Labour Party Prime Minister, Ramsay Macdonald, she treated him to a fine line in political invective, Macdonald regarded by her and Dad as a shameful traitor to the Labour cause. It was an odd meeting between this clever and privileged member of the elite class, and a very ordinary working-class woman; but she was, of course, no ordinary woman, and held her own in ways which should not have surprised me, though it did. Looking back on her now, I am inclined to agree with Marguerite Duras who wrote ' one's mother is, generally speaking, the strangest, most unpredictable and elusive person one meets'.

I was soon obliged to follow her spirited example when I was a guest at a small Ken Scott dinner party, where the guests were mostly influential Young Turks of the British establishment, including the rising Tory political star and economic journalist, Nigel Lawson, judiciously balanced (typical Ken Scott) by the rising young critic of that establishment, Anthony Sampson. An incautious remark provoked a furious spat with the man on my left, who clearly thought me a jumped up meritocrat (read 'grammar school type') who had no idea what responsibilities were involved in being a member of the too-often traduced governing elite (read 'public school and City types'). I was upset by this very public argument and his aggressive disdain: Ken later told me soothingly that he was almost certainly angered by not being placed next to Nigel Lawson.

On the work front, I was getting on by leaps and bounds, as I was nominated to be the next Assistant Private Secretary to the Secretary of State, Duncan Sandys. I would replace the redoubtable Brian Gilmore. The only problem was that Sandys, a hard driving and bad-tempered man, was inclined to eat junior officials for breakfast, so I'd be on probation until he was satisfied with me. I'd had to cope with worse things than grumpy Cabinet Ministers during my life, and I was determined to meet an exciting challenge. A Secretary of State's Private Office was at the very heart and apex of the policy system, a place where politics and bureaucracy merged and had to be reconciled. The Principal Private Secretary was an urbane and experienced man called Nick Huijsman, helped by Peter Moon, a sharp and unflappable diplomat. The two junior Private Secretaries were myself and one Dennis Doble, a quiet and undemonstrative type. The Personal Assistant was the formidable Freda Smith, who had a degree of influence with Sandys out of all proportion to her designated position in the official hierarchy. There were some confidential matters he would only entrust to her, and for these it was at her discretion how she kept official channels informed. She had been with Sandys for many years, and it was rumoured that she was a sometime mistress, though this may only have been unfounded office gossip.

On a typical working day, any adverse publicity might throw Sandys into a grump or a rage. At worst, he might unwisely try to insist on ringing a newspaper editor or even owner, but Freda and Nick were expert at dissuading him from explosive and potentially disastrous interventions in the free press. On one occasion, I was present at a meeting the Secretary of State had with Patrick Keatley, a highly respected journalist on foreign and commonwealth issues. Sandys gave Keatley a note he had asked me to prepare on a particular thorny issue of the day: to my amazement (and part of my education) it appeared in a broadsheet piece three days later, virtually word for word, but purporting to be Keatley's own analysis. Another ministerial trick was to get some political minion, a complaisant peer or ambitious MP, to take a public initiative which reflected the Secretary of State's own preferred outcome, and which he would then use in Parliament as evidence of 'public opinion' being on his side. Interestingly, television was paid relatively little attention in the sixties, compared with the press.

Once the Secretary of State had been calmed down, meetings with various groups of officials would take up most of the day. These would usually involve some attempt to agree a policy decision, or formulate a policy strategy, or prepare for important forthcoming political negotiations. Sandys was now ministerial head of both the Commonwealth Relations and Colonial Offices, though these Offices had separate departmental identities and staffs. One distinct advantage of these regular meetings of senior officials was that you got to know them, and they got to know you: these were the contacts and relationships that could mean the start of a dazzling career, or possibly whip the ladder from under your feet. It was a situation fraught with complexities. As a very junior member of the Office, just starting out in effect, I might have to convey to an extremely senior member instructions from the Secretary of State which might be anathema to him. For example, one of the Deputy Under-Secretaries was Sir Arthur Snelling, formerly a senior ambassador in Ghana (and later to be Ambassador to South Africa), a dyspeptic man with a notoriously short fuse, who generally sported morning dress in the office, a habit already beginning to seem archaic. He had sent a policy recommendation to the Secretary of State. Sandys shoved the memo into my hand and instructed me to tell Snelling to go away and rewrite it on different lines, which he specified in a few pithy sentences. He was on no account to be disturbed further on this (the subtext being that he would not want to discuss this personally any further with Snelling). Sir Arthur, humiliated as much by the status of the messenger as by the message, took umbrage, and visited his ire on me as the hapless go-between. I got angry myself at this bullying treatment and said that I had to get on with my job, and perhaps he had better go and do what he had been told to do. Sir Arthur went a sort of puce colour and at this point was led aside and calmed down by Peter Moon. Afterwards Peter had wise advice for me: "I admire your spirit, but I have to say that I'm not sure you are cut out for this job. Snelling will not forget this, and one day will be able to punish you. You'll need to learn that a diplomat, especially a junior one, often has to bite his lip and keep the peace." He must have taken his own good advice, for he would ultimately be knighted after sterling work in NATO and Washington, a spell at the top of the 'spy' liaison outfit, Information Research Department, and at one point the FCO Private Secretary to the Prime Minister, Edward Heath. Later in his career, he would be High Commissioner in Singapore, with my friend Michael James as his Deputy.

Sir Arthur Snelling was by no means the only senior official to be roughly treated by his political master. The head of the Office, as Permanent Under Secretary, was Sir Saville ('Joe') Garner. When himself a junior private secretary, in the 1930s, his new Minister at the Dominions Office/Colonial Office was J. H.(Jimmy) Thomas, of humble Welsh origins and, a former railways worker, for many years General Secretary of the National Union of Railwaymen. He had asked "What's your name, boy?" "Saville Garner, sir". "No, no, I can't call you *Saville,* don't you have any other names?" "Joseph, sir?" "Right, boy, I'll call you Joe". The name stuck. Joe Garner, some thirty years later a more august and somewhat austere figure, fell out so badly with Duncan Sandys that he refused to enter the Secretary of State's office, and there was a complete stand-off between Secretary of State and Permanent Secretary that lasted for several weeks. Senior staff would give Garner personal briefings, and in turn they would try to convey his advice to the Secretary of State as if it was their own. Sometimes they would try to mediate matters through the Minister of State, Andrew, Duke of Devonshire: the problem here was that the Duke was not only distinctly more liberal than Sandys in his attitudes to some of the decolonisation issues under dispute (he would in the 1980s attach himself to the new Social Democrat party) but simultaneously somewhat self-effacing and self-deprecating, so was no match for the bullying, authoritarian Sandys.

It is worth recalling, with some disbelief, what a world of intertwined upper class and aristocratic class privilege I was moving in at this point in the early 1960s. Duncan Sandys, Secretary of State for Commonwealth Relations and the Colonies, had been Winston Churchill's son-in-law. The Minister of State in the CRO was the Duke of Devonshire, whose aunt, Lady Dorothy Cavendish was married to Prime Minister Harold Macmillan (of whom it has been written 'nepotism held no terrors'.) The Devonshires were also related by marriage to the Lansdownes, and the Minister of State in the Colonial Office was the Marquess of Lansdowne: this was described by Anthony Sampson as 'the cousinhoods who had been interwoven with politics for the past centuries', both having forebears who had held the post of Foreign Secretary. All of these people were Old Etonians, and indeed Rab Butler, passed over later for Prime Minister more than once, believed that he had been the victim of an Old Etonian stitch-up. Despite the significant political and social changes of the post-war period, aristocratic privilege and influence were alive and well in the Macmillan administration, and he himself would be succeeded by another Old Etonian aristocrat, Alec Douglas-Home, who had 11 Old Etonians in his Cabinet. An obituary of the Duke of Devonshire quotes him as saying that his job was down to 'gross nepotism...I think we'd given him [Macmillan] some good shooting'. To remain Prime Minister, Douglas Home was obliged to renounce his peerage, but before he succeeded to that title he was a young Conservative MP in the 1931 election. My mother would have snorted again had she known that he had at that time suggested that unemployed coalminers and their families should be moved to London to work as domestic servants. These two Ministers of State, Devonshire and Lansdowne, had little ability and were not trusted with anything of real significance. My recollection of George Lansdowne, in many Colonial Office meetings at which I was present, is that he stuck pretty firmly, and silently, to his family heraldic motto: *virtute non verbis,* 'by courage, not words'. The writers of 'Yes Minister' would have had a perfect scenario here, and for me it beggared belief that this was how top-level government and policy-making was structured and pursued. I might add that for a period of four weeks I acted as temporary Private Secretary for Andrew Devonshire, and found him a friendly if somewhat distracted master: my reward, shared with the rest of the Private Office, was the wonderful present of a night at the Proms in his personal box at the Royal Albert Hall, followed later by a thumping big cut of venison fresh from his Chatsworth estate. In this setting, my days as a farm labourer's son on an equally aristocratic if distinctly more impoverished country estate seemed more and more like the stuff of fantasy.

But I was also beginning to feel some doubts about what I was doing in this place, and whether I really wanted to belong to it. These feelings, probably submerged by all the glamour and excitements of my first eighteen months, assailed me unexpectedly and in a curious way. In Easter of 1963 on Resident Clerk duty, on a lovely sunny day, I climbed up to the tower on the Foreign Office roof. Overlooking Whitehall, I had a ringside view of what was now a traditional Campaign for Nuclear Disarmament peace march from Aldermaston to Trafalgar Square. I watched what seemed like an endless and colourful tide of thousands of people pouring down Whitehall. Recalling the fear and disbelief of the quite recent Cuban missile crisis, and knowing personally how close disaster seemed to be at that time, questions crowded in. Why am I up here and not down there? Why am I, committed to long-standing and strongly felt Labour Party values, working at the heart of

*Me on top of the Foreign Office, Big Ben in the background, a view available from my flat.*

a nepotistic and class-ridden Tory government? These were invisible worms at the heart of my rose, as yet only dimly sensed amidst the heat and excitement of the disintegrating British Empire.

# Chapter Sixteen

## The Dying Fall of Empire

*Either the British were bowled out (by nationalist and freedom fighters) or they were run out (by imperial overstretch and economic constraints) or they retired hurt (because of a collapse of morale and failure of will) or they were booed off the field (by international criticism).*
Edward Hyam: *Britain's Declining Empire*, 2006

Even for historians of British public life, the cricketing metaphor rules. On the field of play, much of the work of the great imperial offices of state at this time related to issues of decolonisation, as well as substantial post-independence problems in the Indian subcontinent relating to India and Pakistan, and later to Bangladesh; and there were major economic policy issues concerning our trade relations with Australia, New Zealand and Canada, particularly in relation to British wishes to enter the Common Market. There was a lot to get one's head round, and the Private Secretaries dealt with this by each taking lead responsibility for private office management of particular policy areas. I took part lead in principle (and of course under close supervision by the senior Private Secretaries) on decolonisation in Malta and Lesotho, and later in a different capacity on Mauritius, all seemingly small and insignificant, but each offering examples of how problematic clearing up the detritus of empire could be. What this office division meant was that on these issues you would be exposed to the full force of the Secretary of State's scrutiny, and (if he felt things were not going as he wished) bad temper. You needed a thick skin to survive. For a long period my private life almost came to a halt, not only because of the pressure of business, but because Sandys was something of a night owl, and would frequently return to the Office after dinner and work well into the small hours (it was said that he rarely slept much because of the pain caused by a crippling injury from a motoring accident during the war). Nick Huijsman or Peter Moon would often be in attendance, but the junior Private Secretaries were also frequently obliged to take their turn. On one occasion, I was the only minion available and Sandys, trying to sort out some issue I have now forgotten, was less than pleased that the whole Office were sound asleep in bed, making it extremely difficult for me to provide him with information, since most files and papers were also soundly asleep in their filing cabinets. The Secretary of State's irritation was visited on me, the only whipping boy around. When I returned empty-handed and weary after a long and fruitless search, he arrived at a novel explanation for my delays: "Look here, Martin, d'you know why you are so slow? I think it's because you don't walk fast enough". Two days later I went off to recharge my batteries on a week's walking holiday in the Lake District with Quentin and a group of Cambridge friends. When I came back and went into the Secretary of State, he frowned: "Where have you been for the past week?" "In the Lake District, Secretary of State, practising my walk". Sandys stared at me, unblinking, for an unnerving length of time: then suddenly guffawed with laughter. My relationship with him was never close or even cordial, but he actually responded better to people who stood up to him, and I lasted a good deal longer than a trail of previous, quickly jettisoned incumbents of my post.

*With Cambridge friends in the Lake District, reclining after 'practising my walk'.*

You had indeed to be quick on your feet at times, both metaphorically and physically. The occasional visits to Parliament qualified here, for Sandys was no lover of the democratic process and its demands. If he had to make any sort of statement or answer Parliamentary Questions, he would pore over several drafts, constantly amending the offerings from his officials, but rarely improving them. He had his official car, a splendid Austin Princess, ready to rush him to the House of Commons; a favourite trick was at the last moment to demand that you find and convey to him some answer to a subsidiary question he had just thought of, then heave himself to his feet and limp off to the waiting car. More than once I would have to sprint down the steps in his wake, clutching a sheaf of papers, and saved from ignominy only by the wise old regular driver, Charles, who would find some unexpected difficulty in manoeuvring the car until he saw me in full flight. I'd tumble into the moving car in a hail of irritated comments on my dilatoriness from an unrepentant boss. An official history of the Government Car Service (a publication of surprising interest) tells that on one occasion an impatient Sandys poked the driver hard in the neck with his walking stick, whereupon the driver indignantly stopped the car, got out, and refused to continue any further. Good for him.

Once or twice, I acted as the CRO official who sat in the officials' box on the right hand of Mr Speaker. From the front bench the Secretary of State would scribble short and incomprehensible demands for further information. We invariably handled this sort of thing by dint of a list of virtually interchangeable ambiguous responses, meant to fit all possibilities, and reveal nothing about policy intentions. Nonetheless, it was exciting to be inside the Chamber and feel the adrenalin kick in when the ministerial Under Secretary, John Tilney, would lean over Sandys, then slip over to the box with a crumpled bit of paper which might well raise a query impossible to answer. This mattered only in that Sandys might give you a hard time afterwards; the debating and questioning process in the House of Commons was carefully designed and calibrated to conceal information rather than make it available, and it always seemed to me that almost all Members of Parliament, from both sides of the House, comfortably colluded in this institutional stitch up. Once, on the way back to the Office, Sandys said that he wanted to make a private telephone call immediately: I was fairly certain that this would be to some newspaper editor to ensure that the right things were said next day about Sandys' performance that evening. Remember that this was long before mobile phones. Charles, unsurprised by anything, duly found a red call box just off Victoria Street. Sandys lumbered out, and squeezed his large frame into the box. After a minute or so, we saw him apparently punching the apparatus, then half turn to wave me to the box. It turned out that he had no idea how to operate the Button A/Button B call operating system then in place, nor did he realise that you had to insert coins. I proffered a shilling, dialled the number and pressed the buttons; he then virtually shouldered me aside to ensure that I couldn't hear who he was talking to. This was the sort of thing for which they sorted out the best Oxbridge graduates in Savile Row: knowing how to light fires, and teaching Ministers the rudiments of the public telephone system.

In fact, I was given quite extraordinary opportunities to show my mettle, quite apart from my stint as Resident Clerk, and given that it was such an early stage in my career. At this time, Commonwealth and Colonial affairs were particularly fraught and active. Prime Minister Harold Macmillan had delivered in February 1960 his famous 'wind of change' speech in South Africa, anticipating a rapid process of decolonisation in Africa and elsewhere, and this process had been taken forward by a liberal thinking Colonial Secretary, Iain Macleod (another Yorkshire-born Caius historian). During my time at the centre of all this (1962-65), negotiations for the granting of independence, or an associated track at a slower pace for smaller dependent territories, included Kenya, Uganda, Tanganyika (Tanzania), Northern Rhodesia (Zambia), Southern Rhodesia (Zimbabwe), Nyasaland (Malawi), Basutoland (Lesotho), Bechuanaland (Botswana), and Swaziland in Africa alone; in the Caribbean, the troubled colony of British Guiana (Guyana); in the Mediterranean, Malta; in the Middle East, the Aden Protectorate (Yemen); in the Indian Ocean, Mauritius. By 1963, 24 of 40 dependencies were earmarked for independence. My studies at Cambridge, in despite of rather than inspired by Ronald Robinson, had given me a reasonably close knowledge of the colonial history of many of these places, particularly in Africa, and it was fascinating to be involved now in their struggles to be free of metropolitan tutelage. It all seems in retrospect to have been an inexorable and rapidly escalating process in the post-war decades, and so it was, particularly after the disgrace of the 1956 invasion of Suez, but the specific dispositions of individual states was anything but predetermined, each one requiring a solution tailored to its individual circumstances. At the centre of policy, in the Commonwealth and Colonial Offices, ministers and officials grappled with what often seemed to be recalcitrant problems, most obviously where a territory was characterised by mixed cultural groups, whether defined by race, language, religion or a combustible mixture of these defining identities. Decolonisation was most challenging where a colonial territory had been dominated by white settler groups, reluctant to give way to rising African nationalists, as in Kenya and Southern Rhodesia. In the recent past, these differences had not been well handled by the imperial centre: the tragic and bloody transition of India and Pakistan was a case in point, while the brutal treatment of Africans in Kenya by colonial masters and local white settlers had stained Britain's decolonisation record (and continues to do so as more light is thrown on this unsavoury chapter by the release of public records of the time).

In many cases, by the time of my involvement, these issues had been played out politically, and were on the verge of resolution. The focus at the Whitehall centre was on reaching enduring constitutional settlements to give institutional flesh and bones to the new political bodies. The pressures on decision-makers were considerable. Many territories were being brought along at differing speeds, and their differing political, social and economic circumstances made it essential to some degree to find outcomes tailor-made to fit these differences. Making a decision to give a country independence was often not all that problematic; realising that decision by the creation of a whole new set of post-independence institutions that would provide a stable outcome was another matter entirely.

The Private Office staffs had to deal as even-handedly as possible with the Secretary of State, two Permanent Secretaries, two Ministers of State, and an assortment of luminaries of the Colonial Office, as well as our own CRO officials. They included Sir John Martin, then High Commissioner to Malta, who had once been Private Secretary to Winston Churchill and was exceedingly gracious to juniors like me. The Colonial Office Permanent Secretary, the improbably named Sir Hilton Poynton, was more distant and a bit gruff: he was apparently a lover of choral music and someone told me that when he walked home from his train late at night he would be heard singing descants to himself: another Old Etonian, he has been described as 'a patrician civil servant of the old school'. Someone I became quite involved with over the Malta negotiations was a senior Under Secretary, Christopher Eastwood; back-room gossips quickly let it be known that he had a notorious past as the Lands Commissioner in the Ministry of Agriculture at the heart of the well-known scandal over Crichel Down, which had brought down his Minister, Sir Thomas Dugdale, in the mid-1950s. He was never anything but conscientious and hard-working in my experience, always on top of a dizzying array of decolonisation issues: he once commented that so rapid had the pace of such changes become that he always mentally halved the number of years to independence he had first thought of. One day, to my surprise, he invited me to have a drink with him and his wife at his club, which I think was the Oxford and Cambridge club (Eastwood was an Eton and Oxford man). This was a perplexing invitation but one that a junior could not, of course, refuse. My eyes and ears in the Office, Robin Gorham, came up with a likely explanation; he pointed out that an Assistant Secretary on the Colonial Office staff, a pale, perpetually harassed-looking man, was married to Eastwood's elder daughter, the outcome of just such an invitation.

And indeed, on my arrival in the unwonted splendour of the club precincts, I was introduced to Christopher Eastwood's younger daughter, upon which, after a drink, he and his wife made off, leaving us alone. The not unattractive daughter took me off to dinner at her flat, which it turned out she shared with one of my own Private Office secretarial staff. They spent the evening giggling together, casting looks in my direction, and I got the distinct impression that they were trying to decide which of them should be the lucky bride to be. Needless to say, I didn't much feel like becoming a member of the personal entourage of one of my seniors, but we all stayed on good terms. Another introduction to London clubland had come earlier in the year, when I got a telephone call from Sir Gilbert Laithwaite, inviting me to lunch with him at the Travellers' Club, the club of choice for senior diplomats, colonial governors and so forth (and where, writes Anthony Sampson, 'diplomats, with their careful arrogance set the tone' and 'conversation with someone you don't know is virtually forbidden'.) Laithwaite had been a recent former Permanent Secretary in the CRO and a High Commissioner to Pakistan, where he had astonished the locals by wearing morning dress at the height of a blindingly hot summer, the very epitome of the Noel Coward song. Now retired, he liked to keep himself informed about current goings-on by lunching people at the centre of things. Robin, a seasoned observer of office politics, more or less warned me that I could be reasonably indiscreet with such a former dignitary in such a formal setting, but that it would be unwise to accept invitations of a more personal nature. Sir Gilbert had reserved a corner table from which we could see everyone who came in, and he regaled me with gossip about each distinguished diner, while also quizzing me gently about current Office preoccupations. I have to say that I had a delightful time, and if he were indeed an old roué, he never once gave so much as a hint of this.

By early 1964 my stint as Resident Clerk came to an end. This change scarcely diminished the 12-15 hour working days to which I had perforce become accustomed, though it was certainly better than hoeing turnips. Late night meetings going well into the small hours were a regular feature of the Sandys style of negotiation, a style liable to get short-term results but produce fragile and unstable solutions which would quite quickly crumble after independence. Smaller territories such as Malta, Basutoland, and Mauritius could produce intractable problems because of cultural complexities and tensions. It is not my intention here to undertake analysis of the detail of these exemplars, but rather to convey a sense of what it was like to be inside the room while such problems were fought over, played out, and resolved, or very often not resolved.

Malta's war time history is well known, and there was much residual sympathy for them in the post-war period. Britain still had a more than passing strategic interest in this Mediterranean island, and several commercial interests, but found it difficult to handle both defence and political issues in the face of the intractable social and political divisions on the island. The dominance of the Roman Catholic church in Maltese life, and the propensity of the church to use spiritual blackmail to ensure the political compliance of its devout flock, brought headaches for British policy makers more familiar with a clear separation between religion and politics.

The British side sought to get initial agreement on a defence treaty, in their own strategic interest, and in the recognition that this could then be a bargaining counter in the trickier political and constitutional negotiations. Hence we spent many long hours in London, in the first half of 1964, burning the midnight oil over both issues. Night after night Sandys (and the rest of us officials and hangers on) would labour over draft agreements. Refreshments and strong drink were provided and often became a principal focus of Maltese attention. By two in the morning, many of them were extremely refreshed, longing for their beds, and would put their name to anything. Triumphantly Sandys would send them back to their hotel, and we would stay on to redraw the new agreements for presentation and signing off the next day. On arrival, the hungover Maltese leaders would deny any memory of any such agreements, and back we would go to another such night of one step forwards, two steps back, and some fairly heavy strategic drinking. After weeks of this stand-off, a draft defence agreement was signed up to by all the main players, but this still left the more significant political issue: independence? Some sort of continued dependent status? A referendum prior to any agreement on the political side? Elections at what stage of all this? Even Prime Minister Douglas Home was lobbied by well-connected people with links to British expatriates settled in Malta: he commented that Malta was a small but terribly difficult problem. Earlier, Macmillan had written that 'islands can become a terrible bore'.

There was an unmistakable power struggle going on in Malta, and the fingerprints of the Roman Catholic hierarchy were all over the various blueprints proposed. So significant was the influence of the Church that the views of the Vatican were called in, through the personage of the Apostolic Delegate, the Pope's senior representative in Britain. It so happened that

I had been given responsibility for a crucial private meeting between him and the Secretary of State, and took a highly confidential note of the papal preferences, and promises to lean on the Maltese religious hierarchy in order to reduce their political interventions and influence. Later, Peter Moon would be pleased by my summary clarifying the complexities of political-religious interactions in Malta. I'm inclined to think that my mixed religious upbringing, rooted in a combination of superstition and scepticism, had equipped me rather well to understand the Byzantine nature of Malta's religious politics, and the adverse reactions these provoked. At the end of the meeting I shook hands with the most senior Catholic in Britain, and wished that Mum could see me now. Ultimately, Sandys completely lost patience with all the complexity, and was anyway highly disdainful of the petty power struggles which so often evaded his attempts at control. Unable to engineer agreements, he imposed them; then washed his hands of the consequences, controversially giving Malta independence under the more conservative of the Maltese political leaders,Borg Olivier (21st September 1964) only a month before yielding office to the British Labour Party. I have never understood the judgement in one of his obituaries that he was a 'masterful and decisive negotiator'; simply untrue if we are to judge him by the results of his reign as Commonwealth and Colonial Secretary. Leading historians of British Empire judged him 'less clever, more ponderous, more to the right politically than [his predecessors, Iain Macleod and Reginald Maudling] but methodical, a tough and patient negotiator, and forceful'. His former Permanent Secretary, Joe Garner, has described him as 'if necessary, brutal'. Personally, I think 'patient' is quite the wrong description, rather Sandys sought simply to wear people down until he got them to agree with him, and was somewhat an iron fist in an iron glove. He was constantly surprised and irritated when his methods were resisted, or didn't bring the desired results. Tellingly, Indian Prime Minister Nehru remarked that Sandys reminded him of 'the type of Englishman who used to put him in gaol'. His working methods exhausted everyone: himself, his staff, and the opposition. Sir Kennedy Trevaskis, Governor of Aden, and a regular presence in the Office when talks were being held about that colony's constitutional and political future, said that Sandys 'looked wan with fatigue...but not as wan as his red-eyed officials': this may be the only official recognition I have received for those night-time labours. At this time, I recall Sandys walking down the CRO steps with me after a meeting with Yemeni political representatives and saying: 'they really are awfully nasty little people'. This sort of attitude suffused British attitudes to Aden and its Yemeni hinterland for decades, and the benighted people there are currently reaping the terrible fruits of decades of British myopia and miscalculation in that part of the Middle East.

Basutoland was another exemplar of erratic and ultimately fruitless constitution-building. The internal problem was a conflict between traditional and modernising political players, the traditional side represented formally by a monarch, King Moshoeshoe II, but led politically by Chief Leabua Jonathan, ambitious to be head and leader of any newly independent state. These traditional interests were opposed by an African nationalist party with ambitions to establish a more forward looking system of government and more egalitarian systems of land ownership and economic and social development. A complicating factor in these negotiations was the British parliamentary and electoral timetable in 1964. An election had been set for October, with the opinion polls indicating a likely Labour unseating of the creaking and increasingly anachronistic looking Conservative government. Sandys was therefore set (as with Malta) on railroading through arrangements that could not be overturned by an incoming Labour administration, thought to favour the radical nationalist side in Basutoland. There had already been sharp criticism from the Labour front bench, its principal spokesman, Arthur Bottomley, questioning the unseemly haste and Sandys' unwillingness to provide any information on his negotiations. It was against this backdrop that I sat with Sandys and his principal advisers in a make-or-break meeting in Whitehall, late at night, with the Basuto representatives. A draft Independence Bill was on the table, due to be approved by the House of Commons the very next day, but agreement on the main principles still had not been achieved with all the main players; this was brinkmanship with a vengeance. The African protagonists seemed oddly to be physically characterised by their political leanings. The traditional side were short and round, slow in their demeanour and full of gravitas, as befitted their sense of accustomed authority; some wore their traditional chiefly robes. The modernising nationalists, younger and generally better educated, were tall and thin, and soberly dressed in sharp suits. Since there was little meeting of minds between these nationalists and the traditionalists entrenched around the monarchical group, compromise depended heavily on the willingness of Chief Leabua Jonathan, the most significant political leader in Basutoland, to bring both sides along by making concessions to each. As the night wore wearily on, the British side waited tensely for Chief Jonathan to make his move. Suddenly, he raised a hand. "Mr Chairman", he said to Sandys, "the water is running from the glasses", and sat back. We on the British side were momentarily nonplussed, as we tried to guess what this pregnant statement meant; was it a yes, or a no, or perhaps even a maybe? Drawing on my Maltese experience I was the first to divine the meaning, for I had noticed the longing stares at the drinks table across the room: they were ready to enjoy some hospitality before committing themselves to any particular future for their country. I whispered in the Secretary of State's ear and, scarcely concealing his irritation, he called a drinks break. As one particularly large chief crossed the room, he began to shake with belly laughter as he approached the array of bottles and glasses, such was his anticipated pleasure. Soon the whole room was full of little happy groups, rapidly disposing of large glasses of whiskey. Amazingly, this whole episode seemed to dispel the tensions. The traditionalists had a private conclave and stitched up some sort of deal between their respective factions, while Chief Jonathan made last minute concessions to the lean and hungry nationalists. A formal agreement was signed which meant that, as a pale dawn broke over Westminster, Basutoland had secured the promise it wanted of an Independence Day, though some eighteen months in the future. Needless to say, these paper agreements scarcely survived the light of that day, though it took some considerable time for this particular game to be played out, by which time Sandys and the Tory government were long gone, leaving their Labour successors to cope with the prolonged aftermath. As was, with hindsight, somewhat inevitable, Chief Leabua Jonathan ultimately ousted both monarchical and nationalist groups, and staged an authoritarian coup; for them, the water had indeed run from the glasses.

I still had managed to lead a life outside the Office. After leaving my St James's Park residence, I had re-joined my old friends Hugh and James in their new flat in Abbey Road, not far from where the Beatles were operating, but at the rather less salubrious end. We all got on well together. A landlady of faded gentility, distantly related to the lamentable Lord Chancellor, Quintin Hogg, lived downstairs and occasionally invited us for a dry sherry. The house was in a state of disrepair, and one morning a bedroom ceiling fell in on top of Hugh as he lay in bed. In due course, James had to leave: his engineering company had posted him to Hong Kong to work on a huge water scheme, and he would have to make his farewell. Unhappily, the selected celebratory evening coincided with an unexpected long night at the office. Explaining the situation to Nick Huijsman, I was given time off on condition that I returned by 11:00pm to take my share of an anticipated strenuous session of negotiations with Maltese politicians. Predictably, if unwisely, we drank a few too many toasts to James' departure, and left the pub rather the worse for wear. Hugh took charge: hailing a cab, he instructed the driver: "Take this man to Downing Street!" The driver's response was sceptical and unprintable, but the appearance of a fiver as an inducement changed his mind. When I burst smiling and red-faced into the Private Office, Nick took one look at me and hissed "Sit in that chair, don't move, and on no account enter Master's office". To his eternal credit he never mentioned this again, though it might have strengthened Peter Moon's suspicions about my unsuitability for the Diplomatic Service.

James kept us posted about his efforts to bring clean water to the drier parts of the world. After Hong Kong he had moved on to Pakistan, where he was in charge of a large dam-related government water project, under what was at that time a military government, so that he was effectively accountable to the General in charge of the Region. James found himself employing both Indian and Pakistani workers, at a time when tensions between the two countries were very high. Fights broke out on the water project site. Alarmed, James summoned the General, who arrived precipitately by army helicopter. "How many dead?" he snapped as he hit the ground. James faltered: "Well, none dead actually". "Then why are you wasting my time!" demanded the General angrily, climbing back in and zooming off in a cloud of dust. "How many dead?" became a watchword for Hugh and me thereafter, whenever any minor disaster took place.

*Gatehouse to St Bartholomew the Great, Smithfield Square, London where Hugh and I shared a flat.*

Meanwhile, Hugh had found a wonderful new place for us to live, in the Elizabethan Gatehouse of the even older St Bartholomew's Church, bounded on one side by the ancient St Bart's Hospital, and on the other by Smithfield Market (the local joke was always that if you saw a man in a bloodstained white coat you could not be sure whether he was from the meat market or the hospital). St Paul's and Fleet Street lay a few hundred yards away, as did the Old Bailey. It was more or less outside our windows that Wat Tyler had in 1381 famously confronted his monarch, Richard 1, during the 14th century Peasants Revolt, and was unceremoniously slain by the royal party, possibly at the hand of the Lord Mayor of London, William Walworth. Our landlady, aptly named Elizabeth, was an assistant curator at the British Museum, but unhappily we somehow got into her bad books, and we fell out properly when she began to leave pots and pans unwashed in the shared kitchen. After a stand-off, when the small kitchen began to look like a prequel for *Withnall and I*, Hugh and I cracked and undertook an enormous cleansing operation. Thereafter a precarious truce prevailed.

Hugh and I often escaped the London urban scene for a bit of rural calm at his parents' lovely house, Medbourne Manor, in rural Leicestershire. I was warmly welcomed there; Mr Johnson, then Chairman of the North Thames Gas Board, was as stubborn in his right-ish views as my dear old Dad was in his left-ish views, and as equally loved political argument, so we got on famously, while Hugh and I conducted tight-lipped and hugely enjoyable battles on the local golf courses. At this time I bought my first car, a delightful mini Wolseley Hornet, and spent my spare time racing around the streets of London in it. Indeed, I enjoyed over this whole period all that London had to offer. I had always enjoyed theatre, and at the tail end of my Cambridge days had the good fortune to see the newly famous Albert Finney in John Osborne's *Luther* at the Phoenix Theatre; and I now enjoyed the very first West End performance of Joan Littlewood's path-breaking *Oh! What A Lovely War.* I was particularly pleased when Mum came on her WI visit and asked to be taken to see George Bernard Shaw's *Heartbreak House* at the lovely old Victorian Criterion Theatre. She had seen it on television in the late 1950s and found appealing Shaw's castigation of the selfishness and self-absorption of the upper classes during the First World War, characteristics of which she had personal experience. For myself, I was beginning to experience the compelling nature of live performances of classical music in the great London concert halls; on one magical evening at the Royal Festival Hall, Quentin and I were spell-bound as the around-80-years-old Otto Klemperer, propped up by a special support on which he leaned, conducted the around-70-years-old pianist Wilhelm Kempff - I think playing Beethoven - their combined ages being some 150 years. On another occasion Fred Inglis organised a wonderful evening at a Royal

Albert Hall performance of Mozart's *Idomeneo.* I was also glad to be able to renew acquaintance with my old school friend Desmond Gill, just finished at RADA, and acting at the Royal Court Theatre. We met regularly, usually at a cheap cafe called The Stockpot, just off Piccadilly, or at Jimmy's, a Soho basement restaurant of indeterminate but cheap and cheerful cuisine. At a party Desmond gave, I talked for some time to the very young Richard Eyre, not knowing, of course, how famous a theatre director he would one day be. But London was like that in the mid-1960s, a place where everyone felt that they might make fame and fortune one day, and where many people did.

But it was also a time for political change: an outmoded and discredited government had to go. In the October 1964 general election, Labour under Harold Wilson narrowly defeated the Conservatives under Sir Alec Douglas Home. It was an odd and interesting experience to bid farewell to one set of political masters and welcome in another. Despite Labour's very small majority, the end of thirteen years of Tory rule had seemed inevitable by that stage, for the final years of the Tory administrations had been mired in scandals, now well documented, but still astonishing for the evidence of corruption and decadence at the very heart of government. Harold Wilson's promise to bring to bear the 'white heat of technology' on our tired and dysfunctional institutions fell on receptive electoral soil. The spirit of reform extended to all parts of the creaking 'establishment' then just recently anatomised by Anthony Sampson, the young journalist I had met at Ken Scott's dinner party in the FCO a year or so earlier. As government officials we were not allowed to have any formal political involvements, but as a strong Labour supporter I was delighted that I would now work for a Labour administration. I was not sorry to see the back of Duncan Sandys, from whom I got a rather perfunctory handshake, and a pleasant letter of good wishes for my future career: he didn't mention my walk. Now I had to get to know my new political bosses. Principal of these was Arthur Bottomley, MP for Middlesborough East (the seat that Ellen Wilkinson won as the first ever woman Labour MP in the 1924 election that unseated the minority Labour Government). Arthur, an East End working class boy, had made his political career though the trade union movement, local politics in Walthamstow, and the patronage of his then Walthamstow MP, Clement Attlee, who gave him middle level Ministerial office in the 1945-51 Labour Governments. Now Secretary of State, he was supported by the rather more capable Minister of State, Welsh MP Cledwyn Hughes. The kindest thing to say about Arthur is that he was a nice, well-intentioned man, a shrewd and experienced union and party politician, but a poor public speaker and more than a little out of his depth as a senior Cabinet Minister. On their very first morning in office, I had to listen in on a telephone call from Harold Wilson: "Good morning, Commonwealth Secretary," said Wilson solemnly: "Good morning, Prime Minister," replied Arthur gravely: they then broke into what can only be described as a fit of schoolboy giggles. The Permanent Under Secretary, Joe Garner, could also ill-conceal his pleasure; excluded from the Secretary of State's office for several weeks after falling out with Sandys, he was knocking impatiently at the door on the first afternoon of Arthur Bottomley's reign. Arthur quite welcomed this: he told me that on his 1947 Ministerial appointment as Secretary of Overseas Trade in the Board of Trade, he sat alone in his office all day, waiting for someone to come in and tell him what to do, but no-one did. Now, Arthur had got off to another rather unfortunate start when he went to the Palace to kiss hands on his appointment to the Cabinet. He had opted to wear a rather tired old dinner suit, now strained to the limit by his rubicund figure. Bowing low before the Queen, he was (by his own account afterwards) horrified to hear a ripping sound at the rear, and his decision to retreat backwards from the royal presence was dictated by embarrassment rather than protocol.

It was easy to see the change in the way business was now conducted. While formerly, even the most minor decisions had to go through Sandys, senior officials now confidently took back large swathes of policy responsibility, sensing that they were dealing with a more malleable and easy-going ministerial personality. In many cases this actually lead to improved conduct of affairs, for as I have argued, Sandys' bullying and opinionated style often produced flawed policy outcomes, and he had little understanding of or sympathy with the numerous new 'nationalist' politicians he had to deal with from Africa, the Caribbean, and Yemen. While constrained by Macmillan's recognition of the inevitability of decolonisation, as exemplified in his 'wind of change' speech, Sandys' natural political sympathies lay with white settler communities in Southern and East Africa, and with traditional conservative elements in Rhodesia and South Africa. The incoming Labour government took a more radical and determined line in the face of settler resistance and obstruction, and the Rhodesian independence question now dominated overseas affairs. Prime Minister Harold Wilson made the running on this issue, while Arthur was consigned to deal with more routine policy areas. He could be very indecisive and many papers presented to him still remained unresolved at the end of the working day, mercifully much shorter than under Sandys. This meant they would be shovelled into a red despatch box, for Arthur to work on at home. To our surprise these night boxes were dealt with confidently and efficiently, with little marginal notes that we discerned were not in Arthur's sprawling hand. We deduced that another hand was in play here, that of Arthur's wife Bessie, formidable Chair of Walthamstow Council: we didn't intervene, since she was evidently doing a good job.

Arthur still had one priceless moment to endure, when he went off overseas to make a speech at the Zambia Independence celebrations, the political leader there, Kenneth Kaunda, being an old friend of his. Arthur was not at his best on these highly formal occasions, and he stuck closely to the sheets of text drafted for him. Addressing a large assembly of political dignitaries and serried ranks of diplomats and officials, he came to the peroration in honour of Zambia's manifest destiny: "... and so, dear friends, we depart, leaving the future in the hands of you noble..." here he turned to a new page, hesitated as he found himself staring at a blank sheet, and stumbled on: "... you noble savages," he concluded. Happily, given the erratic performance of the public address system, many of his audience assumed that the Secretary of State could not possibly have said what they thought they had heard, but it was a story soon gleefully doing the Whitehall rounds. Arthur did not long survive these ordeals, but kept in touch with me in a most friendly way, and it gave him great pleasure to be translated to the House of Lords in 1984 (the formidable Bessie had been earlier rewarded with a Dame of the British Empire in 1970, presumably for her work in social services rather than on Arthur's Ministerial box).

I'd soon be doing a Whitehall move myself, as the custom was to change Private Secretaries when there was a change of government: and in any case, I had been in this post for a good eighteen months. I had now been elevated to the rank of Second Secretary, and I was told that it was intended that I should go out to Southern Rhodesia to be the aide de camp to the putative new High Commissioner, Sir John Johnstone, who interviewed me and confirmed the position. But at this point I experienced something of a personal crisis, born of a growing awareness of what a career almost permanently overseas would mean. I felt that I would in effect leave my parents and sisters behind: and was keenly aware too that any children I had in this future would on current practise then be sent back to Britain to a boarding school education at a very tender age, a thought I found repellent. A final consideration was a growing realisation that the diplomatic life overseas would not be to my liking, with its emphasis on protocol, and an endless, repetitive social round alongside a

Foreign Office elite still overwhelmingly from an upper class I was not much at ease with, 'the chandelier world of official dinner parties and embassy receptions' as Sampson puts it. That long line of peace marchers had left me with a restless feeling that politically and socially, I was on the wrong side of a significant fence. Unsure what my next step should be, I decided to buy time by applying for a transfer to the Home Civil Service and this was reluctantly accepted once it was clear that I would not change my mind. Most of my friends thought me mad: many people would have fed arsenic to their grannies to get into the exclusive and prestigious Diplomatic Service, at a time when people of my age and level could have reasonable expectations of Ambassadorial appointments. My dear old schoolteacher friends had a different and critical response: how would these elitist institutions ever change if people like me left them? But I was adamant, even though I had to accept a transfer to an unlikely, if senior Ministry, the then Board of Trade, since someone there had won the contest between many candidates to swap places with me. One of the ironies of this situation was that the putative High Commissioner never took up his intended post, robbed of this when Ian Smith unilaterally and illegally declared Rhodesia's own independence. I might well have been obliged to leave the country almost as soon as I had set foot in it.

But I had not done with Foreign and Commonwealth affairs just yet. Quite suddenly and unexpectedly, in the summer of 1965, I was appointed Secretary General of the Mauritius Independence Conference, just about to take place in London. When I recently found (in the National Archives) the file about my appointment, it seems to have been intended to break a deadlock between the Colonial Office and the Mauritian political leaders, the latter wanting an impartial head of the conference administration i.e. someone not attached to the Colonial Office, who for their part wanted someone with appropriate experience of decolonisation and the Whitehall system. I was regarded as fitting the bill because I was serving out my notice of resignation from the FCO, and so at a stretch could be presented as 'independent'. A file minute declares that running a major conference required a strong and efficient character and the ability to work long and exhausting hours: in the margin a scrawled handwritten note says 'we have just the chap!'

This was a fascinating experience, since all my previous involvement had been in decolonisation negotiations masterminded by Duncan Sandys. Now I would have a new political boss in Colonial Secretary Anthony Greenwood, son of the famous Labour stalwart Arthur Greenwood ('speak for England,

*At Mauritius Independence Conference from left, Sir John Rennie, Governor of Mauritius, Anthony Greenwood, Colonial Secretary, me as Secretary General of the Conference.*

*Mauritius Independence Conference at Lancaster House, London 1965.*

Arthur!') assisted by Lord Shepherd, his Minister of State. My job was to sit beside them in various meetings and manage the whole administration and efficient running of the Conference, in consultation with the principally Colonial Office officials with whom I was already accustomed to working. Mauritius, a small Indian Ocean island, presented some difficulty which had created a combustible set of political antagonisms between numerous ethnic groups; Hindus, Muslims, white Franco-Mauritians, a mixed race 'creole' population, and Chinese. The recent past had been spattered with inter-communal conflicts, often very violent. Since none of these groups trusted each other, the Colonial Office imperative was to construct an Independence Constitution which safeguarded ethnic minorities, while allowing effective majority government to be established. We had a leading constitutional expert to advise us, Professor S. A. de Smith, as well as the experienced and canny Governor of Mauritius, Sir John Rennie. Many hours were spent poring over constitutional drafts, in meetings between the contending parties, and all too often indignant walk-outs by one or other of them.

In the event, the independence question was decided at the last minute, and at a somewhat higher level, when a small British cabal, presumably including Prime Minister Harold Wilson, did a secret deal with the

Mauritian majority leader, Sir Seewoosagur Ramgoolam: the British would concede independence if Ramgoolam would agree to hand over to Britain the relatively unknown island of Diego Garcia, henceforth to be titled the British Indian Ocean Territory. In compensation Mauritius would get the paltry sum of £3 million. According to Cabinet records, this ploy had been agreed in principle by both Conservative and successor Labour Cabinets. The real British purpose here was to lease the island to the Americans as an Indian Ocean airbase, a stratagem that would ultimately attract all kinds of obloquy and international inquiries, not least because it meant the forcible displacement from the Chagos archipelago of a number of Diego Garcian inhabitants, whose existence was denied for many years: at least a third of these people were second generation residents, not merely migrant workers, and eventually found themselves living in slum conditions in Mauritius. Despite much international criticism, and legal judgements in favour of these native 'Ilois', the situation now, some fifty years later, is essentially unchanged. For the Americans, Diego Garcia is a significant strategic air base for their varied interventions in the Middle East, and there have been recent claims that political prisoners from Afghanistan and Iraq were the subject of so called rendition (through Diego Garcia) to territories ready to torture such prisoners outside America, but on America's behalf. The secretive British role in all this is poorly documented, but does them little credit, and remains a matter of angry political contention. I am happy to be able to say that while this crucial decision was made under my nose, I had not the faintest inkling of it, being told only that the independence issue was now politically decided, and I could help to draw the formalities of the Conference to a close. The Mauritian opposition parties who had not wanted independence, but some form of continued association with Britain, were angered, and alienated from the Conference decisions. They walked out. Unsurprisingly, when Independence was finally celebrated in 1968, three years on and after violent protests in Mauritius, it was to the sound of British soldiers' boots on the streets of Port Louis, the capital. Three years after that, in 1971, no longer in the FCO but there, as an academic, to assist the development of the new University of Mauritius, it was to find that all the political parties had joined together in a grand coalition, sharing out the ministerial jobs and perks, which generally speaking was what all the acrimony was about in the first place; there's a damning indictment of the corrupt and personalist nature of Mauritian politics at this time in V. S .Naipaul's *The Overcrowded Barracoon.*

Back in 1965, the FCO had not yet quite done with me. Barely had I got my feet under a Board of Trade desk than I was summoned by an old FCO colleague, Tom Astin, to be a member of the Secretariat that would staff the forthcoming (January 1966) Commonwealth Prime Ministers Meeting in Lagos, Nigeria. Here, Harold Wilson would have to face much criticism over Rhodesia, which to many African leaders appeared to be getting away too easily with its self-declared independence under a white minority leadership. In Lagos, on the way from the airport to the luxurious Federal Palace Hotel, we passed several lorry-loads of army trucks packed with grim faced soldiers. There had been serious troubles in the Western Region of the country, and the tensions in the air were palpable. But the Conference of Prime Ministers got under way, and I was too busy taking notes and minutes of meetings to notice much else. My only respite was usually a solitary early breakfast on an enormous garden terrace, but even this became less than relaxed when I was joined by my former CRO boss, Joe Garner, stiff and never really at ease with anyone his junior, though he had the grace to be politely puzzled about my presence, thinking me to have abandoned the Diplomatic Service.

When the conference was over, having decide to expel Rhodesia from the Commonwealth and apply economic sanctions, the foreign bigwigs departed and I was deputed to help Tom Astin wind up the administrative side. I noticed that the hotel was now drowned in top brass uniforms, and that there were soldiers everywhere in the hotel grounds. The next morning I flew out of Lagos, my destination Hamburg, on the way to stay with my old friend Marlis, who met me at the airport, bursting with excitement: "We thought you might be dead!" During my long flight back to Europe, a military coup had erupted in Lagos; the Federal Premier, Sir Abubakar Tafawa Balewa, someone I often saw in meetings, had been assassinated, along with many of his senior army officers, and a General Ironsi had taken power. Some on the government side had been shot in the Federal Palace Hotel itself. I had missed all this by the skin of my teeth, and thought that perhaps the Board of Trade might, after all, be a rather safer place to be.

Safer it certainly was, and tedious to a degree. My heart wasn't really in all the detailed trade and commercial issues which was the BOT's daily diet. I quite soon got on the wrong side of my immediate superior, Elizabeth Llewellyn Smith. An Oxford highflyer, Elizabeth was extremely clever, highly conscientious, but very buttoned up and personally unbending: brilliant on detail, she seemed to have little interest in the wider policy picture. I was the opposite, quick to see the policy implications and nuances, but inclined to brush over any inconvenient detail. We simply didn't see eye to eye. Frustrated by what she saw as an unhelpful colleague, Elizabeth first objected to me wearing a suit not the regulation black (having fallen into the FCO habit of wearing more casual suiting on a Friday, ready for the weekend). When our immediate boss, Assistant Secretary Peter Carey, asked me one day if I had a problem working with women, I was very taken aback, this not having remotely occurred to me. I realised that I had never before worked with a woman supervising me, other than my mother, and I had certainly had problems with her; but on careful reflection felt able to assure Peter that a personality clash was involved here, not a gender issue. I was lucky to find myself working with and learning from his calm decisiveness, and he was quick to give me responsibility for tasks which happily distanced me somewhat from the acerbic Miss Llewellyn Smith. Peter was directly responsible for managing relations with regional Board of Trade offices, and so for a huge swathe of industrial policy in declining areas. I was astonished to discover that he had never once visited the North East or North West where most of these areas were to be found and urged him to do so. When he returned from a subsequent tour, he confided to me: "You were right, it's not at all like Guildford."

I had already become more than a little disillusioned with the excessively bureaucratic ways of working in the home ministries of Whitehall, and chafed at the likelihood that I could not expect to be given any real responsibility for policymaking for at least another five years. I fear my FCO experiences, right at the top and centre of power, had spoiled me for the day-to-day grind of other Whitehall departments, much more bound by precedent and formal procedural rules, more oriented to predominantly legalistic and bureaucratic tasks. I was only allowed to get into Parliament once, to brief George Darling, Minister of State at the Board of Trade (a man after my own heart, a former railways worker who managed to get into higher education, acquired an MA in Economics from Cambridge, and made his way into Parliament through the Cooperative Wholesale Society as Labour and Cooperative MP for Sheffield Hillsborough). The excitement this little spell at the parliamentary coalface generated in me made me realise that the bureaucratic grind was not for me. In retrospect, though, I was extraordinarily fortunate in the people I worked with in the Board of Trade. Peter Carey would become Sir Peter Carey, Permanent Secretary at the Department of Industry and have a famous stand-off with his Minister, Tony Wedgwood Benn, signing a formal note of dissent from his Minister, something of a rarity in Whitehall governance:

on his retirement in 1983 he declared that he had spent two decades trying to convince Whitehall mandarins of the importance to Britain of industry. Someone else I often worked with, a bright young Principal called Peter Gregson who expertly guided me through the complexities of turning policy decisions into arcane bits of legislation, would one day become Sir Peter Gregson, Permanent Secretary to what by then had become the Department of Trade and Industry. My *bête noire*, Elizabeth Llewellyn Smith, rose up the hierarchy to the very senior post of Deputy Secretary, then left the civil service to be the Principal of St Hilda's College Oxford, my sister Sally's college, at a time when it resolutely remained the only single sex college in Oxford: I still cannot imagine her being other than a dour and distant presence there, unless she had greatly changed her spots. But it is interesting now to see what heights were reached by those I worked closely with in my Whitehall years. Most of my FCO contemporaries reached distinguished positions, at Ambassadorial or High Commissioner level. Peter Moon was knighted, as was Nick Fenn, my opposite number in the Foreign Secretary's Private Office. Thorold Masefield, another of our class of '62, held High Commissioner posts in Nigeria and Tanzania and at his retirement was Governor of Bermuda. Stanley Duncan, a charming drinking companion befriended in Central African Office days, was Ambassador to Bolivia and High Commissioner in Malta. My fellow Resident Clerk and Private Office successor, Christian Adams, ended his career as Ambassador to Laos. My fellow junior Private Secretary, Dennis Doble, to my astonishment, became Deputy High Commissioner in Jamaica, then Consul General in the Netherlands: I find it difficult to imagine anyone more buttoned-up English and further removed from the down to earth bonhomie of the Dutch, or the anarchic characteristics of Jamaica's diverse and lively culture. My friend Michael James might have been a more natural appointment to that cricket-mad country, but after varied experiences in Sri Lanka, Guyana, and Ghana, held Deputy High Commissioner posts in Singapore and Barbados. Very fittingly, Robin Gorham's final resting place was as Head of Protocol, a position he seemed to have spent his whole early career preparing for. Another contemporary recruit, Chris Macrae, who once warned me priggishly at an office Christmas party that fraternising with pretty but lower-class secretaries would harm my chances of advancement, held High Commissioner posts in Nigeria and Pakistan, and secured a knighthood: evidently he had followed his own advice.

As for myself I had deliberately chosen to neglect such grand possibilities, and it was time for me to move on. Hugh had now qualified as a solicitor, had been promoted to a junior partner, and would in due course be a mightily successful Senior Partner in his expanding City law firm, Biddle and Co; more to the point, he was soon going to marry Marie-Odile, a young upper-class Frenchwoman, and would leave the Gatehouse. Their delightful high society wedding in Versailles is another story for another time. Quentin was already well on the way to an exceptional and internationally distinguished academic career. As for me, I too would now tread the academic path, as Lecturer in Politics and Government at the University of Kent. I don't know how my lectures on British Government were regarded there: but at least I had some good stories to tell.

# Chapter Seventeen

# Social Difference and Social Change: Back to the Future?

*Condition of England writing constantly reminds us that the nurturing soil of social injustice is inattention, ignorance and unconcern. The moralist calls on the reader to look and to focus.*
Stefan Collini

The idea of 'condition of England' writing originated with Thomas Carlyle, writing in the troubled 1830s and 1840s, responding to what he saw as the deeply damaging social effects of the Industrial Revolution. This theme would later be taken up by novelists such as Elizabeth Gaskell (Mary Barton) and Charles Dickens (Hard Times), detailing the appalling social conditions and poverty of the urban working classes. This response lead on to the notion of a society of 'two nations', with huge inequalities between those who owned land, capital and other institutional resources (a small minority) and an underprivileged, poverty-stricken class of the working poor (an overwhelming majority.) I have deliberately set this personal and family memoir in a 'condition of England' framework, using the lived experiences of one extended working class family to explore more general themes of continued and sometimes deep poverty, and expanded forms of inequality. This is now, of course, and perhaps always was, more properly a 'condition of Britain' question. In this final chapter I identify the persistence right up to the first quarter of the twenty first century of socially advantaged groups and institutions, entrenching a world of unequal social opportunities, life chances and wealth. Over the last hundred years or so, much has changed, sometimes (but not always) for the better, while much has remained the same.

## Shifting classes

The definition of class has always been beset by difficulties in British discourse. The traditional language used to differentiate between classes, and the object of 1960s satire, was itself informed by particular social prejudices: clearly an 'upper' class must be superior to the 'lower' classes, with the rather vague 'middle' class looking downwards with disdain, and upwards with respect. The lower class was expected to show deference to both classes above them: 'I know my place'. But these older certainties have given way to problems over nomenclature, categorisation, and identity. By the time we reach the second part of the twentieth century, we need to be alert to the increased porousness and complexity of class groupings, with considerable movement within and between each traditional class, and no little confusion over self-perceptions of class identity. The notion of a collective 'working class' begins to be strained and unconvincing, or at the very least inclines to be a catch-all category into which we lump together some disparate bedfellows. My initial interest in this memoir, set in the first half of the twentieth century, was to examine the idea of a *rural* working class, the implication being that this would not look like an urban working class. This at once raises issues of difference and similarity, and therefore of comparability. There is a substantial and deeply contested literature on the working class (and thereby on the relations between identifiable classes, and on the institutional structures that produce, maintain and reify class groups). It is not my intention here to rehearse this literature, but rather to reflect on the meaning of my own experiences as someone who grew up in and with traditional working class families, both urban and rural, but moved on to gain some familiarity with other traditional British classes, and arguably 'shifted classes' myself, at a time when classes themselves were shifting and changing.

In 1957, aged nineteen, and at the end of my formal schooling prior to University, I had a strong awareness of contemporary working class history picked up from my parents, and supported by some secondary texts, but this was a patchy and unfocussed sort of learning, the most enlightening sources being Robert Tressell *(The Ragged Trousered Philanthropists)* and George Orwell (*Down and Out in Paris and London; The Road to Wigan Pier).* Both writers chose to write in literary rather than analytical forms, and neither were working class authors, Orwell yet another Etonian, though unusually trying to experience and record the social and economic conditions of one segment of the poor. Given my own links to the mining class, I was amused by his feeling declaration that such hard labour would have killed him in a very short time: and he fetches a telling blow on all those better off classes who would sit in coal fire-warmed drawing rooms and parlours without a thought for those whose dangerous and back-breaking work produced this comfort. I had also read, as part of my sixth form work, the classic historical studies of rural and industrial labour by J.L. and Barbara Hammond, and political essays by the Fabians Sidney and Beatrice Webb. I had a copy of *The Communist Manifesto*, though nothing else by Marx or Engels. Later, in my University studies in the early 1960s, I would read R.H. Tawney's influential *Religion and the Rise of Capitalism,* and Harold Laski's *Liberty and the Modern State*, but few of my studies at Cambridge related to nineteenth and twentieth century Britain. It would be a whole decade later before I would catch up with the significant work of Raymond Williams and E.P. Thompson. While these admittedly eclectic sources were, of course, apposite in terms of a generalised working class historiography, they had a very limited bearing on my own contemporary working class experience.

However significant in the history of British socialism, none of these writers (except Williams) were themselves working class in origin, or could draw on an experience they themselves had lived and could use to inform their work. So it was a seminal moment for me, as it turns out to have been for many others, that I read (while enduring National Service) Richard Hoggart's *The Uses of Literacy: Aspects of Working Class Life* (1958). Here was an account of the working class by someone with genuinely working class origins, in a part of a Northern industrial working class landscape (Hunslet in Leeds) known to me, and who had also been through the socially disorienting experience of a predominantly middle class grammar school, followed by a largely middle class University (Leeds). At the first reading, in 1959, I was struck powerfully by the realisation that here was no middle class intellectual examining the working class through an inevitably distant social telescope: this was someone who had grown up in a working class home and had an emotional understanding of the many facets of a working class environment. On reaching his chapter on 'the uprooted and the anxious', an anatomy of the unease that a 'scholarship boy' would experience as he moved between a working class home and a predominantly middle class educational and social environment, the limits such a dislocation would place upon him, the guilty and anxious feelings that would constrict his ability to achieve a happy and fulfilled realisation of his opportunities, I felt a thrill of recognition. Much of this chapter resonated with my own divided feelings and sense of identity while at grammar school, as it has done with many other successful grammar school boys (there are girls there too if you look for them e.g. Lorna Sage's *Bad Blood,* but although girls were present at Hoggart's grammar school, they find little place in Hoggart's account). Here, clearly, was a man who had been in the same place as me, for how otherwise could he so readily recognise and describe this complicated set of feelings? How could he know, otherwise, the loneliness of this kind of long distance educational runner? And I recognised in myself his claim: 'I am from the working class and feel even now both closer to them and apart from them'.

Some six decades later, I still feel grateful to Hoggart for helping me to recognise and come to terms with my own difficult experiences. But a recent, even-handed, and properly admiring biography of Hoggart (Fred Inglis: *Richard Hoggart: Virtue and Reward:*2014) sent me back to *The Uses of Literacy,* and I found in myself a more critical response. My reservations are principally to do with Hoggart's characterisation of the working class, and emerge from the experiences set out in this memoir. There were some judgements here that were not reflected in my own experience. He implies that those working class boys who were socially upwardly mobile would not all have identical experiences, for those who progressed on to higher levels of education and reward, would be (in ways that are not really explained) what he terms 'declassed': I take this to mean that they would no longer have any attachment to or identification with the working class, while at the same time having no attachment to or identity with the (presumably) middle class into which they were now upwardly mobile. In her introduction to the 2009 edition of *The Uses of Literacy,* Lynsey Hanley comments that 'it is a testament to [Hoggart's] authority that he doesn't have to discuss his own class status'. Speaking from the standpoint of my own experience of challenging social class relationships, I find this surprising. As a scholarship boy he would clearly have had reason to reflect on the differences of his background from those around him, as he would have been in even more of a social minority than I was twenty years or so later. Moreover, he would have been in the same situation at University: even if Leeds was not so class-bound as Oxford and Cambridge, his fellow students would have been overwhelmingly middle class at that time (the late 1930s) as would almost all of his teachers. My own experience of this kind of social movement leads me to think that you never truly escape from the tensions and fragmented identities involved. If you shift between classes, which class *do* you belong to? If your family remains unequivocally and identifiably in the 'working class', do you, in leaving that class behind, inevitably leave your family behind? If you do not leave them behind, or other elements and relationships in your own earlier working class childhood and youth, are you not still in some significant sense working class, even while enjoying the accoutrements and status of the middle class? Or are you now a kind of hybrid social person, able to participate in either social grouping but not completely at ease, or fully accepted, in either? Keeping to my personal interpretation, it is only quite late in my life that these matters have ceased to trouble me, an experience confirmed in other accounts of a similar social journey, and I find it unlikely that Hoggart can have been untroubled by them.

Hoggart clearly remained strongly attuned to the working class and cared deeply about the effects of modern mass communications on working class cultural perceptions and behaviour: and he spent much of his career involved in adult working class education. But he has been criticised for taking a romantic and nostalgic view of the working class, before going on to lament how that older working class culture was in danger of being coarsened, even lost. Selina Todd, in her passionate narrative of the past century of British working class history, recounts her own working class family history, set in the same Leeds industrial district (Hunslet) as Hoggart's and comments: 'their experience didn't reflect the idyll of romantic respectability described by Hoggart' (*Todd: The People: The Rise and Fall of The Working Class* 2015:2). Relying on my own experience of a geographically close but admittedly quite separate part of the Yorkshire working class, I too have difficulty in recognising Hoggart's characterisation, even allowing for the difference in period. Hoggart paints for us a picture drawn mainly from industrial South Leeds. There's no mistaking the bleakness of that setting: Hunslet at that time would have been apt for a Yorkshire Lowry, perhaps exemplified by the town 'moor' made of cinders. But while the physical urban industrial environments of Britain were quite similar, their social make-ups were distinctive and varied. As shown in this memoir, I was familiar with one of these environments, the Tyneside industrial suburban town of Wallsend-on-Tyne, built largely on coal mines and shipyards, replete with row upon row of unlovely back street terraces (as indeed was Leeds). Briefly, I went to school there, in a grim building with the air of a former poor house or prison. Yes, there was here Hoggart's prized sense of the strength and warmth of family, street and community; but I recall just as clearly the signs of poverty and need, the run down physical environment, the distinctive balls of the ubiquitous pawn shop, the anger, the strong and continuing feelings of social inequality and injustice, released in a passionate and articulate independent-mindedness which was the foundation stone of Tyneside's working class politics. The anger, and indeed the politics, seem not to have existed in Hoggart's working class, siphoned off by him to a 'respectable' segment of trade unionists who are not given further analysis. Missing, too, is any real sense of class divisions and tensions, which in the Wallsend case produced a strong class consciousness rooted in the bitter conflicts with the largely upper middle class mine owners and shipyard magnates, not just in the 1920s and 1930s, but well back into the nineteenth century. This bit of the north east of England took part in the long and lone continuation by the miners of the General Strike of 1926; and a decade later initiated the famous 1936 march of unemployed Jarrow workers to London, where Prime Minister Stanley Baldwin refused to meet them. When they returned wearily to Jarrow, many were refused unemployment benefit because they had made themselves unavailable for (non-existent) work. Even in the 1950s, now themselves becoming at last a bit better off, these communities, and families like mine, would still recall bitterly and discuss cogently the poverty and unemployment of those earlier decades, the despair of trying to feed hungry children, the bitter humiliations of the dreaded 'means test'. These were not people who could not handle ideas, or only ones so simplified as to be mere slogans, which Hoggart claims to be characteristic of working class people; and I am pleased to note that a survey of unemployed Welsh miners in 1938 'found unemployed men who discussed philosophy or read Balzac... [while] at Newport the Chief Librarian reported that 50 per cent of the unemployed read books on economics' (Branson and Heinemann: 65).

Here, then, is an example which to my mind gives a rather different picture from that drawn by Hoggart of the Leeds working class. You would obtain another different picture from, say, the heavily Roman Catholic working class section of Liverpool; another again from the mining communities of the South Wales valleys, different in kind (even in some cases in language) from the mining communities of the North East. We see significant cultural differences in the Scottish industrial labour force; and London certainly does not present a picture of a homogeneous working class, given the variations in occupation and culture (think Cockney dockers, Jewish East End tailors, the large group of primarily female domestic servants). In short, there seem to have been, arguably, several urban working classes, not one nationally uniform one, so that generalising from any one example is bound to raise difficulties for teasing out answers to those key questions addressed by Hoggart in the opening chapter of *The Uses of Literacy:* who are the working class? And what is its culture? I do not see how these questions can be fully addressed if class structures, class relationships and class conflicts are set aside. Moreover, in the urban industrial context, these class relationships were in large part expressed by and through political organisation: on the workers' side through their organised unions, on the owner-employer side sometimes by direct local collaboration e.g. local agreements to lock out protesting or striking workers, but at a more strategic level through control and manipulation of the powers of the state, and the related institutions of the policing and criminal justice system. In turn, workers and unions attached themselves to organised parties, initially the Liberals, later the Labour Party, while the better off classes largely supported and inhabited the Conservative Party. Class war was fought out both in the workplace, at the level of local institutions, and at the overarching heights of national political and administrative bodies. There are many examples of how workers might win at the national level, but still lose out at the local and workplace level. An individual example was provided in this memoir of the local squire and Conservative politician vindictively punishing my father for openly acting for the Labour Party in the 1945 election; and again, in the early 1950s when a leading peer of the realm precipitately and for no defensible reason threw my family, including me, out of our house. A more generalised example was seen at the time of the 1906 election, when large numbers of farm workers who had openly campaigned for and supported victorious Liberal Party candidates were instantly turned out of their tied houses by vengeful Conservative-supporting employers.

## The rural working class

> *Agricultural workers are a group of whom most people have little knowledge or understanding* Howard Newby

The biggest change in the working classes over the twentieth century has been the decline and now virtual disappearance of the farm labouring class. In the twentieth century this rural segment of the working class has received relatively little attention from historians, and the focus of this memoir on the lives and experiences of one agricultural labouring family is intended in part to provide some colour and illumination in a historical grey area. The history of this rural working class summons up a sense of oddity and disjointedness, for rural labour and its class relations has received considerable attention and analysis of changes up to the 1830s, but relatively sparse treatment thereafter. The profound changes in British economy and society that we have come to label both the Industrial Revolution and the First Agricultural Revolution proceeded virtually in tandem in the eighteenth and early nineteenth centuries; a predominantly rural and agrarian society and economy was transformed by technological changes and changes in production processes, both for goods and food. Related changes in land ownership and land use resulted in the enclosures of land to the detriment of common rights. Both this loss of customary rights and changes in farming technologies and practices adversely affected the rural labour force, already poorly paid and increasingly casualised or unemployed.

While farm owners and tenants mostly benefited from these changes, farm labour did not. There were two main effects of this. First, rural labour was increasingly sucked away into the growing industrial towns and their factories: second, those who stayed behind rebelled against their declining conditions and opportunities. Both processes have been well documented, with significant work by J. L. and Barbara Hammond, especially *The Village Labourer* (published in 1911, the year of my farm worker father's birth, though he never to my knowledge read it). This volume (the first of three) has a particularly sympathetic account of the so called 'Last Labourers' Revolt' of 1830. More recent analysis by E. P. Thompson,and Hobsbawm and Rude, gives a more radically oriented view of this and other 1830s rural disturbances and machine-breaking, seeing them as having potentially revolutionary inspiration and intentions. This interpretation, of course, precisely reflects that of the governing authorities of the time, and helps to explain their notably harsh responses, with 19 convicted people executed , many hundreds imprisoned, and some 480 transported to Australia.

Was this a version of class war? It is difficult to avoid such an interpretation. The ruling landed class, dominating both the central state and its attendant county institutions, had already used the military (a combination of local Yeomanry and the 15th Hussars) to crush urban protests at the 'massacre' of Peterloo in 1819. A decade or so later they did not hesitate to use the full powers of the criminal justice system to defend their rural interests. Yet this was surely an over-reaction: the 1830 'revolt' might be seen as a particularly deep-throated cry to the ruling class for some recognition for the desperate economic and social hardships endured by rural workers, rather than a call to revolution. Dorsetshire labourers, the famous Tolpuddle martyrs, would also be transported, essentially for daring to combine to ask for wage increases, and were victims of the same Home Secretary, Lord Melbourne. The landed aristocracy dominated government, and were determinedly brutal in these instances of suppression of the labourers who worked on their farms and estates. Both the Hammonds and E.P. Thompson effectively end their fascinating accounts in 1832, as if the Great Reform Act had solved all problems: yet, as we see, it was this same reforming administration which responded to rural protests with such cold-hearted repression, an aggressive state and dominating class response that continued through the troubled 1840s and 1850s.

The second half of the nineteenth century brought a steady trickle of political reforms that also enabled the development of genuine trade unionism and the pursuit by workers of responsible collective action for better wages and conditions for working people. Farm workers joined in, with a rash of regional unions and the most successful, led by Joseph Arch, established as the National Agricultural Labourers' Union. This all ended badly in 1874, with the 'Revolt of the Field ', when farm workers striking for an extra shilling on their very low wages were 'locked out' by the concerted action of employers, testimony, as social historian Howard Newby puts it, 'to the continued strength of rural patriarchal rule'; and Arch's broken Union was dissolved in 1886. But the extension of the vote to most (though not all) adult male workers under the 1884-5 Reform legislation gave an impetus to political action on behalf of all workers, male and female, and including farm workers. The embrace of this cause, first by the Liberal Party and the Independent Labour Party at the turn of the century, then soon the Labour Party, buttressed a political activism that would finally produce Labour governments and the post-1945 welfare state. But while the 'aristocracy of labour' ultimately successfully used trade union power and political influence to win office and underpin a redistributive 'tax and spend' strategy, many working class people were still left behind. This included an ever-declining rural labour force. E. P. Thompson tells us that in 1830, rural workers constituted 28% of all households. While agricultural labour statistics are problematic (depending whether or not you count in part-time and casual workers, or small farmers working their own farms), in 1931 the whole farm labour force stood at some 13% of the total manual work force, and nationally, farm workers were then the largest single occupational group, followed by domestic servants. But by 1948 farm labour was down to about 5% of the national workforce, and in 2015 stood at 1%. In numbers, farm labour fell from just over 1 million in 1901 to 120,000 in 2015. This figure is likely to reduce even further, partly because of the difficulty of replacing an ageing workforce: the average age of workers on farms now, including small farm owners, is 59 years. A 'push' factor was due to technology, as tractors replaced horses and combine harvesters replaced the old horse and tractor-driven binders: in 1950 there were still 300,000 horses on farms, in 1979 only 3,575. We might say that the machine breakers of the early 1830s had been prescient in predicting a real threat to their livelihoods. A 'pull' factor was, inevitably, the attraction of better paid jobs in urban factories.

An Independent Labour Party pamphlet in 1913 described farm workers as 'the most backward class of workers': throughout the nineteenth century, and well into the twentieth century, rural wages reached only half of average manual wages. Patchily implemented reforms in the 1920s and 1930s raised the proportion to about two thirds, and this continued to be the case in the 1950s post war period. The further advance of agricultural technology steadily stripped away labour, leaving agricultural labour unions weak and ineffectual. Tied houses not only remained intact, but were the lot of an increased proportion of the work force (53% in 1976, compared with 34% in 1948) though with the cost of housing constantly rising, tied housing had become a *quid pro quo* for low wages. In 1955 farm workers earned one third less than transport workers, and 40 per cent less than building workers. With more prosperous general economic conditions from the 1960s onwards, the standard of living rose for farm workers and their families (as it did generally) and they continued to benefit from the established 'welfare state' reforms of the two immediate post-war Labour governments. Nonetheless, their incomes remained stubbornly adrift of the national norms for manual workers, fluctuating between 65% and 80% of average national wages over the second half of the twentieth century. Moreover, average weekly wages for farm workers contained a substantial component for overtime, so that these low overall incomes entailed working on average a 47-hour week. Farm workers were described as being, in 1984, the worst paid workers in Britain. It is chastening to find from official figures that in 2013, their wages were still a third less on average than overall national manual wages, much the same as they had been for my father seventy years earlier. Moreover, the 1948 Agricultural Workers Board that had given some protection to the wages and conditions of farm workers was abolished in 2013, with a clear weakening of those protections. Recent research has shown that a significantly casual, largely immigrant workforce has suffered from some shameful, often illegal, employment practices. Meanwhile, owners were, notoriously, 'feather-bedded' in the post war period, increasingly so with benefits from the European Union's Common Agricultural Policy after British entry in 1973.

Later changes to that policy, tying subsidy to the extent of land holdings, gave huge cash bonuses to large land-holders, which included the monarchy (largest of all) and significant numbers of the land-owning upper classes, a reminder of the continuing existence of class-based privilege.

## The persistence of class privilege

> *To those who have shall be given. If you have nothing, even the little you have is taken away from you*
> Amit Chaudhuri: *Friend of My Youth*

The dry statistics that support my outline picture of change in agricultural communities over the past century or so, and the broader canvas of general levels of adult and child poverty in Britain today, tell us little about the painful and oppressive lived experience of poverty, hardship, inequality and social injustice suffered by poor and disadvantaged workers and their families. As E. P. Thompson wrote: 'it is quite possible for statistical averages and human experiences to run in opposite directions'. As so often instanced in this memoir, poverty was not just a matter of income, but of the hard grind that comes with a low income, with never having enough money to meet the most basic needs, the misery that comes with being unable to clothe and feed your children adequately, or to protect their healthy development, and until mid-century the financial burden that sickness would bring. Until the post war welfare reforms in the late 1940s, educational opportunities were almost non-existent, however intelligent or promising working class children might be. They were condemned to the same lives of unremitting hardship and poverty as their parents, and generations of their forebears. My family story suggests what a break in this vicious circle can produce: four of my extended family won places at Oxford and Cambridge, at least a further four or five went on to other universities, and all to successful professional careers. Can we doubt that innumerable talents were lost and unrealised in those preceding generations? I know that my own intelligent parents deserved better treatment and opportunities than our constricted, class-bound form of society was prepared to give them, but there were millions of such people like them who deserved better.

The political reforms of the nineteenth century gave encouragement to industrial trade unionism, which in the early twentieth century produced counterpart political organisation to represent the interests of workers.

War and economic depression combined around this time to produce what a major historian, David Cannadine (1992) labels 'the decline and fall of the British aristocracy', '... a triumphant tale of abuses remedied, hierarchy overturned, privilege rejected, vested interests vanquished, and oligarchy eliminated'. The experiences set down in this memoir suggest that this judgement was not universally applicable. Cannadine's fascinating work shows that the 'ruling class' was still well entrenched in the 1880s around the time of my Irish grandfather's birth, then details how its domination of society, economy and the state was undermined and (he argues) effectively destroyed by the steady decline of agricultural and land values over the next fifty years, and by the social dislocations and changes resulting from two world wars. The decline and demise of the Mowbray and Stourton estate on which both my grandfather and father were employed is a case repeated in many other parts of the country.

But we need to take note of the staying power demonstrated by this aristocracy, as I myself experienced this in the 1960s. At the FCO, one of the Ministers of State I worked with directly, for a short time as his Private Secretary, was Andrew Cavendish, 11th Duke of Devonshire. The Cavendish family had been the political placeholders in my grammar school town of Knaresborough in the eighteenth and nineteenth centuries. His father, the 10th Duke, until inheriting the title in 1935, virtually had in his gift the Unionist, then Conservative seat of West Derbyshire from the early 1920s. As we noted earlier, Andrew Devonshire was appointed to Ministerial office by his aunt's husband, Harold Macmillan. There is another personal link here: the punitive legislation used to crush the 'Last Labourers' Revolt' of 1830 was the work of the 5th Lord Lansdowne: he was also a member of the Special Commission in Salisbury in 1831, which handed down harsh transportation sentences to the hapless protesting farm workers, for which, according to the Hammonds' classic study, 'the chief shame attached to Lord Melbourne, who let the judges do their worst, and to Lansdowne, who sat beside the judges on the Salisbury bench.' In the 1960s, son of a farm worker myself, I would work closely with that Lansdowne's great-great-grandson, the 8th Marquess, in his role as Minister of State in the Colonial Office. Lansdowne still lived on the ancestral estate at Bowood in Wiltshire, and had family links to the Duke of Devonshire, who himself had inherited an Irish estate at Lismore, including many town properties left without inside lavatories and running water, much like the cottages not that far distant lived in by my Irish grandfather's family in the late 1880s. None of us working together in Whitehall knew this at the time, but our histories were in so many ways intertwined. Clearly some social change for the better had been achieved by my very presence at the topmost level of a great office of state: but nothing much had changed in the privileged positions and expectations of the aristocrats with whom I (very delicately) rubbed shoulders. As an entertaining memoir by George O'Brien about his early life in Lismore (1990) makes clear, Andrew Devonshire was only occasionally sighted in the 1950s, and had no intention of rubbing shoulders with any of the locals below the level of gentry, except as servants and estate workers; 'the Duke's dominion was a perfect and apparently indestructible embodiment of the soul of ownership: the dispossessed admiring, the fleeced kissing the shears'. And this, let us not forget, in an independent Ireland which thought itself to no longer labour under a British imperial presence.

Realistically, as Cannadine so ably and entertainingly demonstrates, the dominance of the British state by a few old landed families was already seriously eroded by the end of the Great War. Between the 1880s and the 1920s, the number of new peers increased by 25%, principally drawing much needed new money into the aristocratic system, which became notably more socially fluid. The role of the House of Lords was forever diminished after the 1911 constitutional crisis, while the Labour Party, the party of organised labour, after a number of starts and stutters, moved on to its astonishing and unexpected victory in 1945. The Conservative Party, meanwhile, increasingly sought working class support to buttress its natural upper and middle class constituency. This political progression suggests that class distinction and privilege was a thing of the past, but we need to give class a more nuanced characterisation for the second half of the twentieth century and beyond. My own progression into the Foreign and Commonwealth Office 'high flyer' group in 1962 might be seen as evidence of a new porousness of this elite institution, a new 'democratisation'; except that such an appointment of a man from the lowest rank of the working class was (and remains) extremely rare. In that same year, Anthony Sampson, in his path-breaking 1962 study of 'the Establishment', made much of what he regarded as a surprising number of members of the aristocracy in the Foreign Office, both Ministers and diplomats, and commented on a prevalent aristocratic ethos there; while Cannadine judges that 'in post-war administration ...the most aristocratic part of the civil service was the Foreign Office' . The disdainful and uncaring treatments by landed aristocrats of my forebears, and as late as the 1950s of my own immediate family, can be seen as the dying gasps of an outmoded system. But the inheritors of that system have often survived and prospered on the basis of careful protection of their property and sources of wealth. As you drive around the countryside, you will see the instantly recognisable stone or brick boundary walls of large landed estates at every turn, many still occupied by owners who in effect enjoy a welfare benefit through tax breaks and other public support. Raymond Williams puts it well: 'stand at any point and look at that land. Look at what those fields, those streams, those woods even today produce. Think it through as labour and see how long and systematic the exploitation and seizure must have been, to rear that many houses on that scale.' He might have added that many of those great country and town houses, and the privileges of their owners, were built with capital derived from slave owning plantations or related businesses and investments, a conjuncture now increasingly being laid bare by new research.

The scions of many of these supposedly declining aristocratic and upper middle class families still inhabit Eton and other elite public schools, seemingly untroubled by exorbitant boarding fees; still realise their expected entitlement to places at Oxford and Cambridge, the aristocratic ones at their favoured Oxford college of Christ Church (Charles Stourton one such), which according to Sampson admitted the largest proportion of public school boys (70%) and had the highest examination failure rate (8.2%). Nothing much changes: a 2018 survey of admissions to Oxford colleges shows that Christ Church had the poorest record in admitting non-white candidates. Using our most prestigious universities as a springboard, many upper class people, overwhelmingly male and white, still take up the political positions to which they feel themselves entitled, usually, though not exclusively, in the Conservative interest (I note that some of those enjoying political office in recent government administrations, from 2010 to 2019, are family members of the young Tories so prominent in my 1960s Cambridge years.) This is all unavoidably open enough. But the new 'hidden secret' of the continuation and strengthening of upper class power lies in the worlds of business and high finance, and most notably in the City of London. Cannadine details many examples of upper class men (whether aristocrats, gentry, or from wealthy upper middle class families) who pursue commercial and business interests, hold lucrative City appointments, and still have significant property and land holdings, a pattern that is also detailed in a recent 2014 'anatomy' of the establishment by Owen Jones, though Jones even-handedly excoriates some Labour Party examples . A 2019 study by Shrubsole shows that land ownership in England and Wales - 'our oldest, darkest, best-kept secret' - is dominated still by the aristocracy and gentry, maybe as much as half of the total. The next largest group is what Shrubsole characterises as 'a handful of newly moneyed industrialists, oligarchs, and City bankers', and we know that these seemingly disparate elite groups have many cross cutting relationships and interests. By contrast, only 5% of land is owned by ordinary private householders.

If I peruse a list of my old Caius contemporaries, it will contain dozens who belong to these groups and who have made small fortunes through these channels, just one of some forty Oxford and Cambridge colleges who will have similar profiles. College reunion dinners, I found, are nakedly devoted to raising donations from well-heeled and not always sober alumni: Caius is, by various measures, one of the wealthiest Cambridge colleges. On these occasions I was struck by how much my former college contemporaries were prone to boast to each other about their material achievements and useful connections, a highly visible and self-congratulatory 'old boy's network'. I may stand accused at this point of what politicians on the right like to characterise as 'the politics of envy'. Well, I plead guilty at least to the politics of anger and distaste. The consequence of this self-aggrandising, self-importantly entitled, and complacent elitism, is a system that has worked deliberately to destroy the welfare settlement of the post war period, so significant for my own educational progress; and has sought to attack relentlessly the organised political and economic institutions of working class power which buttressed that settlement, and made lives better for millions of deprived and underprivileged people like my parents. The upper classes have never doubted who their class enemy is: Conservative Prime Minister David Cameron's Parliamentary battle cry of 'Never Again!' to the Labour benches was not only celebratory but knowing and contemptuous, Eton and Balliol crowing over what elite Tories everywhere regarded as their rightful social and political position, their dominant heel on working class necks.

Recent work seeks to explain the economic, political and social crises that have engulfed our society and institutions in the last two decades. Anthony Barnett (2017) judges that blame must chiefly be attached to 'the class system that lies at the heart of Britishness', and points the finger at the continued baleful influence of class divisions; Green and Kynaston (2019) and Verkaik (2017), deplore the 'apartheid education system' of private schooling for the wealthy class which perpetuates those divisions. Alex Renton, reviewing Verkaik (*The Observer* 22.07.2018), comments that we are 'left wondering again how this crony class of bought privilege and vicious self-interest has managed to hold on to the reins for so long'. Worse, inequity is built into the system of financing by a complaisant state: Verkaik calculates that the charitable status enjoyed by public schools confers business rate relief which between 2017 and 2022 will be worth more than £500 million (Eton alone will save an estimated £4 million over a five year period). Meanwhile, as Melissa Benn points out, state schools are not charities, receive no fee income, must pay full business rates, and (unlike public schools) cannot make tax-free profits. The designation of the upper echelons of this system in the 1950s and 1960s as 'the establishment' still holds good today. Sampson had argued in 1962 that it consisted of a series of interlocking circles of groups which were defined by wealth, position, and power, resting on a common social and educational background. While some limited social fluidity has occurred, the nature of the circles of influence described by Sampson - embracing government, parliament, the higher civil service, the judiciary and legal system, leading financial institutions, the media and the Anglican church - remains much as it was in the mid twentieth century, and if anything has accrued an even greater concentration of wealth and power. This class-based system, rooted originally in land, money and political power, has also rested on its binary opposites: dispossession, poverty and inequality.

## The persistence of poverty and inequality

> *He knew well the price of poverty and the crushing of the human spirit that it often brought.*
> Alan Titley, Introduction to Mairtin O' Cadhain: *The Dirty Dust*

Studies of the poverty of rural labour had a significant and lasting influence on British studies of poverty and inequality more generally. The Quaker philanthropist Seebohm Rowntree's path-breaking surveys of poverty in York tell us about the causes and extent of 'measured' poverty in the first half of the twentieth century. His 1901 survey would have included the household of my great grandmother, for it surveyed *all* of York's working class households, a significant proportion then working in agriculture in York's rural hinterland. This survey found that at least a third of the wage-earning classes lived in 'total poverty', i.e. not far short of destitution, the primary cause being desperately low earnings. With large families the norm, malnourishment was a major consequence. Rowntree's second, 1936 survey, confirmed that a third of wage earners continued to live in poverty, now described as 'primary' poverty, defined as an inability to meet the most basic needs; but the main identified cause of poverty in the inter-war years is unemployment. The much lower poverty findings of a third Rowntree survey in York in 1950 have been disputed, producing estimates that range between 4% and 14% (Gazeley: 2003); but the new primary cause of poverty is identified, in the immediate post 1945 period, as old age. From this point, with real incomes rising and low unemployment, together with the social cushioning offered by the new 'Welfare State', Conservative Prime Minister Macmillan seemed justified in his late 1950s claim that British society had "never had it so good". It came as something of a shock, then, when the rediscovery of poverty was announced in the mid-1960s, with the establishment by Abel Smith and Townsend (1965) of a new measure for poverty based on the idea of relative deprivation, and 'the principle that the minimum level of living regarded as acceptable by society increases with rising prosperity'. On this (now fully accepted) basis, almost 18% of households, or 7.5 million people, were in 1960 regarded as living in poverty. While 35% of these were pensioners, and 23% on welfare benefits, 41% were wage earners with low incomes (this would have certainly included most agricultural workers, and my own parents). The 7.5 million included 2.25 million children. Abel Smith and Townsend's publication in 1965 of *The Poor and the Poorest* coincided with the launch of the Child Poverty Action Group; child poverty would henceforth become the principal signifier of social need, and social and economic inequality, in due course something of a political football, as it is today.

General levels of poverty under this new 'relative' definition averaged around 10% up to the 1980s, but the Thatcherite years, which produced de-industrialisation and high levels of unemployment, escalated these levels. By the turn of the century, according to the respected Institute for Fiscal Studies, some 4 million children were living in poverty, one in six of those experiencing multiple levels of deprivation. This process was reversed for a time by successive Labour administrations, committed to a targeted reduction of child poverty. But in 2015 the new Conservative administration scrapped Labour's child poverty target and intensified the austerity programme begun under a Conservative-Liberal Democrat coalition in 2010. In 2017, half of the children in single parent families were classed as in child poverty, and health professionals reported 'seeing problems that seemed to belong to a bygone era'. A later IFS report showed that the total figure of children living in poverty was still around 4 million, but estimated that this figure would increase to 5.2 million by 2021-2022, largely as a consequence of planned reductions in welfare benefits. This new estimate calculated that 37% of all children will, in 2022, be living in relative poverty, 'the highest percentage since modern records began in 1961'; and this rising trend was confirmed recently for the period up to 2023-24 (IFS, November 2017; Resolution Foundation, 2019). The educational consequence of child poverty is that by GCSE examinations, there is a 28% gap in achievement between children on the lowest income levels and their better-off peers. In a class of 30, nine of those children will be poor, i.e. on free school meals (FSM) benefit (CPAG, March 2018). Meanwhile the poorest third of the population found their incomes reducing relative to the rich as a consequence of either unemployment, or benefits reduction, or both. A leading authority suggests that Britain is moving back to levels of inequality in wealth and poverty last seen in the mid-1960s; we now have a 'new super-rich and new extreme poor mimicking (but not as great as) inequalities at the start of the [20th] century... in this sense we are back where we started' (Dorling, 2003).

We need to recall that poverty experts like Townsend (1965, 1979) and Donnison (1982) judged that relative poverty meant exclusion from the average living standards, lifestyles and fellowship of one's fellow citizens, an exclusion to be remedied through welfare payments; but a study for the Joseph Rowntree Foundation of *100 years of poverty from 1901 to 2001,* points to a clear and growing gap between what is regarded as an appropriate poverty line, and how much in practice government is prepared to give to people on benefits. The key determinants of poverty in 2000 are not unemployment alone, but a range of other factors: low income while working, casualised and insecure employment, single parenthood, and disability. The authors comment that in 1901, women comprised 66% of the poor, and in 2001-2, 54% of the poor, so 'women were, and are, more likely to be poor', (Glennerster et al, 2004). Others note regional disparities, and high levels of disadvantage for some immigrant groups (Dorling 2003).

A further recent measure of increased poverty in 2013-2019 is food insecurity, registered by the growth of charitable food banks, described by the largest provider, the Trussell Trust, as 'a broad index of social hardship'. In 2017-18 the Trussell Trust provided 1.3 million three day emergency food supplies, a figure that included 484,000 children, and represented a 13% increase over 2016-17 (Trussell Trust, 2018). In April -September 2019, 823,000 food parcels were issued, an increase of 23 % over the same period a year earlier. Low incomes, benefits changes, and benefit payment delays accounted for the majority of Trussell referrals. A National Audit Office report (NAO, June 2018) established that a major cause of such problems was the controversial and much delayed 'rolling out' by the Department of Work and Pensions of Universal Credit, a reform bundling all welfare benefits into one single benefit; the report found that a quarter of new claims were not paid in full on time, with delays of 11 weeks for 40% of claimants , while 20% had to wait for five months, a disaster for people already on low and wholly inadequate incomes: little wonder that a report by the Food Standards Agency found that 4 million people 'regularly struggled to put food on the table'. There are unavoidable echoes here of the soup kitchens in my mother's home town of Wallsend in the mid-1920s-1930s. But back then, the poor who resorted to soup kitchens were striking or unemployed; now many who resort to food banks or who are homeless are in work, a scandalous phenomenon in our social welfare history. These lowest levels of 'the poor' have been labelled 'the precariat' (Standing 2011), enduring insecure employment, poor housing, low incomes, and constantly shifting living standards well below the norm: they come at the bottom of the most authoritative recent analysis of British social class groupings which contains seven categories, the 'elite', naturally, being at the top (Savage, 2015).

The reality of extreme inequality in Britain is supported by official figures showing that by the measure of average household annual *income*, the top ten percent is 6.8 times higher (£68000) than the lowest 10 per cent (£10,000); while by the measure of *wealth,* the average of the top 10 percent (at £1.5 m) is 315 times higher than that of the lowest 10 percent (ONS surveys of wealth and assets, 2014-16). Meanwhile, the richest one percent in the UK held just over 20 percent of UK wealth.

Dorling (2003) rightly suggests that in considering such inequalities while using a standard of relative poverty, we must recognise that there has been an enormous increase in general living standards over the twentieth century, such that the lowest third of the income distribution would expect to afford the full range of consumer durables such as washing machines, refrigerators, central heating, even cars; in these terms, poverty was no longer the same in 2000 as it was in 1900, or even in the 1950s. But he argues that, while the broad structure and relationships of poverty and wealth have remained much the same over the twentieth century, inequalities of income and wealth between different social groups have widened. Since these wealth gaps seem to have accelerated in the first part of the twenty first century, the implicit trade-off between a decent general standard and continued inequality between social groups is now under severe strain. The scenario where the rich are getting significantly richer, and the poor are getting significantly poorer, may well produce political and social tensions and conflicts reminiscent of the darker parts of the twentieth century.

This situation is compounded by unsympathetic public attitudes towards the poor, and those on benefits, redolent of traditional prejudice against 'the undeserving poor' (Seabrook, 2013). This Victorian-era moral stance is now seemingly replicated in government policies and in a hostile popular press, the poor condemned for their alleged behavioural characteristics, including having too many children, cheating on benefits, being unwilling to get out of bed and go to work in the mornings, and daring to want televisions and holidays. Yet a new and imaginative analysis, based on comparisons of actual standards of living across all classes, confounds such myths. They show that a wide range of items and activities is seen as 'necessities' across the whole range of classes: that in these terms a large proportion of households suffer clear levels of deprivation and social exclusion; that many people who want to work are unable to find secure or other than low paid work; and that 'most children in poverty live with both parents, are in families with one or two children, and have at least one person in the household in full-time work' (Lansley and Mack 2015). We also know that damaging beliefs about the extent of benefit fraud or the welfare dependency of immigrant communities are far removed from social realities. Government-directed austerity strategies since 2010 bore most heavily on those most in need, so that the burdens of wider economic and financial failings perpetrated by those at the top of the system are borne by those at the bottom, victims of a brutal and unfeeling austerity regime initially designed by a Cabinet full of millionaires, and led by an Old Etonian Prime Minister, emblematic of a 'ruling class'.

The relentless neo-liberal assault from the 1980s onwards, both on traditional industrial sectors, and on the institutions of the post war welfare state, has itself had many damaging consequences for the working classes, not least the steady erosion of the rights and powers of trade unions. But the damages are to the whole society, as spelled out by Polly Toynbee and David Walker, in the tellingly titled *Dismembered: how the attack on the state harms us all* (2017). The attack has been spearheaded by an ideology that proposes the superiority of the market, and a sort of zero sum practice that attempts to replace state institutions with market institutions. The collapse of an overweening and deeply unethical financial and banking system in

2008-09 gave way to a savage austerity programme, over the next decade and beyond, of deep cuts in state spending and services. As this has played out in the public sphere, major areas of social policy, in the NHS, in education, in welfare provision, and in housing have been mutilated to such a degree that the old, benevolent welfare state model has been traduced. As we have seen, social misery has increased, and poverty is steadily rising as deep cuts to welfare benefits kick in. Real income levels for most wage earners are still some 6 per cent below levels a decade earlier, as the economy experiences what has been termed 'wageless growth'. The signs of social distress are there for all to see, in the spread of homelessness and the growth of food banks; in some schools, teachers are providing food and clean clothing to children who turn up at school hungry and unwashed; levels of mental depression and suicide are worryingly high among young people.

Successive governments since 2010 have persistently based a defence against this critique on claims that unemployment keeps hitting historically low levels. But these claims are deeply flawed and fundamentally dishonest because the terms 'employment' and 'unemployment' conceal harsh realities. Employment is often partial and limited, not 'full' employment. The jobs market has increasingly been characterised by exploitative, often inhumane employment practices, and a high incidence of temporary, part-time and so-called 'zero hours' contracts This all too often means that you may be 'employed' or 'self-employed', yet still be living in conditions of real poverty. Many of the growing cohorts of homeless living on the streets are in work, but work that is impermanent or badly paid. A Rowntree Foundation report in early 2019 noted that 56% of those living below the official poverty line are in a household where someone is working. In short, 'unemployment' is not the real issue; the real issue is in-work poverty.

In November 2018 a special investigation and report by the UN Rapporteur on Extreme Poverty and Human Rights, based in part on recent studies cited in this chapter (IFS,NAO etc), and incorporating two weeks of interviews with benefits claimant groups, charities, and government Ministers and officials, declared that levels of child poverty in the fifth richest country in the world were 'not just a disgrace but a social calamity and an economic disaster' characterised by a 'punitive, mean-spirited and callous approach' to spending cuts and welfare reforms. He found 'a striking and almost complete disconnect between what I heard from the government and what I consistently heard from many people directly, right across the country': Ministers and government officials were 'in denial'. As if to reinforce this view, the Work and Pensions Secretary of State attacked the report's 'extraordinary political language' while the Prime Minister's office said they profoundly disagreed with the analysis. But a Guardian leader (Guardian, 19 Nov 2018) thought it 'unpardonable that the costs of austerity have fallen so disproportionately on the poor, women, ethnic minorities, children, single parents, and people with disabilities'. A report by the UK Equality and Human Rights Commission later in November 2018 essentially duplicated the UN report's findings and confirmed that these consequences of government policy were a political choice, creating 'alarming backwards steps' towards a 'two-speed society'. We see here glimpses of the destitute poor of Seebohm Rowntree's day: in terms of resources and opportunities there is a gap between the wealthiest and the poorest as great now as it was a century ago. As George Bernard Shaw wrote: 'Do not bother your head with social problems: what is wrong with the poor is poverty' (quoted in Gazeley: 2003)

## The self-serving rich versus the undeserving poor: who wins?

> *The process of catch up never seems to result in any catching up*
> Danny Dorling

A question that naturally arises from my account is: are things better now than they were then? Have the social inequalities and injustices that I record disappeared? What has happened to what we have come to label 'social mobility'? How would a boy or girl from my lowly working class background fare now, compared with myself seventy years ago, or my sister sixty years ago? A clue to the way in which we need to conduct this debate lies in Dorling's judgement in his survey of social policy and deprivation over the whole twentieth century (Dorling 2003), that 'although there was enormous social progress in absolute terms, there was also remarkable social rigidity in the basic structures of society, particularly in its inequities.' In other words, there has been considerable social and economic change for the better, but the structures and relationships of social class have not changed, with the poorest third still stuck at the bottom, and the wealthiest 10 per cent not only still at the top, but now opening up a still wider disparity with the rest, including much of the middle class. Within and apart from the top group is a small number of super-rich: the infamous 'one per cent', standing so far above the rest as to constitute a different social and economic universe. The political response to complaint about this hugely unfair system of socially entrenched privilege has always been summed up in the phrase 'social mobility', the supposed ability of all to aspire to what is enjoyed by the few. One clear marker here should be change in the educational opportunities open to poorer members of the community, broadly that bottom one third of the total. By one standard, the opportunity to access higher education through universities and other degree-awarding institutions, there has been considerable change and improvement. In the late 1950s only 4 per cent of my age group went to University; the creation of several new universities in the 1960s, then from 1992 the translation of most polytechnics and many higher education institutions to university status, means that higher education was in 2018 available to just under 50 per cent of the age group, and there are many examples of young people who are the first members of their families ever to reach this educational level. Has this corrected a historical marker of inequality?

Some serious caveats must be entered, to do with the system of schooling, and its links to university admissions. A major change here was a substantial translation of the old tripartite secondary modern/technical /grammar school system into a comprehensive school system, the predominant type in the state school system. But this was a muddled reform, for in some local education authority areas grammar schools were retained; while the private sector (public) schools also continued to exist. The public schools represent only 7 per cent of school children, yet through charitable status reap tax advantages worth £2.5 billion a year, while only 1% of their pupils pay no fees. These schools, and a number of high performing grammar schools, have dominated admissions to the best universities, notably Oxbridge, and what has become known as the Russell Group. Since these schools overwhelmingly represent both the traditional upper classes, and the newly expanded middle class, considerable disadvantages and inequalities still dog children from the less privileged parts of society, and we need here to link the discussion to the social and economic inequalities identified earlier in this chapter. In a trenchant analysis, Diane Reay, from working class origins herself, suggests that 'social mobility' has 'an iconic place in English political discourse', and compares the situation in the 1960s with that in recent decades. She judges social mobility to be a form of 'cruel optimism' because working class people who strive to escape the limitations of their backgrounds form 'optimistic attachments to the very power structures that have oppressed us, and our families before us'. This damages both ourselves, and the communities we leave behind, so that in 'deeply unequal societies like England [social mobility] has come to feel much more like a social ill, one that harms both the socially mobile individual and the communities they grew up in'. Her analysis of her own feelings in this situation, as she moved between classes and socially difficult, even distressing experiences, pretty much reflects what Hoggart has to say (though surprisingly she does not reference him). But, as I have tried to do, she emphasises the conflicted feelings about class identity, that 'in a strongly classed society like the UK... a sense of belonging to the working classes carries connotations of being less' (Reay:2017).

This issue of class dislocation is compounded by the very constrained practice of social mobility. Numerous reports from the Social Mobility Commission, the Resolution Foundation, and the Sutton Trust make clear that a supposedly meritocratic educational system is a delusion. A recent University College London research study of 5 years (2010 – 2015) of misconceived and dysfunctional schooling reforms initiated by the Conservative-Liberal Democrat coalition government of 2010, describes 'a chaotic process of centralisation' that has fuelled educational inequality, with a decline in the numbers of the poorest (FSM) children going to high performing schools, and rising numbers of these children being concentrated in poorly performing and resourced schools. Conservative Prime Ministers proclaim social mobility as a policy objective, but in practice have shown no interest in realising it and have in effect side-lined the Social Mobility Commission. To its everlasting discredit, the Labour Party has at no time shown any appetite for the correction (or elimination) of the clear inequalities and social injustices in our mixed public-private system of education, proposing only a sort of lame tinkering which envisages that private schools and elite grammar schools will somehow drag poorly performing schools along in their privileged wake. The reality is that the already disproportionately advantaged children of the upper and middle classes reap most of the rewards of the national higher education system.

If we take entry to Oxford and Cambridge to be the summit of the educational mountain that all children must scale, we find that those from a private school background have an advantage out of all proportion to their numbers. They represent 7 per cent of the age group, but for most of the post war period, and well into the twenty-first century, have commanded around half of Oxford and Cambridge admissions. While state schools still send large numbers to these elite institutions, the majority of these entrants will be from middle class backgrounds. A very small minority will come from genuinely underprivileged homes, and this itself needs to be subdivided, for in contemporary Britain, we have to pay regard not just to class but to black and ethnic minority groups, many of whom will also be in the lowest income groups, so doubly disadvantaged. A 2017 study cites figures showing the average parental income levels of Cambridge colleges in 2009: it was no surprise to me to find my own old college, Caius, second highest on the list with an average parental income of £96,000. If we are to take income as the touchstone for class position, there will be an enormous mismatch between the poorest students and the rest: average annual incomes in the lowest group in 2009 were probably not much more than £10,000 to £12,000.

Admission to Oxford and Cambridge is a significant measure of genuine mobility, not only because these universities are regarded as the best in the country, but because their graduates also secure the majority of high level jobs and related incomes across a range of professions. In relation to the Russell Group of universities (which includes Oxford and Cambridge), recent research shows that in the early 21st century only five per cent of UK working class children obtained admission, and that the poorest category (FSM children, i.e., those provided with free school meals) accounted for only 0.9 percent of admissions: meanwhile, private school students were '55 times more likely than FSM students to gain a place at Oxford or Cambridge': scarcely a new millennial dawn for this least privileged group, or for "social mobility". Many from the two least well off working class groups will still go on to a university education, but at universities which are widely regarded as second or even third rate in an over-expanded higher education sector. Implicit here is that working class students should be grateful to have a 'second best' which is good enough for them, and will lead on to inferior jobs later, also good enough for them: in 2013, 47% of recent graduates were working in non-graduate, mainly low-skilled jobs.

A further disincentive for working class children and their parents is what is now the enormous personal financial cost, with tuition fees generally set at £9,000 a year, and maintenance grants just recently terminated in favour of even greater dependence on loans. For the poorest students and their families, the prospect of graduating into what is an increasingly uncertain jobs market with debts of more than £50,000, much more if postgraduate qualifications are required, must be extremely alarming. Further inequality arises in relation to competition for attractive jobs, particularly in the arts and media, where recruitment is often through unpaid internships, a luxury that children from poorer backgrounds cannot afford. The blatant inequality in financial resources available to the different social class groupings suggests that the idea of meritocracy in access to higher education is a fig leaf to cover up the naked dominance of the system by those with the deepest pockets.

If I look back to my late 1950s and early 1960s family experience of the 'meritocratic' system, what comparisons could I draw with the present day? When I was accepted for Cambridge (in 1957) and my sister Sally entered Oxford (in 1964), we were certainly in that category that would now be labelled FSM, the 'officially poor' (though we would not have cared to be so labelled). Our parents constantly struggled heroically to cope with the costs of our school years, but the provision by the state of university funding of fees and living costs for high performing children (the lost and almost unimaginable world of State Scholarships) was a considerable relief to them and allowed us to take full advantage of real opportunities, especially because in terms of employment and income we then benefited from the extra cachet that our leading universities conferred, our working class background finally no longer a handicap. It would have been a wholly different story had they (and we) been faced with meeting full fee costs plus living costs, and the prospect of enormous debts thereafter. In the present day, even middle class parents and children are struggling with these issues, so it will not be surprising if many working class families and their children, even more so the poorest, come to see higher education as an unrealistic and unaffordable prospect. When we recall the Institute for Fiscal Studies prediction that by 2021-22, 37% of all children will be designated as living in relative poverty, there is little room for optimism about their educational life chances; while the children from the wealthiest 10 per cent of the population will continue to monopolise both elite educational opportunities, and (as now well attested) all the major employment providers, in government, law, business, the media, even in the performing arts. The proportion of children from the poorest sector of the working classes who succeed in rising to these elite levels will be no higher, and may well increasingly become lower, than it was in the middle of the twentieth century. Unhappily, at the time of writing, these disparities may well be enormously increased by the effects of the Covid-19 pandemic, which are predicted to damage or restrict even further both the educational opportunities and the career expectations of those on the bottom rungs of the social ladder ( Education Policy Institute,2020; National Foundation for Educational Research, 2020).

## Back to the Future?

> *He was grateful for the illusions that had held him steady all his life*
> Barbara Everett: *Six Poems*

In his 1971 account of growing up in urban working class Salford, *The Classic Slum,* Robert Roberts tells the following story passed on by his elders: '... a man with a large family [was] struggling to keep his sick father with them. At last the old man insisted he should be taken to the workhouse. They set off, the wife picking up his few belongings, and the father on his son's back. En route, they stopped to rest a while on a stone seat. "It was here" said the old man, "I rested too, carrying my father to the workhouse". The son rose, took the burden on his back again, and turned with his wife for home. "We'll manage somehow" he said.'

I first read this story many decades ago and was reminded of it recently, quoted in A.H. Halsey's *Change in British Society.* It still moves me, for it captures not only the extreme misery and low expectations of the lives of endless generations of working people, but also the bravery and steadfastness of those who, across the centuries, resolved not to accept such circumstances unquestioningly. I see the heroism of this son in the lives of my own parents, and the same determination, for when the question arose in the early 1950s as to whether my very hard-up parents could afford for me to stay on at school, and beyond that university, my father uttered those very same words: "We'll manage somehow". I recall too that people of my grandparents' generation were still fearful of 'the workhouse' in the 1930s because once you could no longer work, you would have no money, and the workhouse would be the most likely destination. Ironically, my Irish grandfather would, at the end of his life, be admitted to the grim and much feared old Knaresborough workhouse, but now transformed by the post war Labour government into an NHS hospital. His son, my father, gave up lifelong farm work, and village life, when my parents were in their sixties. The English village has always been something of a nostalgic construct, as fondly presented by writers like George Ewart Evans (*The Farm and the Village; Ask The Fellows Who Cut The Hay),* or George Bourne (*Change in the Village):* at least the clearer-eyed Ronald Blythe acknowledges 'the grim old tradition of labour without money' (*Akenfield).* By the 1970s this 'traditional village', with its supposed basis in an occupational community related to agriculture, was being replaced by a middle class commuter version with few connections to declining rural occupations. This memoir has detailed the earlier life of a Yorkshire village in the 1950s and early 1960s, showing how a strongly etched community life still then played out, almost all of the inhabitants coming together to share social events: dances, whist drives, Women's Institute activities, Coronation celebrations, village cricket, even the fun and games of a parochial election. But the occupational structure was already loosening then, the first middle class incomers were arriving, a trickle which developed into a flood over the decades after my family departed. Our old tied house would be 'gentrified' and sell for more than a million pounds (to my mother's chagrin) to a celebrity footballer, the village now a highly sought after commuter enclave, the fate of villages across the country. My father did not really leave agriculture, it left him, his old proud skills no longer required, the physical side now too demanding in his advancing age. This lifetime of farm labour had brought him scant financial return: for the greater part of their working lives my parents lived in or on the edge of poverty. But the socialism to which they were so committed finally brought some reward, not least in the social opportunities opened up for their children.

The workhouse may have gone, and there is no doubt that there have been significant changes in the shape, character and cohesiveness of the traditional working class, but no doubt also about the poverty, inequalities, and social deprivations suffered by many of its members over the long twentieth century (say the 1880s to the 2020s). While the ways in which we define these conditions have changed, and considerable social transformations have taken place, more than a third of our population (and rising) still experiences familiar conditions of need, suffering, low incomes, poor housing, social exclusions, and political powerlessness. All of these people are at the bottom of the social heap, just as the old manual working class used to be in the first half of the twentieth century. Their plight is disregarded by a dominant, wealthy, and socially distant political and financial class, too often aided and abetted by selfish and largely uncompassionate middle class groups, an implicit coalition that fails to recognise that their privileged ways of life depend on the labour and social involvement of other much less well rewarded groups (a truth also brought home by the Covid-19 pandemic). Professor Danny Dorling has rightly anathematised this abuse of power, writing that 'it is a sign of the duplicity of our times that institutions that often claim that they are against elitism do much to promote it, that governments that say they aim to reduce social exclusion actually create it'.

This family and personal memoir tells a story of changing social and educational opportunities as they played out in the middle of twentieth century Britain, and explores some of the difficulties and dilemmas then created by movement between clearly defined social classes, though such movements and opportunities turned out to be relatively rare for those from the lowest income groups. We might then, echoing Auden's judgement about the 1930s, inveigh against the low, dishonest decades of the early twenty-first century. Buttressed by wealth and social power, the upper sections of our increasingly unequal society (perhaps some 10% of the whole) continue to monopolise economic and social resources. For those without access to such resources, maybe as many as 40% of the whole, the notion of 'social mobility' must appear as a cruel hoax. The dominance of the already privileged is all too visible, not least in its perpetuation through a private education system and the closeness of its linkages within a social, economic and political elite recently described as a chumocracy to which the normal social and political rules do not apply(and see highly critical report of the Johnson government's procurement decisions by the National Audit Office: NAO, November, 2020). This elite, judged by recent studies of its membership and sources of wealth and patronage, is no more porous now than it was seven or so decades ago. While a very few from the lowest ranks will be granted entry, the vast majority will continue to experience the most restricted of life chances: for them, 'social mobility', indeed talk of a classless society, will be experienced only as a cruel delusion embedded in an intentionally manipulative rhetoric. While the composition and identity of social classes has changed significantly, the erosion of the cohesiveness of working class groups has left them ill equipped to fight what is in effect a continuing class war. As a recent (2018) study of social mobility concluded: 'we are missing out on the biggest talent pool, fishing in the same small pond, generation after generation. Low mobility's legacy is a self-interested and self-perpetuating elite that neglects the rest of society'. Yet it cannot, in the long run, be in the interests of the dominant social classes to preside over the destruction and immiseration of such large swathes of our society. This is a 'condition of England' question (though properly of Britain) which requires a moral response, something the competitive market model has, time and again, shown itself incapable of providing. a failure underscored by the Johnson administration's inept responses to the Covid19 pandemic.

As I recall the optimism that came with the new post 1945 dawn of the British version of socialism, its realisation of a welfare state that would create a world for working class heroes like my parents, I am certain that the present, increasingly restive and newly disadvantaged younger generation will demand a reformulation of Britain's present broken social and economic system, and a return to the moral values on which our still too narrow and self-serving elites have turned their backs in their pursuit of an economic and political ideology that broadly preaches 'devil take the hindmost'. Those moral values are straightforward enough, and in a wealthy country like ours would be indicated most clearly in the willingness to respect social differences, to share out more equally and justly the fruits of our economic system, and above all to protect those who enjoy the least of those fruits, though they play a full and essential part in producing them. I would like to look ahead to a world in which all our children and grandchildren, regardless of the diversities of class, race, ethnicity or gender, can enjoy the protections, benefits, and opportunities that I and my sisters enjoyed under a benevolent welfare state, so representing a return to a more caring society, a world in which no one needs to say 'we'll manage somehow'.

# Sources Used

## *Primary sources*

Since this is a family memoir, it is necessarily based substantially in personal memories and papers. These include a substantial (unpublished) account written by my father on his retirement, setting out in detail the working life and social times of a farm labourer in the first half of the twentieth century: such sources on rural labour are rare, compared with those from the urban working class. My mother also left a variety of papers, including memories of domestic service, of household life during the 1939-45 war, and a number of poems. I am grateful to my cousin Tom Minogue for giving me access to his excellent and informative family genealogy; and also to Linda Burns, my cousin Joe's wife, for useful material relating to my mother's family genealogy: both are labours of love. For Chapters 1 and 2, I used limited public documents relating to the Mowbray and Stourton estate.

## *Secondary sources*

This is a personal selection from a very wide range of secondary sources which provide background, context and analysis for the periods covered by the memoir; some are referenced in the text.

Abel Smith,B., and Townsend,P. *The Poorest of the Poor* (G.Bell, 1965)

Barnett,A. *The Lure of Greatness: England's Brexit and America's Trump* (Unbound, 2017)

Benn, M. *Life Lessons: the Case for a National Education Service* (Verso, 2018)

Benn, M. *How do we end the class divide?* (Guardian, 24.08.2018)

Benson, R. *The Valley: A Hundred Years in the Life of a Yorkshire Family* (Bloomsbury 2014)

Blythe, R. *Akenfield* (Penguin 1972)

Boroughbridge Historical Society *A History of Boroughbridge:A Historic Yorkshire Town* ( Croft Publications,2018)

Bourne,G. *Change In The Village* (Penguin, 1984)

Branson,N., and Heinemann,M. *Britain in the Nineteen Thirties* (Panther Books,1973)

Brendon, P. *The Decline and Fall of the British Empire 1781-1997* (Vintage Books, 2008)

Briggs,A. *A Social History of England* (Weidenfeld and Nicolson, 1984)

Brown,J., and Lewis,W.R. Eds., *The Oxford History of the British Empire, Vol IV: The Twentieth Century* (Oxford University Press)

Cannadine, D. *The Decline and Fall of the British Aristocracy* (Picador 1992)

Child Poverty Action Group:*Poverty:The Facts* (6th edition: CPAG London 2017)

Child Poverty Action Group: *Report, March 2018* (CPAG, London)

Cobbett, W. *Rural Rides* (1830: 1967 edition, Penguin Books)

Darvill,P. *Sir Alec Clegg:A Biographical Study* ( Able Publishing,2000)

Devlin,S. *Agricultural labour in the UK* ( Working paper, New Economics Foundation 2016)

Donnison,D. *The Politics of Poverty* (Wiley-Blackwell,1982)

Dorling, D. 'A Century of Progress? Inequalities in British Society 1901-2000' in Gilbert *et al*,(2003: 31-53)

Dorling,D. *Injustice: Why Social Inequality Still Exists* (The Policy Press, revised edition, 2007)

Ewart Evans,G. *Ask The Fellows Who Cut the Hay* (Faber and Faber, 1956)

Ewart Evans,G. *The Farm and the Village* (Faber and Faber, 1969)

Ewart Evans,G. *The Crooked Scythe: an anthology of oral history* (Faber and Faber, 1994)

Farman, C. *The General Strike 1926: Britain's Aborted Revolution?* (Panther Books 1974)

Freese, B. *Coal: A Human History* (Arrow Books 2006)

Gardiner, J. *The Thirties: An Intimate History* (Harper Press 2010)

Gardiner, J. *Wartime Britain 1939-45* (Headline Book Publishing, 2004)

Gazeley,I. *Poverty in Britain,1900-1965* (Palgrave Macmillan,2003)

Glennerster, H., Hills, J., Piachaud, D., Webb, J. *One Hundred Years of Poverty and Policy* (Joseph Rowntree Foundation, 2004)

Gilbert,D., Matless,D., and Short,B. *Geographies of British Modernity: space and society in the twentieth century* (Blackwell, 2003)

Green,F., and Kynaston, D. *Engines of Privilege: Britain's Private School Problem*(Bloomsbury, 2019)

Halsey, A.H. *Change in British Society* (Oxford University Press 1986)

Hammond, J.L., and B. *The Village Labourer* (Longman 1978, ed. G.E.Mingay)

Hanley, L. *Estates: An Intimate History* (Granta 2007)

Hanley,L. *Respectable: Crossing The Class Divide* (Penguin Autobiography, 2017)

Hargrove,E.T. *History of Knaresborough with Harrogate* (Hargrove, York, 1798)

Harrison,M.J. ed., *Living History In The Ainsty* (Ainsty Villages History Group,2010)

Harrison, Tony *Selected Poems* (Viking 1984)

Hart-Davies, D. *Our Land At War: A Portrait of Rural Britain 1939 – 1945* (Collins 2015)

Hartley, D. *The Land of England* (Book Club Associates. 1979)

Hattersley, R. *Borrowed Time: The Story of Britain Between the Wars* (Abacus 2009)

Hennessy, P. *Never Again: Britain 1945 – 1951* (Jonathan Cape 1992)

Hennessey,P. *Having It So Good: Britain in the Fifties* (Penguin, 2007)

Hickman, T. *The Call-Up: A History of National Service* (Headline Publishing 2004)

Hobsbawm,E. and Rudé G. *Captain Swing* (Penguin, 1973)

Hoggart,R. *The Uses of Literacy: Aspects of Working Class life with Special Reference to Publications and Entertainments* (Penguin, 1958)

Horn,P. *Life Below Stairs in the Twentieth Century* (Sutton Publishing, 2003)

Hutchinson, K. *Images of England: Wallsend* (Tempest 2005)

Hyam, E. *Britain's Declining Empire: the Road to Decolonisation, 1918-1968* (Oxford University Press, 2006)

IFS: Institute of Fiscal Studies: *Research reports on poverty, inequality and living standards* IFS,1999; IFS,March 2017; IFS,November 2017: IFS,March 2018: IFS, February 2020.

Inglis, F.C. *Richard Hoggart: Virtue and Reward* (Polity, 2014)

Inglis,F.C. *Radical Earnestness: English Social Theory 1880-1980* ( Martin Robertson 1982)

Jackson, D. *The Northumbrians:North East England and Its People* (C.Hurst,2019)

James, S. *Diplomatic Moves: Life in the Foreign Service* (Radcliffe Press, 1995)

Jennings,B. ed., *A History of Harrogate and Knaresborough* (Harrogate WEA Local History Group 1970)

Jennings,P. *The Living Village* (Hodder and Stoughton, 1968)

Johnson,A. *This Boy: A Memoir of Childhood* (Corgi Books, 2014)

Jones, O. *The Establishment and How They Get Away With It* (Allen Lane, 2014)

Kellett,A. *King James's School, Knaresborough 1616-2003* (King James's School, Knaresborough,2003)

Kightly,C. *Country Voices: Life and Lore in Farm and Village* (Thames and Hudson, 1984)

Kineally, C. *A Death Dealing Famine: The Great Hunger in Ireland* (Pluto Press, 1997)

Kynaston,D. *Austerity Britain 1945-51* (Bloomsbury, 2007)

Kynaston,D. *Family Britain 1951-57* (Bloomsbury, 2009)

Kynaston,D. *Modernity Britain 1957-1962 (*Bloomsbury, *2015)*
Laski,H. *Liberty in the Modern State (*Pelican, 1937)

Lansley, S. and Mack, J. *Breadline Britain: The Rise of Mass Poverty* (One World, 2015)

Lawrence,F.' *Fear, hunger and dirt: Lithuanian migrants on life as chicken catchers'* (The Guardian, 10.08.2015)

Light, A. *Common People* (Penguin 2015)

Longmate, N. *The Real Dad's Army: The Story of the Home Guard* (Arrow Books 1974)

Maconie, S. *Long Road From Jarrow: A Journey Through Britain Then and Now* (Ebury Press, 2017)

MAFF *Statistics on Agriculture Fisheries and Food, 2014* Ministry of Agriculture, Fisheries and Food, 2014

Mckenzie,L. *Getting By: Estates, Class and Culture in Austerity Britain* (Policy Press, Bristol, 2015)

McKibbin, R. *Class and Cultures: England 1918 – 1951* (Oxford University Press 1988)

Mingay, G.E. *Parliamentary Enclosure in England: an Introduction to Its Causes, Incidence and Impact* (Routledge,1997)

Morgan, K.O. *Labour In Power* (Oxford University Press 1985)

Morgan, K.O. *Britain Since 1945: The People's Peace* (Oxford University Press 2001)

Morley, F. *The Great North Road* (Hutchinson,1961)

Nabakov, V. *Speak, Memory: An Autobiography Revisited* (G.P.Putnam, New York, 1966)

National Audit Office (NAO) *Rolling Out Universal Credit* (NAO, London, June,2018)

Newby, H. *The Deferential Worker: A Study of Farm Workers in East Anglia* (Allen Lane 1977)

Newby, H. *Green and Pleasant Land: Social Change in Rural England* (Pelican 1985)

Newby, H. *Country Life: A Social History of Rural England* (Weidenfeld and Nicolson,1987)

Orwell,G. *Down and Out in Paris and London (*1933:Penguin Modern Classics, 2013)

Orwell,G.*The Road To Wigan Pier(*1937:Penguin, 1962)

Overy, R. *The Morbid Age: Britain and the Crisis of Civilisation 1919-1939* (Penguin, 2010)

Prothero, R.E. (Lord Ernle) *English Farming Past and Present* (Heinemann Educational Books 1961)

Pugh, M. *We Danced All Night: A Social History of Britain Between The Wars* (Vintage, 2009)

Purkiss, D. *The English Civil War: A People's History* (Harper Press 2006)

Reay,D. *Miseducation: Inequality,education and the working classes*(Policy Press, 2017)

Rebanks,J *The Shepherd's Life: A Tale of the Lake Distric*t (Allen Lane, 2015)

Roberts,R. *The Classic Slum: Salford Life in the First Quarter of the Century* (Penguin,1971)

Roberts,R. *A Ragged Schooling: Growing Up in the Classic Slum (*Fontana/ Collins, 1978)

Royle, T. *The Best Years of Their Lives: The National Service Experience 1945 – 1963* (Michael Joseph, 1986)

Sage,L. *Bad Blood* (Fourth Estate, 2001)

Sampson, A. *Anatomy of Britain* (Hodder and Stoughton, 1962)

Savage, M. *Social Class in the 21st Century* (Pelican Books, 2015)

Saville, J. *The Labour Movement in Britain* (Faber and Faber, 1988)

Scarth,B. *We'll all be union men: the Story of Joseph Arch and his Union*( Industrial Pioneer Publications, 1998)

Seabrook, J. *Pauperland: Poverty and the Poor in Britain* (Seahurst, 2013)

Shrubsole,G *Who Owns England? How We Lost Our Green and Pleasant Land and How To Take It Back* (Harper Collins, 2019)

Standing, G *The Precariat: The New Dangerous Class* (Bloomsbury, 2011)

Sutherland,D. *The Landowners* (F.Muller, 1988)

Tawney, R.H. *Religion and the Rise of Capitalism* (Pelican Books, 1937)

Thompson, E.P. *The Making of the English Working Class* (Pelican, 1968 edition)

Todd, S. *The People: The Rise and Fall of the Working Class.* (John Murray, 2014)

Townsend P. *Poverty in the United Kingdom* (Penguin, 1979)

Toynbee, P. and Walker, D. *Dismembered: how the attack on the state harms us all* (Guardian Books 2017)

Tressell, R. *The Ragged Trousered Philanthropists* (1914; Wordsworth, 2012 edition)

Trussell Trust *Report on annual statistics, April 2017-April 2018* (Trussell Trust, London)

United Nations, *Report on UK* by Philip Alston, Rapporteur on Extreme Poverty and Human Rights (UN, November 2018)

Verkaik, R. *Posh Boys: How the English Public Schools Ruin Britain* (Oneworld, 2017)

Vinen, R. *National Service: Conscription in Britain 1945-1963* (Allen Lane, 2014)

Wade, F. *Square Hunting* (Faber, 2020: epigraph to Acknowledgements cited in review by Susannah Clapp, London Review of Books, 29, Oct 2020)

Wilkinson, E. *Jarrow: The Town that was Murdered* (Left Book Club, Victor Gollancz, 1939)

Printed in Great Britain
by Amazon